SHEYMES

SHEYMES

A Family Album
after the Holocaust

Elizabeth Wajnberg

McGill-Queen's University Press
Montreal & Kingston • London • Ithaca

© McGill-Queen's University Press 2014

ISBN 978-0-7735-4459-8 (cloth)
ISBN 978-0-7735-9695-5 (ePDF)
ISBN 978-0-7735-9696-2 (ePUB)

Legal deposit fourth quarter 2014
Bibliothèque nationale du Québec

Printed in Canada on acid-free paper that is 100% ancient forest free (100% post-consumer recycled), processed chlorine free

McGill-Queen's University Press acknowledges the support of the Canada Council for the Arts for our publishing program. We also acknowledge the financial support of the Government of Canada through the Canada Book Fund for our publishing activities.

Library and Archives Canada Cataloguing in Publication

Wajnberg, Elizabeth, 1947–, author
Sheymes : a family album after the Holocaust / Elizabeth Wajnberg.

Some text in Yiddish. Issued in print and electronic formats.
ISBN 978-0-7735-4459-8 (bound). – ISBN 978-0-7735-9695-5 (ePDF). –
ISBN 978-0-7735-9696-2 (ePUB)

1. Wajnberg, Elizabeth, 1947–. 2. Wajnberg, Elizabeth, 1947– –Family.
3. Daughters – Québec (Province) – Montréal–Biography. 4. Children of Holocaust survivors – Québec (Province) – Montréal–Biography. 5. Holocaust survivors – Québec (Province) – Montréal – Biography. 6. Jews, Polish – Québec (Province) – Montréal – Biography. 7. Immigrants – Québec (Province) – Montréal – Biography. 8. Jewish families – Québec (Province) – Montréal – Biography. 9. Jewish families – Poland – Biography. I. Title.

FC106.J5W24 2014   971.4'270049240092   C2014-904881-5   C2014-904882-3

In memory of my parents and my sister

לברכה זכרונם

CONTENTS

INTRODUCTION

Sheymes, or "holy fragments," is a Yiddish term for pieces of the Torah which, when old or damaged, are not to be discarded or burned but buried in consecrated ground. The fragments are holy because each one may bear the name of God. *Shem* means "name" in Hebrew. The Yiddish pronunciation "shey" and ending "es" makes the word plural, with the colloquial meaning of "pieces."

I have seen those stitched-up Torahs, shredded by the Nazis, and just barely recovered, their wooden arms lacerated with a number. They are too fragile to read from, but can be carried around the synagogue to be kissed. My parents and their generation of survivors were living *sheymes*; human beings once intended for disposal so radical that not even their memory would be left. Haunted by the families they lost, the unspeakable acts they had undergone, as well as the heroic acts which cost them nearly as much – the survivors faced another, different struggle. Whether they found themselves in displaced persons' camps or stranded behind the Iron Curtain, they had to leave their countries of origin. They had to emigrate.

To no other people, perhaps, is the act of memory so crucial as it is to the Jews. Torn from a charred community of which they were the only direct memory, the remnant of European Jews managed to collect all they remembered about their decimated towns in Yizkor or Remembrance books. The act of memory has become an act of faith.

This memoir marks the history not of the wartime events but of my parents' *telling* of the war. I was born after the war and my lifetime measures the time of the telling. As I grew up, I became the repository of my parents' fragmented memories. My telling includes the context in which those fragmented memories emerged, how they formed our postwar family life, their hold on my parents and sister and into the next generation. "Pick up the bags," my mother said. I picked up the bags. This was the burden I was privileged to bear. I gathered these fragments to stitch them together into a narrative that others would remember.

I gathered their memories until my parents themselves became living *sheymes* to me; until they themselves became fragile and were seen as expendable. We are told not to destroy or discard old or tattered pieces of the Torah but to bury them. That is, to treat them as we would treat that which is most sacred: living beings. Everybody who lives long enough becomes a tattered being. My parents in their journey through time became old. They joined another group: the old, the weak. They became, so to speak, doubly Jewish. When I felt my parents become vulnerable again I stopped being the collector and became the protector.

A NOTE ON THE
TRANSLITERATION OF YIDDISH

Reading transliterated Yiddish, or any other language, does not mean reading Yiddish. If you want to read a Yiddish book, you either read it using the Hebrew alphabet in which it has been written, or you read a translation. Transliteration is the means of eliciting the corresponding sounds of one language from its target audience, which in this case, is English speaking. The accent is on the spelling for the target audience. My aim was to render the Yiddish in such a way as to allow English readers to pronounce it the way it sounds, as well as to capture my parents' particular Polish Yiddish dialect. Ultimately, I am writing down what I heard.

Although Yiddish originated in the German spoken along the medieval Rhine, it is written with Hebrew letters, not Roman. Our ancestors transliterated Yiddish into their language of literacy, so one of the ways to reach English-speaking readers is to take a detour through Hebrew to convert it back into the Roman alphabet. The standard for Yiddish transliteration, established by the YIVO Institute for Jewish Research (founded in Vilna, Lithuania, before the Second World War) attempts to express the sounds of the Hebrew alphabet, letter by letter, using the Roman alphabet. This detour through Hebrew occasionally renders Yiddish words already familiar in North American English unrecognizable, such as *chutzpah*, which in the YIVO spelling would be *khutspe*.

Words such as *chutzpah* (Hebrew) and *mensch* (German) that have entered the North American lexicon have either been intuitively spelled the way they would be in English, or are natural for English readers to pronounce because of the Germanic components they share with English, while YIVO transliteration filters them through the Hebrew alphabet.

Hebrew stands on its consonants (the Torah is inscribed without vowels), and it is in the pronunciation of the vowels that my parents' Polish Yiddish accent most differed from the Lithuanian or "Litvak" dialect. Polish Jews pronounce the *-ei* in Germanic words, such as *klein, shein,* and *nein,* the same way in Yiddish to rhyme with *mine, wine,* and *Weinberg.* The YIVO spelling, however, uses *-ay* to represent this sound, as in *klayn, haym,* and *nayn.* The Litvaks pronounce these same words to rhyme with *main, rain,* and *Spain,* and YIVO uses *-ey* to represent this sound as in *kleyn, heym,* and *neyn.* This may seem backwards to the English-speaking reader, but the diphthongs *-ay* and *-ey* are also the universal, phonetic representation for those sounds in all languages, including English.

Besides using these diphthongs, I have left the many Yiddish words and phrases that have entered the North American English lexicon as they are. They already elicit the correct pronunciation from English readers and for consistency I followed through their spelling elsewhere. For example, I have retained the *ch-* in *chutzpah* instead of using the standard YIVO *kh-*.

I have retained my parents' and their community's pronunciation wherever it differed from either the YIVO or Americanized Litvak spelling. My parents said *shmeeze* not *schmooze, mayven* not *maven, chuchem* not *chacham, git* not *gut, gezint* not *gezunt,* and *mishpucheh* not *mishpocheh.* They also softened the *r* sound at the end of words to render the grammatically correct *eyer* as *eyeh, mir* as *meh, der* as *deh.*

My parents also used Polish and German words for the Holocaust process created in those languages. As these words are written in the Roman alphabet with their own diacritical markings, I will not embark on respelling for the English reader. The letter *w* is pronounced as *v* in both languages: *wald* is pronounced "vald," *Buchenwald* is pronounced Buchenvald. There is no Hebrew *w* at all.

These are *klaynekeiten,* or "trivial matters," as my mother would say.

Yiddish is more than the sum of its German, Hebrew, and Slavic parts. It constitutes a unique compound of these and several other languages because, like the Jewish people, Yiddish has a unique history that has made it flexible and adaptable while remaining inimitably itself. It is itself a language-making process that comments on itself as it speaks. No transliteration or translation can capture it. Perhaps that is why I nevertheless felt compelled to write out its sounds in this book.

Chaja Wajnberg's zeyde (grandfather).

A school photo from Demblin before the war.
Chaja Zylberberg is seated in the front row, third from the left.

The staff of Demblin's Jewish Free Clinic in the 1930s.
Chaja Wajnberg is on the right.

Chaja Wajnberg as a young woman.

Chaja Wajnberg with Toba (known as Lusia postwar Poland), 1939.

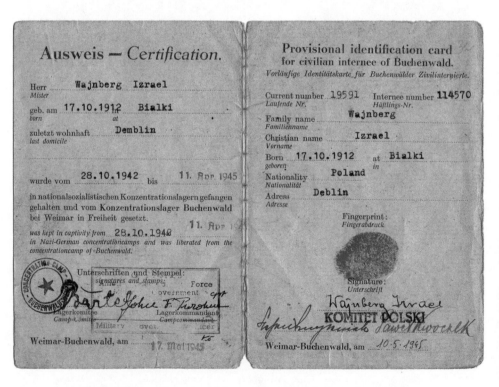

Srulec Wajnberg's concentration-camp ID card from Buchenwald, 1945.

Postwar banquet. Chaja, wearing a white blouse, standing centre.
Srulec and Lusia are seated, fifth and sixth from the right.

Lusia and Srulec, Lodz, 1946.

Elizabeth and a bear, Lodz, 1949.

Elizabeth with Chaja in Lodz, 1949.

The family in Lodz, a few years after the war.

Chaja (top left) and Elizabeth (bottom left) in Israel, 1950.

The family as recent immigrants to Montreal, early 1950s.

Yonah (Hebrew for Toba) Hashomer Hatzair summer camp, Canada, 1950s.

Yonah, on her graduation from McGill University, 1960.

Elizabeth with her parents, summer camp, 1962.

Elizabeth in Montreal, 1967.

Elizabeth with her parents,
on her own graduation from McGill university, 1968.

Lusia in Israel, 1972.

Elizabeth with Srulec in Montreal, 1993.

Elizabeth with her parents in Montreal, Chanukah 1993.

Srulec sewing alone at home.

Chaja.

SHEYMES

Chapter One

MY FATHER'S VISIT, 1983

He came, he saw, he conquered. My father, that is. The first time he
came to Paris was when I said I was not coming home. Every Passover
on their way to Israel from Montreal, my parents stopped in London
to see my sister. Now they stopped in Paris to visit me. After the war,
my parents emigrated from Poland to Israel and then to Canada only
to have their daughters move back to Europe. I stayed with him in his
hotel room that time so that he would not see the maid's room I lived
in. This time he stayed in a quiet hotel set in a garden, which was near
the sixth-floor apartment in the Latin Quarter that I shared with my
boyfriend, Benjamin. It was a challenge being on the streets with my
father each day without tiring him, carefully choosing the few times
for him to climb up the six flights *sans ascenseur* to our apartment.
Even with my stopping and telling him a *mayseh* on every landing like
I promised, it still took him a half hour to recover.

One afternoon he lay on the bed while I tried on my birthday
dress for him, which I thought would not be warm enough to wear
out to dinner, but he liked it, so I wore it under two sweaters. Then I
cooked my infamous bouillabaisse. An entire *rascasse* went in, its head
swimming in wine and saffron and its tail poking out from under the
cover. The only restrained eater in the family, my father had one bowl
and had enough. The French bread, however, was a different story. Had
to ration him or he would have eaten nothing else. And the croissants!

"Lizzie," he says reading the newspaper in a café, "Get me another one please. They make like this in Israel, but not so light." Not a sybarite, my father, but judicious.

Benjamin took us to Chez L'Ami Louis. "I will take lamb," says my father summarily. After that, he looked around, chuckling at the scowling waiters, enjoying the scene. In the wine-dark, old-wood setting, he and Benjamin, bent over a menu, looked like figures in a Rembrandt painting.

Seventy years old, he hops out of the shower to open the hotel-room door with a big grin, bare, youthful chest, and a towel over his genitals.

But the toughest hurdles are his sudden mood shifts. Through the cracked grin and twinkle-eyed chuckle, I can feel his vitality ebbing in a dismaying withdrawal. This is when I call him back. "Daddy, explain to me the economy. Daddy, look at that baby on the next park bench."

If my mother aroused terror for what she had gone through, my father aroused grief. He confessed that when they were in Israel, my sister jumped on him for "speaking softly." "What's the matter?" she demanded. "Are you sick? Then I shouldn't have come." I could see my father shrinking even further at the attack and – in this lay his weakness and his strength – enduring it.

Anything I say about my mother or sister is news to him: supporting three females has not left him much leisure for character analysis. Nor, in the end, would it have made much difference.

I turn my back on him for a moment in a café then see him swallowing a coloured pill with his *café crème*. "Valium," he says, "because my hands are shaking." He has been urging me to call my sister the way I used to write to her, whether she reciprocates or not. He calls my sister to ask her if she will accept a visit from my mother. He looks at his watch to see if it is time to call my mother in Israel. I take his hands and ask him to take a deep breath.

The comedy of my teaching him yoga breathing every day in his hotel room: Along with *The Bowel Book*, I ordered *Yoga for the Elderly* and have been teaching him from it. Eventually, after he's read the *Herald Tribune*, I give him the book. And he reads it. The joy is, he is *teachable*, always my first and last miracle.

We buy perfumes, not at Michel Swiss, the Polish Jew on the Rue de la Paix like last time, but where it's really Jewish, on the Rue des Rosiers in Le Marais. On the Rue de la Paix, they brought us demitasses of coffee. The cup rattled in his shaking hands. He put it down and took a piece of paper out of his pocket which he carefully unfolded, on which my sister had written, in order of preference, a list of her favourite perfumes. When he tried to drink from the demitasse again, coffee splashed over his coat. Finally, I grabbed the lapels of his coat to cut the circuit and demanded, "Why are you so nervous?" I let go, immediately ashamed. Who was I to talk?

I take pictures of my father writing postcards in the Place des Vosges. The character in my father's face and his slightly formal elegance suit the red-gold banquettes and Renaissance arches of the oldest square in Paris. I lead my father through the heart of the medieval Jewish ghetto on the way to a Monet exhibit. We go down the narrow winding streets, which were made a ghetto again in 1940, past the craftsmen's courtyards from behind whose doors the Polish Jews who had come to France to start a new life were rounded up first.

"France was the first country in Europe to grant civil rights to Jews," my father said. Only now I learn that his first attempt to leave Poland after the war had France as our destination. He had distant cousins in Paris who vouched for our visa. "At the time France would let us in, but Poland behind the Iron Curtain would not let us out." It was only because the recognition of a Jewish homeland in 1948 applied some international pressure on Poland to let its Jews go that we got out of Poland at all. In 1950, we immigrated to Israel. I was five when in 1953 we marked time in Paris for six months before finally leaving Europe and taking the boat to Canada. I might have been a Parisienne! Or at least spoken French like a native.

Suddenly he remembers an Orthodox Jew in the *pletzel* who sells perfumes. Sure enough, a few doors down, between the kosher butcher and baker stands a Jew in a black hat among outsized bottles of Patou, Ricci, and Dior. In two seconds, my father breaks into Yiddish, and on either side of him ladies carrying eau de toilette bottles break into Polish and Hungarian. Everyone with survival stories, helping the shopkeeper add up the prices on a slip of paper. The perfume seller is missing a finger, "by Hitler," and the lady next to us survived how? "*Goyishe papiren*," she shrugs. Gentile papers.

The perfume seller has two pieces of advice for me. "Buy the big size, *narishe* [silly], it's cheaper!"

"But I don't need," I protest, frightened by a huge bottle that will outlive me.

As we go out the door laden with presents for the clerks at the bank and the switchboard operator at Canadian Outfitting, the perfume seller gives me the second piece of advice. "Never trust a *goy*." He comes running out on the street after us and gives me his card. "If you are ever in trouble, you come here. Not to buy perfumes," he waves a finger, "just to talk. Here is *haymish*."

Then further along the street, in the heart of the *pletzel*, we come to Goldenberg's with its herring, vodka, and red banquettes – pure 1930s Warsaw. It felt like Old Warsaw soon after I arrived when armed guards were patrolling the door in the wake of a bombed synagogue. "Two Jews and four innocent people were killed," was the newspaper headline the next day. Neither the *krupnik* (barley soup) nor all of Monet's blooms warm my father, so we take a taxi from those damp, narrow streets to the broad boulevards of St. Michel and St. Germain and the Café Cluny where there is life before the eyes.

The café where we ate an omelette and the museum across the boulevard he remembers from his short visit here two years ago, when he stood there marvelling at me marvelling at the tapestries. The café has some of the North American insulation that he likes. His back is always cold from where the Germans whipped him. But what brings the twinkle to his eyes are the streets, the girl in the camera store, the bears in the Jardin des Plantes.

On busy St. Germain he picks up a shoelace from the sidewalk to measure my shoulders for a winter jacket, tying a knot where they end.

As we start climbing a narrow street he gazes back down the row of adjoining restaurants. "How do they all make a living?" I steer him out of the way of the *clochard* asleep on the grate on the Rue Linné. Dismay spreads over his face. "In Canada," he whispers, "you would never see a person on the street without a place to go."

He is in a different mood when Benjamin brings us sandwiches in the park. "I will walk with my father in the Jardin des Plantes among the spring blossoms," I had been saying for weeks before. My father is hunched on the bench in his coat and tie, quickly vaporizing again. He answers in absent monosyllables, his temperature sunk to flat tepid. I see Benjamin's usually cherubic face fall in dismay. "Daddy, do you want to see the bears?" I ask, my own voice faltering. He's about to shrug violently – no! – when, to please me, he takes my arm and puffs along. Fatigue, the coefficient of despair. And I am glad I coaxed him: somewhere I learned that the first step out of it is to take the first step. Because in five minutes he is my other Daddy, chuckling at the bears. That night he changes into the vivid blue shirt I gave him – spiffy, twinkling again. This is how he is better; to please me, he takes the first step out of it.

Puffing along, he exhales like a runner now just to walk a little farther. Yet on the last morning, when I make a move to help with his heavy suitcase, he grabs it and toddles toward the taxi, "Look! I can fly with it!"

I push back the wad of a thousand Canadian dollars he brought me, saying, "Play with it in the stock market for me."

"Will that make you feel good?" he asks and takes it back reluctantly. He helped my sister buy a flat so that she would have a decent place to live. Me, I know he expected to get married. I am no longer rebellious enough to tell him not to count on it.

At the airport gate I burst into sobs. "Oh, Lizzie, maybe you are not happy here," he says, never dreaming that it's because I miss him. I cheer up fast while he takes out a hankie to wipe his tears. His face red, he breaks out into one of his ear-to-ear grins. "Write me letters," he says, "I like your letters."

Came home, did not go up right away, cried and ate fruit in the street.

Chapter Two

PARIS IS THE MOST BEAUTIFUL CITY IN THE WORLD

———

On an October night in 1942, my mother sprang out of a window of a Polish farmhouse with her child. She jumped to her death and instead they both lived. The other women, her mother among them, were sent to Treblinka. Since then, my mother's most nightmarish actions have been right and twisted wrong at the same time. She did not want to see her child being killed. Since then, she has wandered the earth as if she is sightless.

Forty years later, in Paris, I take pictures of my mother eating an orange. From under her downturned eyes there is a glimmer of a complicit smile, and a few blunt strands of hair hang loose over her forehead. I take pictures of her putting on her shoes, in a nightgown over the body that has frightened me off womanhood, the huge breasts pulling her forward as she reaches from side to side. I have a picture of her waiting at the window, one hand pulling the curtain back, the nightgown open on her bosom leaning on the windowsill, her face very old, very soft.

She is smiling in the photo because the moment she catches sight of me is the moment I snap the picture. I revisit my mother in an endless suite of her drinking tea in a café with mirrors and worn wine-red leather banquettes. Second by second, her head bends to the cup in an eternity where she becomes another, a stranger, herself.

I photograph her from the front, the back, the side; I am closest to her when I let her be not my mother. I am rendering her silent homage, my mother, an homage she can never allow herself to hear.

I am adding that silent seeing for which there is no place between people, which you cannot avow without disturbing the river from which it flows. Because there is no way to be with her other than to be away from her. With the camera between us, I can keep her for a little while longer the way she does not permit herself to be. Unguarded, present, vulnerable.

There is no order to these photographs. There is no order to her stories. The patience to judge perspective is gone. She tells stories stored as mental tapes and recited blindly by heart, stories that lose and gain by being recited. Snatches of them run around in a loop, especially the phrases in English, even if no longer true or she does not believe in them. The recorder broke down in 1942.

Her stories are so untouched by what came later they might as well be pieces of their time. They are all alive and spinning and retrievable, including the postwar stories that even at the time gave not so much an illusion of recovery as the signs of desire for it. And this desire was welcomed even then only as a sign. It was enough to make a story. They were stories to keep whole, while time showed not only all that was irrecoverable but also the further unimaginable damage, the cracks that widened, the nightmares that awoke her and blackened her days awake. My father places events in historical context, but not my mother. The stories do not fall into perspective. Because in the light of the ovens, tell me, what can any of them mean?

"Speak English!" she whispered when I hugged her off the plane at Charles de Gaulle. She was stopping to visit me on her way to Israel, where my father and sister would join her for Passover. I greeted her in our usual Yiddish. "Why aren't you speaking English?" she demanded, because my American boyfriend was there. I introduced them, and Benjamin, choosing that moment to show me how easy it was to resist the most mythical personage of my life, went right on reading the *Herald Tribune*. Then we couldn't find her bags because she was standing right next to them and didn't recognize them, and we had to store most of them because she was carrying with her half the household and enough cans of BC salmon to feed the entire country.

"*Nem*. Take up the bags."

On the walkway outside, the wind that morning blew dust into her eyes. They flickered, blinked, and teared. From her bag she took out one of those big checkered handkerchiefs from Poland and wiped the corner of her eyes.

"It's nothing. A piece of ash."

Her eyes were still tearing when I left her resting in her hotel room. She liked the tree outside her window waving its shadow on the rose-flowered wallpaper. Europe!

"Ma," I said, loosening her girdle with attached money belt, "Why didn't you get traveller's cheques?"

"What good would they be in an emergency?" Sometimes hard currency was not hard enough. I brought her tights when I went to meet her the next morning, because it was raining and my feet were always wet and cold in Paris. Youthful legwarmer tights that were completely alien to her, and she put them on. She who wore nylons buttoned into her girdle, she let me take care of her. That's the good thing about her, the unselfconscious side that does not notice to disapprove.

"You're the only one who shows me warmth, which is what I need," she said, as we sailed into the grey drizzle.

She was well disposed toward Benjamin that night at dinner. At least she had not yet found anything bad to say about him, unlike my other boyfriends, even my first one, the Canadian Jewish medical student whom she liked. She complained that he answered the telephone with an accent. She was so overjoyed when the English one left me, she wanted to send him flowers. Not that one had to like the person one married, she said. In life, one had to compromise. It wasn't as if she had been crazy about my father.

"He was not my level," she said; he was "in trade," as if she were in a Jane Austen novel rather than in a pot of potatoes herself. But there were eight hungry siblings at home, and, village beauty though she was, my father was the only one who would marry her without a dowry.

This was the story she clung to for over fifty years.

That night at the restaurant near the Place du Panthéon, while the violin played, the table shook with my mother's bottomless sighs. My mother has an operatic soprano voice that used to project the four syllables of my name through the neighbourhood. When the violin played she hummed – a high piercing melancholy that plunged into a throaty sorrow. When we came to Canada, she sometimes broke into song at the kitchen sink while I did my homework. I held my breath at the miracle of my mother forgetting herself.

She could not, however, forget the lights of the Champs Elysées. Long before she saw them, they were the light by which Warsaw and every other European capital saw itself. She could never forget the smell of the earth in Poland, the taste of fresh butter, the country's *wiosna*, springtime, which nothing can rival. It *shmekt!* She waited under the trees for my father to return from the forest. She parted the branches and looked out, her black hair parted down the middle showed her white skin, her black dress parted on her bosom, her eyes were violet. He was late and she was anxious. Why was she anxious? She must have loved him.

He was seven years younger than her, independent, and wore his handsome clothes with ease – a prince, the townsfolk said when he came to call. He married my mother because he chose to. The thirty-three-year-old bride, according to her, went reluctantly to the *chuppah* in a wedding fashionably held in Warsaw. Since I was the same age then as she was when she married and lacking a biological clock of my own, she would have to drag me too.

"There is something Old World about you," Benjamin said when we met, as if I were a piece of rare porcelain. Benjamin was not the first Jewish-American boyfriend who prided himself on avoiding Jewish, or in his case, "American" girls. What was I, then? I was a European immigrant sufficiently exotic to them that they didn't recognize that this was also what Jewish looked like. If my mother wanted me to marry a Jew, I would have to inform her that it was the men who were the obstacle.

Benjamin was nine years younger than me, but I was incompetent in so many ways he would have to be younger still to feel out of his depth. All the same, he had that unspoiled American innocence that disarmed the French. Still I was floored when he arranged for us to meet Céleste Albaret, who was still alive and living in the country in 1982. This was the woman whom Marcel Proust allowed to watch over him as he wrote in bed. Céleste called Benjamin *jeune homme* too.

Our first Proust adventure was months before that, however. On the day before Christmas, we took the train to Proust's childhood paradise, Illiers-Combray, the most remembered town in literature.

It was raining, we were the only visitors. We waited while the *gardienne* opened up Proust's aunt's house. In the book his memory, sparked by the narrator's dipping a biscuit in tea, unfolds the entire nine volumes. The reality was disappointing, as Proust might have predicted. The furniture, beds, tables, a madeleine biscuit under glass, retreated further into their materiality the harder I tried to match them to the book: here was the staircase where he waited for his mother's goodnight kiss, the little bell that announced guests. "The person on whom Swann was based never visited here," the *gardienne* corrected me, "neither did the maternal aunt and uncle." In order to include them in Combray, Proust had assimilated his mother's Jewish relatives into his father's Christian family. As an artist, of course, he was free to select, transform, or suppress irrelevancies such as the absence of his beloved Jewish mother's extended family from French village life and certainly from the chivalric images projected on his bedroom wall.

We wanted to stay overnight in town, but there was no room in the hotel. Oddly, it was Benjamin who got the creeps.

"Come on, you don't think it's because we're Jewish ..." I said, laughing.

"Well, look around," he said. "The hotel is not exactly hopping with customers. And who else but two Jews would be wandering around on Christmas Eve?"

We took the train back to Paris.

One afternoon while still under the Proustian influence, we went walking in the Parc Monceau where Marcel was taken to play as a child. We stopped on a bridge under which lushly feathered ducks floated by. Elegant ducks, I could have sworn I recognized them. If not from Canada then where? It had to be the park where my mother used to take me when I was a child in Lodz. That's when I remembered I wasn't the older woman; I was my mother's youngest child, more trembled over than any generation of children in history.

My mother, perhaps remorseful at turning us off marriage, decided to make up for lost time. Smiling at me gamely as she hauled herself up the six flights by holding on to the banister, when I asked her if it was too much, she shook her head, "I am a force of nature." I set the table, moving but not removing Benjamin's typewriter. Benjamin, thinking to endear himself to her, talked about that winter's Polish

Solidarity movement against the Communist government that started in the Gdansk shipyards. While he went on about his admiration for the Polish people, my mother held her head in her hand and gazed at him with her glittering blue eyes.

"You don't know the Polish people like I do," she said finally. "I would tell you more," my mother said to Benjamin, dropping her hands, "only I have not the passion."

"The patience," I say. The passion. For her it is the same thing. Patience would demand more of her than the most extreme passion. She would rather jump through the window than wait. My mother told him nothing more. There was too much to tell. Her passion had burned out the patience.

◆ ◆ ◆

"Elizabeth," she said in an ominous tone of voice, when I'd taken her back to the hotel and undone her girdle and had her snugly ensconced in the rosebud-flowered sheets. "You think your father wanted to marry me? Give Benjamin an ultimatum. I gave your father an ultimatum."

Woman to woman. My mother looked up at me with her bright eyes from the pink-flowered pillows. *Ool-tee-matum*. It sounded even more Latinate and diplomatic in Polish than it did in English. She had trembled over our safety, but she had so little noticed our rites of passage that a teacher had taken it upon herself to buy me my first bra. Mortified, she sent me back with a box of chocolates.

I turned off the lights except for the rose-coloured bedside lamp. My mother's beautiful eyes shone up at me from among the fresh pillows in the lamplight, her Mediterranean features powder-soft with the blur of old age.

The next evening in our apartment, when I came in from the kitchen to set the table, she was saying, "The duke and duchess of Windsor." After I had told her that Benjamin was nine years younger than me in an effort to discourage her, my mother was naming illustrious couples in which the woman was older than the man.

"Elizabeth Barrett Browning."

Since I could not be trusted to do anything for myself, she was courting Benjamin for me.

"Queen Victoria."

I did not know Queen Victoria was older than her consort, but I never questioned my mother's knowledge of royal British genealogy.

"How about Elizabeth the First?" I said. My mother shot me a murderous glance. Fortunately, Benjamin was smiling. But then, her ploys were transparent compared to the subtle manoeuvres of other parents, who knew better than to interfere. She pulled my baby picture from her purse. She makes it no secret that I have deteriorated since then, and believes this memento of the last time I seduced her will seduce Benjamin. "You were the most beautiful child in all Lodz."

So soon after the war I must have been a rare Jewish child in Lodz – it was enough that I came with a head and a tail for me to be a phoenix.

"The woman in the next bed wanted to matchmake you for her son."

How beautiful can a newborn be?

No, she was not biased. It was not because she was my mother that she thought I was beautiful. "'All children are *śliczny*,' one Polish woman protested to another, 'you've seen one, you've seen them all.' She came closer to look at you. 'You're right, this is a *śliczny dziecko*.' Tell him what a *śliczny dziecko* is."

"A lovely child," I say, numb with rote response.

"We gave you a royal name."

They had me examined by the best doctor. "You can't be sick," says my father about my sickness, "when you were born, the best doctor in Lodz examined you and he said you were a healthy child."

"Look what has happened to you," my mother said. She gazed at the flickering candle. Her eyes glittered and flickered.

I never saw her *bensh licht*, bless the candles. Never saw her with kerchief on head press her hands to her eyes in the meditation that welcomes the feminine Sabbath, the wandering forsaken bride of God.

◆ ◆ ◆

"What are you wearing?" my mother asks when we meet the next day. "It smells so good."

I am wearing her favourite gardenia perfume.

My mother becomes self-absorbed in front of a mirror. The astonished salesgirls fell out of her way in the Rue Saint-Honoré boutique with a perennial sale on cashmere sweaters. She stationed herself in front of a mirror in the storage room in the back. As I handed her another sweater with a décolleté neckline, she pushed my hand out of the way. Whom did she see?

Did she see the huge bosom, the hands always folded beneath? Or could those brimming sightless eyes gaze through the mirror and into the young woman who had jumped out of a window? If she was remembering herself, that vision was static as in photographs, because in movement she became clumsy. When not folded, the long hands fall uselessly by her side. After the war, her hands forgot how to hold a baby. She was afraid she would drown me in the bath. Any time I lost my mother on the street, it was because she had bumped into a mirror and was standing in front of it, mesmerized and lost.

In one of my earliest memories, I am three years old and beside myself. I am standing at the knees of a woman who is sitting with her hands covering her face, crying. I don't know how to make her stop. She is beautiful. Her black hair parts over a shimmering white face. Who is this? I am astonished. She is my mother.

"It's nothing," she says.

She bent over, elastically folded in half so I know the source of my flexibility, to rummage in the suitcase open on the floor. My parents packed quickly, a suitcase for the ghetto, a bag for the *lager*. I know how each one packs now: my mother in a rage of chaos, my father skilfully knotting rope with long practice, so that in any post office in the world I can pick out his parcel.

There is nothing my mother cannot take out of a suitcase. A piece of coral necklace from Poland she has rethreaded. A child's knitted red beret: mine. Pictures: A picture of her, a brunette beauty, that we have only because her uncle took it to America in 1930. Although I was born there, pictures are all I know of Poland. Standing at a bookstall in Paris, I saw the people of the town where I was born in photographs that German soldiers had taken as souvenirs. A kerchief with berries on it: She brought it home from downtown one icy day, walking all the way, her face red and rigid with cold, her cheeks streaming with tears, "Look!" These things transported west across the world, then east, to be transported back west again. The suitcase my father has ingeniously packed for her is a field of rubble. I stand knee-deep in my mother's chaos, created by her heedless, sightless drive to find something. The scene will be repeated the next time she searches for it, if only because it is easier to flounder, tear, rip through the contents than to pay attention to where she put it last. Easier in the short run. My mother has no long runs.

We sat in the Luxembourg Gardens. She loved *die Natur*, for which, like company and art, she claimed to be starved in that Canadian wasteland, and for which my father had no feeling. "I am a product of the European *Kultur*," my mother says. Nannies wheel elegant children in the sunshine, mothers push baby prams. She is staring at a bird on the grass so bitterly that if the bird knew, it would drop dead.

"Ma, this is Europe! Not only that, it's Paris!"

"In Poland, in March when you were born, it was *wiosna*, spring, the cherry trees were in bloom ..." The lights on the Champs Elysées stretched eastward all the way to Poland and choked in smoke.

Farshtinkene Poyln. Romantic and stinking Poland. Her forests, her birds, her air, her mushrooms. They shot at concentration-camp survivors returning home after the war. When it was all over, it still wasn't over. She straggled back to Demblin with my sister, ducking shots from her compatriots.

The bird on the grass hops and twitters. She loves birds! Flowers! Cherries! Kerchiefs with flowers and berries.

Please remember when you took me to the park every day in Lodz and I asked why I couldn't have a baby to play with instead of such a big sister.

Please remember that when you went into labour with me, Daddy ran out to get a droshky, I came on so fast I was nearly born in it. It was *wiosna* and the cherry trees were already in bloom, I was so beautiful that the woman in the next bed wanted to matchmake me to her son. You gave me a royal name. You were so healthy that the doctor included you when he said, "All my strong ones in the new wing!"

She is always someplace else. She is in Europe where she wanted to be and it is someplace else. Right now she is taking in the fact that though I am all hers, the world is so made that children leave their mothers and go to work. And that nowhere on this earth can she find refuge. She is completely dependent, how much she denies. Since 1942 she has learned nothing; she doesn't have the patience. Besides the fact that she is helpless by herself, forwarded like a package from one airport to another, she can't be left alone. "I can't be alone." Alone, there are no distractions. She stares at the bird sightlessly.

Because that place could be only one thing, all places after were made in the image of Treblinka.

◆ ◆ ◆

"You don't wear lipstick? Lipstick makes a woman," my mother said when I came to take her out to dinner. She used to say that lipstick would wear out your lips and make them purple and old.

"Is Benjamin coming to dinner?"

"No."

"Then I'm not hungry," she said. "I'm too tired to go out. Elizabeth –"

"Not now, ma."

"I want to ask you something."

My mother did not say I was worth a million Benjamins; that he was not worth my little finger, such a pearl diamond star as I was, there was no brighter star in the firmament. She was disgusted with me.

"Where is Benjamin?" demanded my mother, as if I'd hidden him.

"He's busy."

"Ah."

"He's got better things to do."

"What does he do?"

"He's a journalist. He's interviewing a Polish filmmaker."

She could never say of Benjamin, as she said of my father, that he had no feeling for art.

"The last art he took me to," I said (it was a concert of avant-garde cacophonous squawks), "I jumped over the back of two theatre stalls to escape." And like my mother, I am no athlete. "He says I have no patience, I should open myself up to the experience. But to a painful experience? 'If there's one thing I learned from my mother,' I told him, 'it's that you don't sit still for painful experiences.'"

"Elizabeth," my mother said in that relentless tone. I wish she'd given me a name with fewer syllables or given me a nickname. "Elizabeth, you are digging a grave for yourself. You are doomed. You have ruined your life. That's all I'm going to tell you. You were the most beautiful child in Lodz and you have been on a downhill road since then. You are digging your own grave."

"Why won't I get married? Because I wouldn't want anyone to come between you and me, Ma!" I said, putting my arm around her.

My mother's bosom heaved. "*Gay avek.*" She threw off my daughterly arm. "Get away from me. I am one nerve, a deathly sweat pours over me and you sit there *tsapping* my blood."

"But people still survive if they don't get married!" I said.

My mother bristled. If she had had a wet dishrag handy, she would have smacked me with it. She refuses! She refuses!

"You are digging your own grave and nobody will save you."

My own brand of living death, I am dumb, numb, my fingers have gone white in the spring sunshine. I stuff them in my pocket before she notices and blames me for them too. Whether I "looked good" or not meant was I – her child, her pearl, her diamond, her star, her sun – going to die? A fury at vital signs that refused themselves, a fury at anything of hers dying. *Shaynheit. Shtern. Zin.* My beauty. Stars. Sun. Perele, Rivka, Estere, she called me by each of the names of her murdered sisters. And then she called me the most beloved private name that she also had not given me: Shayndel. Her mother's name. "Look at those hands!" *Smack.* "You are green like a corpse! *Ich ken nisht kikin.*" I can't look.

On the third day, I did not rush off to meet her at her hotel. I took my time. Not that I was late. To be on time is to be late, only to be early is to be on time, and sometimes even that's not enough for her not to be seething with impatience. I had to push the clock back before I was born. The angry goddess was banging on the walls while I gulped my coffee. *Let her wait*, I steamed.

"Don't drink it so fast," said Benjamin, who claims he picked me out of a roomful of people by my palpable nervousness. "Your mother can wait for five minutes."

"No, she can't, there's one thing she can't do is wait. She'll panic, she'll think I'm dead, she'll drag the Seine for me."

"She must have waited sometime in her life. You're exaggerating. You're as bad as she is."

"You don't understand. She can't wait. She has no nerves left to learn anything. She'll start walking the streets in her nightgown calling my name." I could hear the four-syllable aria beating up from the traffic to our sixth-floor window. The faster my eyes skimmed the print of the *Pariscope*, the angrier I got at her or myself; it made no difference which anymore.

"You must be crazy, you need a psychiatrist," my mother said smugly the time I called her twenty times in a row to tell her why I couldn't call her twenty times in a row to tell her where I was. An exorcist was what I needed. She had entered into full possession. My nerves sang to hers.

Everything in me is derived to the second power. The nerve-shrieking emergency was my mother shrieking in my nerves. From now on everything will fall out of my hands, I will become true to every one of her predictions. In return for the nine months she carried me, I have carried her all my life. What if she is out running around the streets of Paris in her nightgown calling my name? *Let her wait*, I steamed.

"E-liz-a-beth!"

In mid-breath my lungs burst, my mother's voice can freeze the life processes. How she had the patience to gestate me nine months I don't know.

I grabbed my coat. "Sweetheart," said Benjamin.

"Get out of my way," I hissed. I tripped over myself running out the door and fell a flight headlong out of the six flights down. In mid-tumble it flashed through my mind that if I cracked my skull, who would tell my mother why I was late? I ran bruised and shrieking to the hotel.

"I'm coming! I'm coming!"

◆ ◆ ◆

"I don't see what you see in him, whatsisname? He has an ugly build. One thing I can say about your father, I never have to be ashamed of him on the beach."

The waiter has poured us cups of hot chocolate with scalded milk from the pot.

"It's hot. Wait for it to cool down," I say.

"Now may I?" she asks, smiling. Her cheeks are pink like a young girl's. Any barb I take in dissolves. For two minutes we are in harmony.

My mother lifts up the cup and looks out the window. Outside the window a tree hovers with the buds scarcely showing; a tree with skeleton branches in the grey light still barren with the look of winter. She stares at it until her eyes glitter and – crashes down the cup. She gulps down the scalding liquid; suddenly nothing is too hot for her boiling blood. Her eyes glittering, blinking furiously. She no longer sees me. She sees an invisible landscape.

"And when I came back, there was a corpse in front of the door. Hanging above the stove, there were three corpses, I had to cook with, never mind …"

I wonder if anyone in the café knows where we are.

She stays an extra night, and climbs up the steps again to sleep in our bedroom. There is the same small smile of gameness, as she accepts a ham baguette sandwich from Benjamin. Watching her in her housedress munching on the sandwich, he makes a ravishing comment. "Your mother has a lot of soul," he says.

I, who don't get any sleep because of her final admonitions, think: *Oh sure, soul that gnaws at my entrails.* I wished my parents were more like his, blandly assimilated American Jews who drove around Europe with bathing suits and matching thimbles of pre-dinner scotch. Yet I was perhaps naively surprised to discover that despite their history, how much more open to others and the world my parents were.

I am sending her away. Benjamin belatedly turns up at the hotel to take her to the airport. He smiles pleasantly. My mother barely recognizes him, both her sympathy and antipathy forgotten. He has dropped into that mass of underlings – sometimes I am one of them – from whom she deigns to take instructions. She is on unseeing *fur aus* autopilot now. "You want me to sit here? Should I take the luggage?" She has been up and ready for hours.

The lights were flashing in the Place du Châtelet as we passed in the taxi. It was silent. My mother looked from side to side out the windows. "Paris …" She leaned over to my boyfriend and her blind eyes brightened. "Paris is the most beautiful city in the world."

Halfway across Charles de Gaulle airport, the receding squat figure all alone on the bench steamed at me. I was at the counter filling out her formalities for which she had no patience and which her glare said was just another tactic for me to suck her blood. The woman in her seventies looked shorter and shorter, leaving the child for whose sake she claimed she would get slaughtered without saying goodbye. Why? Because I would not give Benjamin an ultimatum? Without saying even the minimal tearless goodbye she throws my father: *Zay gezint.* Be well.

Go, she nods. *Go. You're young.* Bitter nod.

I look back from the airport counter at her glare receding on the horizon, the small squat figure, a plume of anger like smoke rising from her head. The beaten face like a hatchet to the wind and the enormous bosom. The bitter nod. I turn around and ask for her blessing in going. I turn to wave and my hand withers in her stare. "Go, leave me here." I am abandoning her in the camp. Children abandon their mothers and save their own children. And it is even right that it should be so. I refuse. I refuse to have my own strength used against me as it was used against her. I would reverse all biological laws to show her it isn't true. I would save the mother. "She refuses! She refuses!" I refuse. There will be no more saving of children.

Nem. Take up the bags.

She is leaving. I am sending her away. "Is it here I am supposed to go?" She walks blindly forward. My mother lurches ahead of me up the walkway, condemned head thrown back. I am sending her away. Just before we part at the barrier, she has a word for me. She stops, pulls my elbow.

"Elizabeth, I want to tell you something. I want to tell you something."

A last mother-to-daughter word. A torrent of twisted love soot smoke rotting words pour out of her mouth.

"Elizabeth, I'm going to tell you something that nobody else will tell you except your mother. I'm telling you this because I am your mother. You were the most beautiful child in Lodz. The stars above may as well have hid their faces when you were born. There was not another like you and there will never be again another like you. And now, I don't know why, I don't know how it came to be, you look terrible. I can't look at you. You are yellow like a corpse. You are dying again, Elizabeth."

On the last day, I had led my mother round and round. We walked up the picturesque Rue Montagne-Sainte-Geneviève, down the picturesque Rue Mouffetard, and back again. She rocked from side to side, each footstep a sigh. One hand under my arm, I lead my mother round and round the neighbourhood. They'll never *feer* me to the *chuppah*. They'll never lead me to the canopy. Instead, I lead my bridal mother round and round. You be the bride, I'll be the mother. She leads the mother in honour. I lead the *elterin*, the parents, in honour.

"We're almost there," I say, desperate to console her.

She smiles shyly, ironically. "We're almost there?"

Round and round. Hers is the face that accepts the next step. What next? Tearless face raised to the wind, she does not feel or think in that blasted Polish heath, she goes forward. *Fur aus.* The trees shiver, the clouds move. To go on is to get married. To get married is to have children is to save the child and abandon the mother. To go on is to go on. Within this hopeless lurching forward, there are no questions and no impatience. To be strong is to have your own strength used against you, to abandon the mother, to be pushed and push the weaker into a gas chamber. Onto a bus. Into the fields. No one humbler than that unbowed head. All is consumed, all yes or no is consumed in forward movement. She walked through fields of corpses in the dead of night carrying her child. She turned her back to receive a bullet, but it did not come. So she walked. When they deported one camp to the gas chambers, she walked to another. She walked from camp to camp. She walked with a rifle butt in her back. She walked from Częstochowa to Demblin in the path of fire. I am but the puniest expression of my mother's sentence to go on living, and the miraculous proof of her having passed through the fire alive. She loves me like God loves the Jews.

Nem. Take up the burden.

Chapter Three

WOOD

———

"*Ich – Ich bin ein tischler*. I – I am a carpenter,' I said, I had no more strength to walk. I had scarcely strength to say it." My father pauses to catch his breath; he has been puffing a little as we climb the road planted with cherry trees toward the hotel. We stand under a cherry tree and he turns to me with a touch on the elbow. He is telling the story I have heard since I was a child – how he survived the end of the war in Buchenwald. "They took away our clothes and left us naked during the freezing night. Then they gave us a rough piece with nothing underneath, no underwear – you know what kind of clothes." I knew only from a *Life* magazine photograph of Buchenwald prisoners taken in 1945: a row of sunken-cheeked grizzled men in striped pyjama-like uniforms, one with a rag around his head, behind barbed wire. I searched the faces for my father. I tried to place him in that country where I did not want to find him.

"They gave us wooden shoes that you could not walk properly in, you could only shuffle … I was swollen and weak." He is telling my childhood story that has in common with fairy tales a happy ending.

Every time there is a detail I have not heard before, a detail that opens an entire realm of possibilities in that place and time about which you cannot predict the smallest detail.

My father was recalling the war that spring in 1985 when he was seventy-three, I was thirty-eight and we found ourselves suspended in the Swiss Alps. Schweiz was my mother's current idea of heaven. This was where they were stopping on their way home from spending Passover in Israel. My father and I met in the sanatorium-like hotel in the woods above Zurich, the Hotel Waldberg, which someone had recommended to my mother. The hotel was so high up that once when we were returning by bus, we found that it had snowed in our absence, and we kept going round and round the city, until my father finally stood up and pointed upwards, "There it is!"

All I saw was whiteness. "Where?"

"There." This Jungian hotel, with its huge white doors marked "BAD" in red letters, had been especially recommended to my mother for whom, until she is in it, somewhere else is always heaven. Perhaps it would remind her of the *kurort,* cure places, the resorts in the Polish Tatra Mountains we frequented when I was a baby. My mother was not the one who had been sent to Germany during the war. In my mother's blind drive to go "there," because "there" might be better, she was liable to end up landing us smack in *gehennom*. She had landed us in Germanic Switzerland. We were in heaven, all right, and I was not sure I liked it. She always rained upon us that good health was to be found only in the mountains, the *berg*.

"When we took you to Zakopane you bloomed, but when we took you to the mineral springs in Krynica you turned yellow like a corpse." My mother cut short the virtues of any watery climate. During his nervous breakdowns, my father found the ocean most soothing of all, but my mother's nagging is so strong we both succumb to it. Everything on these Swiss hills rhymes with our name. The most opulent department store in town and one raffish café bear our name plain: Weinberg. Our Jewish names and language descend from our sojourn along the Rhine in a land we named Ashkenaz. That was also once our home.

Perhaps it is also this conflicting recognition that stirs my father's memory; there are few parts of Europe that have not composed him as well as tried to destroy him.

His choice of immigration country composed me. For me, northern woods mean Quebec's Laurentian Mountains where my parents began to take me in the polio-ridden summers of the 1950s. When my father got his first car, he drove us "up north" with me carsick in the back, and as on each side of the road the woods parted to reveal a lake, my mother would shake her head: what a rich country Canada was! Forests she knew from Poland, but so many lakes! To step out of the car and inhale the pine air in relief – my nose may as well be my father's when either of us smells wood. Wood and whatever steeps in wood in order to mature: wine, brandy, pickles, herring, your body lying on a wooden dock slapped by the lake.

The Laurentians remind me of the Polish forests I no longer remember except through my father and our photos. We keep displacing the world as the world displaces us, so we no longer know which is essence and which is nostalgia. One summer in Paris I got so homesick for Canadian forests, I ended up in Austria.

My affinity for wood and wooded places arises from my father's. Before the war, he was a lumber merchant in Poland. The portion of countryside that was as much his as any land could be to a Jew in Poland was the neighbouring estate Sobieszin. "It was in a beautiful place with pine trees. The air was very healthy," he told me. Most lumber merchants were Jewish; this was one of those intermediary functions that the aristocracy had invited Jews from western Europe to perform at the end of the Dark Ages.

Around Demblin he bought wood from the aristocracy and sold it as far away as England. He was a born entrepreneur; there was never a time he was not thinking on his feet. "Your father was always a worker," my mother conceded.

"Was wood your first business?" I once asked him. At fifteen, he managed a grocery store. Then he entered into managing a mill. In joining his elder brother in the forest, he found his vocation: beech, spruce, fir; forests and wheat fields and mills. In the fragment of any love story that I can glean, my parents met at a mill in the countryside where my father was working in the forest and my mother was visiting friends. He lived for entire seasons in the forest, sledding from one campfire to another.

In August 1939, he entered a bid for a large quantity of exceptionally fine oak veneer from Sobieszin. Recently married, with a child born the year before, he must have thought he was in for a run of good fortune. The theft of his largest and finest shipment of wood on its way to Danzig signalled the end of his life as a lumber merchant and the first shots of the Second World War.

Although he would deal in other materials, such as herring and textiles in Lodz after the war, wood remained the material he knew best.

During the first bombings of Poland, my father hid my mother's family with the forester of Sobieszin. When the smoke cleared, he read the notice on the town's bulletin board: "For the Jewish instigators of war there will be no place in Europe."

In Buchenwald he had the chance to extend his expertise in wood.

"Who is a carpenter here?" The German demand burst into the bunk.

"We were squeezed like sardines, so many we could not stand up all at once, we lay eight or nine on planks of wood. I thought to work might be better."

Here and there my father picks out the rare person whom you did not expect to be good. The German *meister* was a communist prisoner who used his administrative position for minimal acts of resistance that had maximum impact.

"To encourage us, he said that we would not be working for the Reich, but for our brothers arriving from all over Europe by the thousands, who otherwise would be left outside to freeze." He could have refused to care, to work, and hence to live. He could have lost the creaturely desire to receive. My father got up from the bunk and volunteered.

"After all," he said, "*wood* I knew."

Neither did he forget the brother-in-law, Feivel, pulled along with him from the first escape to the last call in Buchenwald.

"'And my wife's brother, he is a carpenter too,' I said."

The events that stick together for a coherent telling are the bright spots: the resistant German, the gift of bread, and the mad rush to the end. "At the end of the first day of work, the *meister* took us outside the camp and gave us – it must have been German rations – soup with pieces of meat in it." Then he gave them a Red Cross package that contained a treasure: bread. But such bread: packets of dry toast, easily digestible; as good as medicine for the dysentery ravaging his townsman Gradmann's adolescent son. "'Take, because I am full and I will have the same thing tomorrow.'

"Everyone went to the toilet in the same place. So I saw that Gradmann's son was emptying out his guts. I left the package with them in the morning. They were so honest that when I returned they had not touched it."

My father still marvels at the special quality of the packaged bread. In forty years, it has suffered no diminution. It was dry and light, deli-cate-*essen*, like Melba toast, says my father.

"Give it to your son," he told Gradmann, "if they see he is sick, they will kill him." From the edge of the latrine the SS guards amused themselves by taking pot shots at the prisoners who drowned in excrement.

"A piece of bread for the whole day. A piece of bread that you could eat right away and it was as if you had eaten nothing, you would still be just as hungry. Some people bit a little then saved the rest for later. Others ate the whole piece right away to feel as if they had eaten."

Over the Buchenwald gates the Nazis hung a sign that read, "*Jeden Dann Sich.*" Every Man for Himself. He and the Gradmanns were more familiar with another, thousand-year-old motto: "In a place where there are no human beings, try to be one." They were in a place where to be a human being, a mensch, was harder than to be a superman, a hero, or a saint.

What would a Buddha have done in Buchenwald, I wondered, *what would a Jesus Christ?*

In actual time, the miraculous job as a *tischler* and the bread it brought lasted only for a month out of the four he was imprisoned in Buchenwald. But this was all he told, this and the story of the liberation.

Suspended here in the rarefied air of these Swiss woods he began to tell me more. We had never spent two weeks like this, with him not rushing off to work. Every morning he checked the slips of paper, or *kivtls*, that he kept in his pocket to remind him of his obligations. His stories were like those *kvitls* folded up one within the other, each one containing another detail that opened up another story.

That night as I scanned the supper buffet, I noticed an absence of meat (no vegetarian main course either), and of wine. My mother had no idea she had sent us to a hotel affiliated with a Christian sect that believed austerity was good for the soul but they had been good to the Jews. Corralling some soup and side dishes, I brought the tray to our table. It was only when my father, who never complained about what was missing, caught sight of the cabbage swimming in vinegar that his face cracked in laughter. "In Buchenwald on a day we got a potato, that was paradise. That we called 'Canada.'"

Their discrimination impressed me because they could have called it "America." I will be older still before I learn that at the time concentration-camp inmates measured the smallest reprieve by the most abundant creation: "Canada," the country that would not have let a single one of them in.

At the end, the Americans put the prisoners in the SS bunks and my father was given bread to distribute. "Some of the others wanted to punish the Germans," my father added with a shrug, "I couldn't."

Usually when you tell a story it is over. This is the implicit gift my father telling the story carries, that the events in it are over. Would that you could stop the process by telling it. This is why in the camps they dreamed of telling the story, but they woke to the anguish that nobody was listening. Even their dreams would not allow them the future past tense in which stories are told.

Anyway, my father had no one left to tell. They all carried the knowledge into the gas chamber.

Until I was born, "after."

◆　◆　◆

Although my mother strained toward Europe ever since we came to Canada, in recent years she had settled for these layovers during their Passover trips to Israel. While she prolonged her stay in Israel, I came to meet my father. When I arrived from Paris and knocked on his door at the Hotel Waldberg, we had not seen each other for over a year.

"Well, Lizzie," he said, throwing back the covers, "we go and have lunch?" He is hungry and has been waiting until I arrived.

It is not until we are seated downstairs that I say to his bent head under the lamp, "I love you." He does not look up at me. "I love you, Daddy," I say a little louder.

With his head bent, not moving, he still does not look up but I can see the edges of his face crack. "I heard. I heard."

Unpacking, he picks up a huge transparent plastic bag full of jostling pill boxes. "An *apteik*, an entire pharmacy, no?" he laughs. Three kinds of pills for his "nerves" and now there are three for his heart. He monitors a diurnal mood drama I know little about. He glances frequently at his watch – I have not made him forget himself – or is he self-conscious because he is not at work? I meet again the mystery of where he goes when he slips into a frown where he is hidden from me, and the challenge of keeping him here with me. As a child I would tug on his hand, *Come back.*

Walking hand in hand on immigrant Sunday *shpatzirs* along Montreal's Fletcher's Field (he was forty-two, I was seven), he argued with himself out loud in Yiddish, as one of a people who needed to talk to somebody so badly we invented an invisible God. My father had just entered Jewish time-space, where you could consult with *chuchems* (sages) from across the millennia.

The question my father asked himself was: should he go off alone to Newfoundland where high wages were paid for labour? Eventually he would stop and *shmeeze* with the men in front of the Jewish Public Library, and in the tradition of talking Torah on the Temple steps, they talked about how to make a living. It was all one discussion. The body of laws was called Halacha, literally translated as "a way of walking," because it emerged from everyday practical problems. For example, our walking was done on Sunday, because everybody had to work on the Sabbath.

"Na." My father shrugged emphatically. In his middle age, my father, the Buchenwald survivor, was going to pioneer in the Canadian north. But he could no more leave his family, not even in thought. *Come back*, I tugged at his hand.

◆ ◆ ◆

He is on vacation now, but every morning he goes through the little cards in his pocket to read his messages to himself. My favourite time with him: breakfast at the window with the sun streaming in. He is wearing a tweed jacket this morning. I have brought him a canary-yellow sweater and a blue polo shirt to loosen him out of shirt, tie, and jacket. I have never seen my father lounging around in shorts and an undershirt. He is always spiffy, *habillé*, ready to work and meet people. When we came to Canada, a *landsman* – a fellow townsman from

Poland – sat him down at a sewing machine, "but I had no talent for it." He found a job in Pascal's Hardware store on Park Avenue. On my father's first day, another clerk criticized him for tying up parcels the wrong way. He, who was expert at packing for transport. Eventually, he became a prized worker (Pascal's had a reputation for personally helping customers), and the manager wanted to groom my father to replace him. He turned it down. He said he wanted to try something on his own.

He bought a Buick and became a peddler. From being a lumber merchant in Poland, he became a throwback to an earlier Jewish trade in Canada. Since the 1800s Jewish peddlers had roamed the backwoods of Quebec bringing goods to isolated cabins. Big companies like Eaton's would give peddlers a stake of inventory on credit to sell. A lowly business, but his own.

I thought of my father climbing up the curving Montreal steps and knocking on doors. He went door to door practising the new French words he learned in night school.

His customers liked him, he said.

"Breakfast gives you the foundation for the whole day," he repeats to me the message I brought home from the New World along with B vitamins to sheathe his nerves.

Breakfast turns out to be the hotel's glory, served in an elegant dining room bathed in light from gabled windows. We choose a table under one these windows and look out at the waves of mountains flecked with the blue-green of budding trees. There is a buffet of chees-es, yogourts, berries, brioches, and a smiling hostess delivers eggs to our table cooked just so. The fresh rolls make a lump in my father's cheek. "Pour my coffee, please, Lizzie, because my hands are shaking." I pour his coffee and when he is not looking, I flick the elegant curls of butter off his plate. "But it's Swiss butter," he protests. "I never eat butter at home."

His shaking hands are a side effect of the lithium he takes, he explains. "You know how they discovered lithium?" We are leaning over the veranda looking at the lake. "Once there was a place where nobody was depressed, nobody was nervous sick. And they asked how come? Then they found in the water, which everyone drinks when they are thirsty, particles of this substance. It is something I am missing from my body that makes me sick."

My father discovers that I have been living in Paris without a watch. "How can a person go around without a watch?"

"Everyone else has a watch," I say, "then I don't need one." I behave as if I have drawn the logical conclusions of his experience into my bones. No watch. Very little luggage.

I did not want to be reminded that my parents' bodies were once worth less than what they had on their backs or in their teeth. Valuables meant ransom. I could never be unencumbered enough. Nothing makes sense in light of the event that outmoded common sense. But my nihilism is humbled by my father's acceptance. "I will forget I ever had anything," he told himself starting over in Canada for the fourth time in his mid-forties.

"I want to buy you a watch," he says. "I had a very good watch in Poland. I had it for thirty years." Up and down the Bahnhofstrasse we go, into a department store where he draws the frigid clerk into the story: "This watch from Poland was of such good quality. A Schaffhausen, perhaps you have heard of it? I had it with me for thirty years and then I lost it." He buys me an Omega watch and we choose the plain leather watchstrap together.

"Come, Lizzie, I want to have lunch where is good for your stomach." It begins to rain and my father tells me, laughing at himself, how he lost his umbrella. We buy a new one. We have lunch in a restaurant in the Paradeplatz.

"I have to call Mummy," he says, checking his watch. My mother has remained behind in Israel and is waiting for his telephone call.

"You will be sitting on *shpilkes* until we can get to a telephone," I say.

"I will not," he promises. He is as good as his word. He relaxes. I order two glasses of white wine. "The Americans," he says, "put us on a special diet. You should see how they dismantled the camp. They put us in SS quarters and they gave me bread to distribute." He adds a new detail. "Many people ate too much at first and got sick and died. I didn't overeat because I told myself that now I would not starve anymore. But I got sick anyway."

I offer him *spargele,* spring asparagus with a Yiddish diminutive, but he is not crazy about it. He likes better the rolls. *Broyt!*

◆ ◆ ◆

From the next room in the hotel, I hear footsteps; he cannot sleep. In pyjamas and slippers, he shuffles to the dresser in his room for a glass of water.

He could have turned his face to the wall and not gotten up. He could have refused to care, to work, and hence to live. Not in Buchenwald, but twenty-five years later on another continent, he awoke to the apathy of the living dead. I, who was born just after the war, was in college when he fell sick. His head hung with empty eyes and sunken cheeks. He lost weight rapidly. For the first time in his life, he couldn't go to work. He went to see a doctor who could find nothing wrong with him. Then somebody told my mother about "a doctor for the nerves."

"It is obvious what is wrong with you," the psychiatrist said. "They have only to look you in the eye. You are wearing a depressive mask." My father's eyes were the eyes of those prisoners in the camps who everyone could tell were as good as already gone.

In the fifties and sixties, applications were being taken for German reparations based on health damages. The German name for this process was *Wiedergutmachung,* literally Making Good Again. Less in a spirit of contrition than one of continuing punishment, each case was contested like an adversarial legal suit. There seemed to be no admission of what a concentration camp *was.* The German government demanded medical proofs such as bullet wounds as if they had been combat soldiers.

Letters airmailed on onionskin paper passed between the German government doctors and my father's. All documents had to be translated into German. This was accomplished with the aid of the United Restitution Organization, which was formed to help Jewish victims follow German orders to the letter. My father's claim was filed on behalf of his inflamed bronchi. The arguments went back and forth as to whether my father's respiratory troubles were due to innate or environmental causes, with the Germans taking the innate side.

Dr. Kral wrote the Germans a letter. "Before the war, this man was a lumber merchant employing hundreds of people. His business was taken from him. Here he started over. He became a salesman and now because of his illness he is unable to work more than a few days a week. Depression is anger turned against the self; an overwhelming anger that no doubt he is suppressing."

If his depression was caused by his internment, the Germans countered, why should it only show up now? It was obvious he had inherited this illness, which would have surfaced anyway. Jews had a greater genetic propensity to mental illness to begin with; this was why the German state had tried to purge Jews from the gene line.

"The patient became so ill he was about to be hospitalized," Dr. Kral continued in his report on my father, "but he became alarmed and ran away to Saratoga Springs."

Mineral baths! Krynica! I could hear my mother: "What you need is *luft, menschen*, a resort, a *kurort!*" Dr. Kral prescribed different sorts of pills to take at certain times of the day. When my father regained some spring in his walk and went back to work, he bought Dr. Kral several handsome shirts of the finest quality he could find.

When we walk in the forest behind the hotel, my father names the trees to me in Polish. *Brzoza.* "Birch?" Birches with their *biala kora* white skin, are Polish trees. *Sosna* and *świerk* sound as fresh as evergreen pine. The *demb*, the magnificent oak tree, was reserved for the finest hardwood dance floors. "Demblin was named for the oak trees which grow between the Vistula and the Wieprz Rivers.

"The town was called Irena in the last century, for the Russian governor's wife," my father says. "Poland was divided three times." He knows the Polish plaint by heart. With every heaving of the map, Jews found themselves along different ethnic fault lines, but always lumped with the "not us." At the end of the First World War, jubilation at Polish independence was cut short by the pogroms, which turned out to be part of the national celebrations.

Irena-Demblin's military fortress, its railroad station, and its airport, none of which employed Jews before the war, became the sites for German labour camps that slightly delayed their death sentences.

◆ ◆ ◆

It has taken me to middle age to fit my father's stories to a map. The county of Lublin was in that central portion of Poland which remained after parts on either side of it were annexed by Germany and Russia, and was named by the Germans the General Government. There the Vistula River itself cuts the country in half. "Visluv, we say in Polish," my father says, and traces with a fingernail how the Vistula rises as a little stream in the Carpathian Mountains, passes Cracow in the south-west, Auschwitz is a blink away, running north near Lublin farther up, splits Warsaw, and finally empties into the Baltic. But nowhere on the map can we find Demblin.

"In relation to Lublin, where was it?" I ask. Flanking the city of Lublin on this World War Two–era map I see Treblinka, Sobibor, Belzec, and Majdanek: the east just before the Russian border was well supplied with concentration camps. Two million Jews lived there and more were dumped there from the rest of Europe. My father moves his finger a little to the south to show me Demblin.

"We belonged to the Lublin SS," says my father.

On a rainy day in November 1940, my father, mother, and sister were driven into the back alleys of Demblin, exchanging their apartment with Poles. My father was chosen to be on the Jewish Council ("and I was so young!"), those councils that were often later subverted by the Nazis to enforce rulings against their own people. But after being beaten up by the German police for a Jewish misstep, my mother called a stop to his political career, and he resigned. "I *asked* to resign."

In 1942, the final solution was officially announced. "With the first Demblin deportation of May 6, they took 2,500 – half the town's Jewish people," my father said. *Wysiedlenie*, the Polish word whose meaning I guessed as a child now expands to *ausdiehlung* (leading out) as my father excavates the German term for "deportation." In another time, he retrieved one of those details that suddenly opened up a new per-spective on the very scale of what could be left out. Cysts: we were talking about the familial tendency to form cysts when half again the population of the Demblin ghetto rose up from a phantom bump on my father's head.

"Oh yes, I also had a cyst once, on my forehead," my father said. "It was many years ago. A Czech doctor took it out and showed it to me, this little sac."

"Where, Daddy? Where and when was this?" I happened to ask. And in one of those retrieved details, he resuscitated 2,000 Slovakian Jews who, as human material assembled faster than could be "processed," were sent to fill the place of the first half of the Demblin ghetto residents who were deported in May 1942.

"Even seeing what they did, it was still hard for us to believe that the Germans would take away a whole city of men, women, and children only for the sake of killing them. It was still hard to get that through our heads." Until they could glean further information, the sight of the Czech Jews raised a hope that the first group of deported Dembliners were also still alive.

"Among these Czech Jews were about twenty doctors. We made rooms for them to take care of the sick. There was little they could do, as we had no medicines."

Between October 15 and October 31, 1942, thirty deportations left the towns of central Poland for Treblinka. My father was on good terms with the Polish work inspector. My mother and sister were sent with other women to work on a farm.

On October 15, the remaining Demblin Jews in the ghetto were ordered to assemble in the marketplace within the hour. On October 28, the Germans came to round up the women and children at the farmhouse from which my mother escaped with my sister.

As Demblin had military installations in its railroad and airport, the German army requisitioned Jewish labour from the Lublin SS. These two labour camps were the only places left where Jews were still allowed to be alive.

My mother, having escaped the roundup for Treblinka, found her way into the railroad camp. My parents did this several times, escaping from one camp to let themselves in another. In five years they compressed several thousand years of Jewish history to its logical end, running toward an ever-receding vanishing point.

Meanwhile, my father had been sent to Sobieszin to sew uniforms for the Hitler Jugend, or "Youth." "You are a tailor?" said the astonished Poles who knew him.

"Yes," said my father, "I used to be a lumber merchant, now I am a tailor."

("It is good to have a trade," repeats my mother, who has none.)

However, my father did no sewing. There was food, but he could not eat. "We had it in our minds that we would not live." Two days after the deportation, they brought them back to the town. "There was not a Jew in the street, not a Jew on the road, not a Jew in a shop. They wanted to make it so that not a Jew should be left. It was, you see," my father pauses, "they wanted to make it –" he finds the word in German, "*Judenrein*, clean of Jews."

He was dropped in the railroad camp where my mother says she "met" him. "In the ghetto we worked for nothing, in the labour camps they gave us to eat. But so little, it was enough practically not to live. These were not death camps where they gassed people. But people died, because they did not have enough to eat and they were not good dressed and they were beaten. The younger ones survived. I was young."

"The SS ordered the German military to whom they lent us as labour to give us less food, as their aim was to *farnichten* the Jews. Once a boy took a bit of food from a house he was told to clean. They hung him and left his body for eight days to teach us a lesson." *Farnichten*, that sounded as soft as snuffing out a candle came from the German word *vernichten* – to annihilate.

One step ahead of the gas chambers. But they could only allow themselves one step. In July 1943, my father was doing heavy work on the railroad when my mother's brother, Feivel, who had gone to fetch a piece of wire, came running back breathless with the news. He had seen a locomotive and guards on the tracks. "They are taking out the Jewish people."

"I took his hand and I said to run."

My mother, on cleaning duty in the barracks, grabbed my sister and almost within sight of the guards, tore bleeding through the wires.

"It was July," says my father, "the corn was high." My parents had made a tryst that in case of liquidation, they would each try to escape and meet in the fields near the cottage of a Polish engineer to whom my father used to sell wood.

"The corn was high." Wheat, I think. "Corn" in Europe is wheat. During the day the tall grain hid them. My father was afraid to show himself to the Polish friend knowing that he would put his friend in danger. Finally, they asked him to hide their daughter, Toba. My mother changed her mind and took her back. "We can't stay here." All night they wandered in the fields, my mother and sister separate from the men. "The Germans used automatic weapons on any escaped Jew," my father said.

With the liquidation of the railroad camp, they came to the remaining labour camp near their town – the *flegehaus*, the airport. "Go and see if there are Jewish people there. There we are allowed to be alive a little longer." By day they stood at the gates of the camp to ask entrance and by night they hid in the corn.

"Go away from the fence," warned the work foreman, "because when night falls the German guards who check for escapees will shoot you." They had to account for their status. What excuse did they have for being alive?

My father thought of an excuse. He wrote a note to the commandant saying that on the day of the deportation, he had been away on an errand to this larger camp to arrange the weekly showers. "I had this *Bescheinigung* – this shower-arranging permit – I still had this piece of paper." The commandant told the *Arbeitmeister*, "Let them in."

"In the ghetto things were bad. In the labour camps things were worse. They sent us to Częstochowa, it was worse. They sent me to Buchenwald, it was …" My father thinks for a moment –

The worst, I want to say.

"When we got to Buchenwald, it was …" He pauses. The ellipse of time between our sentences has redeemed a word. "Worse," he says.

◆ ◆ ◆

When the Russians reached the Vistula in February 1944, the Germans sent the Jews in the Demblin camps farther west to Częstochowa. When, a year later, the Russians crossed the Vistula, he was sent all the way into western Germany, to Buchenwald. The next day, the Russians liberated the women and children.

My father had his initiation ahead of him: one and a half days in the wagons without knowing where they were going.

"They counted us," says my father. "Every night they called us out for the *Appell*, the roll call, and we stood in the cold and dark. As there were so many, 1,000 to a block, it took hours. Sometimes it took all night. Many, the older and weaker, fell over. Sometimes men on either side of a sick prisoner held him up until the SS man passed. It was anyways impossible to escape. They did this especially to keep us like dogs. But a dog is free. In the morning, there were corpses on the ground ..."

Once I have started to ask, he tells me, each day reconstructing the concentration-camp universe as if he cannot trust the listener, with events intervening, to have retained or believed it.

"They counted us."

"It's me, Dad," I say, dismayed, "don't you remember you told me?" But with the smallest ellipse of time, the same is not the same; it has survived the events in between, and has suffered a change.

"Let me tell you the rules and regulations. Let me tell you the coming in." Every day of our visit more and more German words surface: *Häftling* (prisoner), *eintlausung* (delousing).

One and a half days from Poland in the wagons without knowing the destination. Buchenwald within western Germany became a dumping ground for Jewish prisoners evacuated out of the way of rescue by the Russians advancing from the east.

"In Buchenwald there were people from all over," says my father. "Hungary, Poland, Czechoslovakia, France."

One thousand to a block. So that it took another day and a half waiting naked in the cold for the initiatory bath, the baptismal *eintlausung*. "Until then, in the labour camps, we wore what we had on our backs. They took away –" my father struggles to list all the things that were taken away, it is immense, and many did not survive the shock and disintegration of entering this world, "shoes, shirt, pants, belts. They cut the hair, not only on your head but everywhere. If you had a piece of paper with a name on it they took that away. They made us wash with lye that took away the skin. They took away –" my father grasps for the words. He is looking at his outstretched arm holding the imaginary piece of paper and looks at his wrist. "They took away my watch." It comes to him: "I had a watch." Every person has a watch.

"I fainted in the bath," he says as he turns to me. "Yes, I fainted and my friends hid and revived me so the Germans should not see."

There were captured French resistance officers who arrived in Buchenwald and, seeing the 35,000 men gathered in the *Appell Platz*, they said to each other that this must be where the Nazis interned madmen.

Within two weeks the French officers looked exactly the same.

◆ ◆ ◆

The next time we walk in the forest, my father tells me what each kind of wood was used for. "The pine made the houses of Polish villages. You know, in Poland not only houses but very old synagogues were sometimes made completely of wood. The birch made – you know what it made?" he says. "Matches! Yes, toothpicks! The oak was the finest quality wood. The first three or four metres, the round ends of the trunks went whole for the veneer on tables, chests, drawers; farther up, it made blocks for parquet floors. Higher than that, where the branches notched off, it made barrels for herring and for wine." I have never before heard him speak in such detail about trees and wood, although to me he is an expert on all humanly worked materials: the cut of a coat, the joins of furniture, the workmanship of a watch or a pair of shoes.

We were walking *im wald,* in the forest. In German, and of course, in Yiddish, *wald, vald,* means "forest." He has never needed to tell me this. Yiddish is my mother's tongue, which I retained to speak to her long after she would learn nothing new. With my father, I speak in English, not his language of ease but the language he carved out of necessity.

"In May 1939, a big wind – a tornado in Poland – put down some of the finest oak trees." I wondered whether these felled oaks made up his final shipment.

My father pursued a claim for his last shipment of wood for the rest of his life. Sixteen wagons of wood were taken off the tracks leading to Danzig and rerouted to Germany. There was no way to claim reparations for sixteen wagons of relatives. The wood seemed to represent everything that was taken from him: his brothers and sisters, his pre-war life, his identity, his place. Years of correspondence with lawyers and witnesses passed during which most of the witnesses eventually were gone. "You remember the people who welcomed us in Israel? They were the children of Mr. Eidel, a man I knew in Poland before the war." Mr. Eidel had been an importer-exporter from Warsaw, and the last living witness to my father's stolen shipment of wood.

"I am sorry to hear of your ill health," began a letter from the lawyer in Germany. The claim for the wood spanned thirty years, but was most active in the sixties, when my father fell sick.

"Will you write me a few words in English, Lizzie?" my father used to ask his high school daughter.

Was the wood taken from him as an anti-Jewish measure? Witnesses from 1939 testified that the distinction between Jewish and Aryan businesses had been mandatory and that Jewish businesses were to be destroyed. Moreover, it was well known that the lumber trade in Poland was transacted by Jews.

What was the quality of the stock, veneer or ordinary wood; was its circumference forty or forty-five centimetres? The Germans said inferior material would not have been sent to Germany.

"It was from Sobieszin and of such high quality that it was bought by an English furniture maker. That kind of wood could be used for furniture or," he hesitates, "airplanes. War materials." The shipment was supposed to travel to the free port Gdansk or Danzig, whence it would be shipped abroad to England. The dispute over the free port of Danzig triggered the first shots of World War II. "When it arrived in Dirschau, a railway station before Danzig, I received a cable from the station master saying the goods could not proceed 'due to technical difficulties.'"

He falls silent then says softly, "You know when that was? August 1939."

He blinks, and squeezes his eyes shut so tightly that one might think for a moment he has fallen asleep. But then he opens his eyes, and begins again. "The week that you were born ..." he continues. In that short gap, an aeon has passed; in a blink of his eyelids, my father has elided the years between 1939 and 1947, a blink-time in history.

We have come out of the woods and sat down in lounge chairs on the terrace. Behind us on this Swiss mountain the birds cheep in the woods, and below us the town and river spread out like an eighteenth-century etching with waves of mountains and, now and then in the distance, a cow. My father, in his tweed coat against the early spring chill, pauses to sniff "the good air." On Sunday afternoon, tourists and townspeople come up to take tea on the lookout terrace. I awaken in a garden chair to hear my father in conversation with a young American couple, perhaps on their honeymoon trip, from the Midwest. They are asking him about Germany; the husband will be stationed there.

"We were there during World War II," the young man says.

But this man couldn't have been born then, I think in my drowsiness, *he must mean "we Americans."* I try it out. We Americans who in 1939 turned the refugee ship the *St. Louis* back to Germany? We Canadians who refused to let them in because "none would still be too many"?

The only time my father ever said the word *we* with confidence in an unquestioned commonality was when he spoke of "we *Häftlings*" in Buchenwald. "They treated us like dogs. We stood all night. A dog was free, but we, we were not free."

The young couple is spooning a dessert with whipped cream, in the posture of people being entertained.

"Germany has a wonderful climate, so bracing," I hear my father say. I open my eyes to look at him.

"Beautiful forests," he says.

Chapter Four

THE FOREST OF BEECH TREES

———

Mountains were healthy? Then why stay in the city when we could go to the mountains? "Don't take me to a wilderness," was my father's one request. From Zurich we took the train, boat, and funicular to the village of Appenzell.

There was not a soul besides us on the glassed-in funicular. Once we got on it, the windows automatically sealed shut and we began to rise vertically along a cable. My father looked underneath us at the receding water, and forward at the oncoming slab of rock. My mother had slapped us on this airless Schreckhorn, which a doctor could reach only by mountain goat. How could my father breathe when I couldn't?

There was nobody in the village. We were the only people in the restaurant. It was too early, or too late, in the season, which is a good time to visit only the Mediterranean. An immaculate autobahn-like road cut a swathe through the few houses. The happy *fröhlich* mountains were holding the air prisoner; not a breeze to flutter a leaf, nothing bent, not a blade of grass.

"Just tell me when, and I'll get you out of here." In my mind I am already rewinding our journey. These suffocating mountains are not *haym*, at all.

Forewarned of how much the present is made up of the past, I took up a position in the future. I wanted to make, however belated, some bits of a past that the future would also include. The tense I lived in with my father was the future perfect: the perfect café, the perfect mountain.

With a tact absent from my mother, he did not say he would rather I paid some attention to my own future.

I want my father to be where he feels well. Three kilometres east or west, north or south, a fingermark away on a map can make all the difference. My father is less drastic.

"We will see how it is tomorrow."

The next morning, I climbed up to see where the road blitzed to the horizon. On my way back down, I saw my father, a man alone sitting at a table and chair on the edge of an immaculate highway. If not for this or that accident, he wouldn't be here. Because the past made me take up a position in the future, I already missed my father. He so much might not have been that I was apprehensive that very soon again, any moment, he might not be. Between the mountains we were cut off from any movement of air. Not a leaf or blade of grass stirred. Looking down, I saw the huge airless chamber of the outdoors press in on my father. The still air branded a frown on his forehead, and squeezed his heart.

I packed our bags and we reversed the journey.

◆ ◆ ◆

If northern landscapes meant home, home was the place we had to leave.

I took my father south across the Alps to a resort on the shores of Lake Maggiore, in Italian Switzerland, and found this southern Europe also familiar. Already lush with flowers, we could have been on the Mediterranean with its shorter plane and olive trees scaled as if to classical civilization's human proportions, if not for the snowy peaks rising vertiginously behind. "This is the most beautiful place I have ever seen," said my father. The mist rose from the lake like a sea in humid puffs, breathing into the nerves a Riviera languor. Because many landscapes had touched my father, and none of them alone summed him up, I found bits of his world scattered everywhere. When I took his picture against a Visconti wall, it seemed the character in his face found its natural setting among the mellowed princely stones.

We walked along the broad lakefront with its cafés and plane trees. I chose postcards. He chose postcards also. I swam in the rain and he waved at me, without warning me I would catch pneumonia.

"Do you want to take a boat ride on the lake, Daddy?" Although my father grew to love the ocean most of all, this stopped short of sailing vessels. Who ever went on a boat except to emigrate?

I took a picture of him in a jaunty cap, scowling in the rain when I coaxed him into a boat tour of the Borromean Islands. Boats were not pleasure cruisers for my family. Whatever fuelled the ship to Canada, Dramamine got my mother and sister through the Atlantic crossing. I did not see them for a week while they were seasick in their cabins. Apparently, somebody had put us in first class. I kept my father company, promenading up and down the deck, and sitting with him, a happy five-year-old, at the dinner table.

We sipped cappuccino in Stresa, the first Italian town when the boat crossed a liquid border. "On the boat to Canada, do you remember?" he said. "You were afraid you would not have a birthday because we were *between* places."

On the lake the ferry boat gently swayed past the rust-coloured and lush green reflections of Renaissance villas in the water. I never dreamed I would visit the poets' Italian Lake District with my father.

We got off the boat to visit the two islands, Isola Madre and Isola Bella, which seemed to have exchanged each other's names.

I took a picture of my father under an umbrella pointing at the purple flowering trees on Isola Madre. It should have been called Isola Bella, Beautiful Island. Isola Bella itself had been appropriated by eighteenth-century aristocracy. Following tourists through the rococo palace attended by bewigged mannequin footmen, my father tugged at my elbow. "Meanwhile, the ordinary people who lived at that time were *starving*."

The best picture was of him in an Argentinian restaurant in Locarno. He is leaning toward me over the table, his eyes twinkling. I took a picture of him on a cobbled street with mountains rising above. In the middle of the square where four streets meet, looking at home among the Renaissance stones, he takes out one of those *kvitls* and unclips his pen from his jacket pocket.

"What are you writing?" I see a wavy *L* then an *O*. *L-o-c-a-r-n-o*. He is writing down the name of the place. "Because I will forget."

We have been in Italy before, in the port city of Genoa, he says. We have even been in Marseilles. When we left Poland we took the train across Europe with our papers in his briefcase, which when wrapped in a coat, doubled as a pillow under my head. In Genoa, we were waiting in a train compartment and my father was late. I remembered my mother's rising worry, the whistle blowing, the crowds milling. His briefcase was under my head, but where was he?

On the return trip through the Alps, we have the train compartment to ourselves. "How do they make a living in the winter?" asks my father looking out the window at the snug mountain villages. My father is wearing his yellow pullover. We eat the sandwiches I have made with the fresh Italian cheese that reminds him of Poland. I take pictures of his cracked grin while he tells me the story of my fortunate birth.

If to my mother I represented *shaynkeit* (beauty), to my father, I brought good fortune. The week that I was born, he tells me, he transacted the luckiest stroke of his career.

"Wait, how did you get back to Poland from Buchenwald?"

"We jumped on trains returning to Russia. Every country in Europe made provisions to bring back their surviving prisoners except Poland. "It was me and the Gradmanns together. Jump!" my father said as he jumped on a train. Gradmann's son tried and could not make the jump. My father jumped back off. "You do this for us?" Gradmann said.

He returned to Demblin in search of his wife and child. He found all the survivors huddled in one house for protection. "The Germans shot Jews on orders," my father said, "the Poles shot Jews on their own initiative."

My parents went with others in the house to the nearest big city, Lodz. "There we started a new life," my father said.

I have been so protected by the happy myth of my birth that it is not till I am middle-aged that I learn Lodz had a ghetto second in size only to Warsaw. This is where I was born.

In the week that I was born, my father continues, he heard that a platform of scarce wool cloth was on sale by a government official.

"Lodz, you know, in woollens used to be like Manchester." He launched a hectic search through town for capital, asking this one and that one. "Meet me in front of the bank on the main street at noon," he asked and raced off.

"What's the rush? Wait, Srulec," they said.

"I don't have time to wait," he said.

So after wood, there was cloth. No, before the cloth there was another venture. "You mean the herring," says my father. With private grocery stores closing, there was a lack of herring in central Poland. A Baltic country like Poland without herring is like a Mediterranean country without olives. He rented a truck and ran it to the once-again-Polish port of Gdynia to pick up a catch of fish. The herring venture was based on the Poles assuming he was a Polack. "Oh, yes, and I took an airplane for the first time. There were no seats, only chairs." For the money to rent the truck, he asked a friend who had hidden some in his mattress. The friend listened to my father, astonished less at the idea than at my father's initiative in conceiving it.

"If you think so, Srulec."

"And they came and they came and they came." My father waves at the incoming tide of people who showed up at the last minute at the bank to invest in the cloth. "When I saw the cloth – white, soft *shtikelech* – it was of better quality than I expected." We go under a tunnel, and my father continues to speak in the train's rattling darkness.

"I had no place to put it so I brought it home. It took up the whole hallway and the vestibule." We have come out of the tunnel on the other side of the Gotthard Pass and as he speaks, I see first one, then two …

"There was so much of it and it was so soft …"

"Look, Daddy, snow!" White feathers thick as whirling cotton fly in through the window.

"… that sometimes you fell asleep on bolts of cloth."

A gift, an effulgence so abundant that flake by flake it transformed the world.

"People came to buy it and carried it away in bags. They had to walk on their tiptoes," my father says with a chuckle. "If they said a word, your mother scolded them. Couldn't they see the child was sleeping?"

As the wind blows the snow in through the window, he unconsciously folds his coat in the space behind his back. We have come into northern Europe.

My father the herring-mover and forest-runner is the same man who, when sent on a carpentry errand outside Częstochowa, traded a coin for half a loaf of bread and tried to smuggle it in to his wife and daughter. "I put it between my stomach and pants." On the return, he was searched. "Fifty lashes!" They told him to lower his pants. Two Ukrainians concurrently lashed his spine with lead-tipped whips over the kidneys where it hurts the most. Then he was left lying unconscious in the snow.

"In June of the year you were born – you don't remember? – I took you, your sister, and your mother to Karpacz, where the climate is so good people go undressed in the snow to get a tan. Two years after the war my family was in the best resorts." He rented the most comfortable suite, the one reserved for government functionaries. On the balcony overlooking the mountains, my father was smoking a cigarette and fell into conversation with a Pole. They were both leaning over the balcony side by side; the Pole gave my father a complicit look straight in the eye.

"It's much nicer here now, isn't it? Before the war there were too many Jews."

"How did we get out of Poland after the war?" I ask. "As a Communist country, didn't it refuse to let people out?"

"Poland wasn't letting anyone out, but with the creation of the state of Israel in 1948 the other countries put pressure on Poland to allow some Jews to go." We went on a dilapidated World War I freighter with bunk beds. "The Jews had a boat!" my father said.

"Why didn't we stay in Israel?" I asked, mostly on behalf of my sister who bloomed in the desert.

"At the time there was no way to make a living," he said. He fell like a fly in the Middle Eastern heat. He carried me on his shoulders up the hill – the "tel" – to a lone white apartment building. My mother, longing for a green onion, broke down and asked me to pick one from a neighbour's plot. My father said: "I told a friend in Israel we had a visa to go to Canada. He shook his head and said, 'Oh, there you will have all the cold you can stand.'"

◆ ◆ ◆

"Lusia I mean Lizzie," my father will call me long distance with a question. "I was worried that you might not have enough." Enough what? Enough food, enough shoes, a coat, boots for the snow. He will call me, I will be in yet some other place, and he will ask out of the blue, "Is your watch still working? I dreamed that you are again going around without a watch."

I have often stayed glued to a series of three photographs taken in 1946. The photographs are different angles of guests around a banquet table brilliant with glass, fruit, and spirits. The main photo features this magnificent table spread lengthwise to the people who have stood up and grouped themselves at one end. The other two pictures are close-ups of this group where my parents can be found. Among the women with the big shoulders and big hair of the 1940s, I find my mother, narrow-shouldered in a white blouse, her oval face bare, her black hair pulled back in a bun. My father, young and gaunt, is sitting with a child on his lap whose cadaverous face peering over the table I barely recognize as my sister. "After, soon after, you were not born yet."

Looking at my own childhood photos a year later you would never guess anything at all had happened just before: My mother in an embroidered Carpathian jacket with a walking stick. My mother, father, and sister pushing a baby carriage on a street topped by mountains. My mother with me in her lap and my sister beside us in a horse-drawn sleigh. It was my father who brushed my hair and tied a ribbon in it, because my mother did not have the patience. It has taken my lifetime to catch up with those photos – and for the effects of the war to catch up with my parents.

My lifespan measures the time "since," the time of the telling.

When I was twenty, my father turned his head to the wall. Only when my hair begins to turn grey do I learn, in an aside, that my father's family was among the population marched from the neighbouring town, Ryki, through Demblin to the train. "I am alone, you see. I am the only one who survived."

Back on the *shpitz* in Zurich the trees rustle in full foliage, releasing flocks of birds into the sky. I don't even know how many there were in my father's family, let alone their names. I think perhaps because my mother takes up all the room, she never gave him a chance to talk.

Below us from the Hotel Waldberg spreads the river and the city with waves of mountains rising behind. Around us, Sunday strollers push baby carriages, young and elderly couples have come up to take the air. We could be on Mont Royal in Montreal where my mother dragged me off the streets as a kid to get some *luft* in the summer; where my parents still go on Sundays, although my mother sighs that now you no longer could see a single Jew.

My father is in his withdrawn mood, absent, silent. If a stranger came by, he would light up and talk. Doves are flying through the air in front of us, mating and cooing when I ask him, "How many sisters and brothers did you have?"

"Five," he says with emphasis. "They took them to Sobibor and they gassed them, I don't want to talk about it!"

He got up and left the park bench.

On May 7, 1942, the Jews of Ryki were marched through the forest to the Demblin train station. Among them were his brother Moishe, his sisters, and their families. The Ryki Jews, whipped and beaten, were marched four abreast holding their children. On either side, German guards fired at old people. They ordered the Jews to run and at the same time they ordered them to sing.

◆ ◆ ◆

My mother spits out the war; my father carries it silently in his body that does not sleep. I measure by my lifespan the history of the telling. At first, I was told only the end of the war, because you tell a child a happy ending. I realize he was not trying to tell me a fairy tale; this is what stuck together for a coherent telling. The boundary of a story is how much the mind can take at one time.

I don't remember when my father started to tell me about his liberation from Buchenwald. He told it to me over and over as Jews tell the same story every year at Passover. In every generation we are commanded to tell the story of the exodus from slavery. The Telling. Haggadah. Passover is a ritual of transmission, in which the children ask questions and the adults take all night to answer. Although I am the youngest and the only one of the family who was born after the war, when he told me this story I asked no questions. On the contrary,

I was in unbearable suspense. "Hurry up and get to the end of the story," I tugged at his hand, "so that you can come out alive."

Unlike Passover, we cannot tell this story in unison. The community is gone and so almost are the survivors. It has to be told singly, one by one. Each story is different and it is different each time it is told. Somehow my father's body always stored up a detail to be revealed at some other time, in some other place. Still each time his historical voice recounted the larger events that he might not have known at the time.

"When the Russians massed on the Vistula," he says as his fingertip shakily traces the river that divides Poland, "they moved us to Częstochowa," his finger moves west. The Russians massed on the river in July 1944 and they waited. I didn't realize until much later how accurate my father was. If they had crossed the river then instead of the following January, my parents might have been spared the Nazis' end-stage deportations west to Częstochowa and Buchenwald

Every time my father gets to this point in the story, the Germans whipping along their half-dead prisoners to the disadvantage of their own retreat, his voice rises with amazement. "This is where I fit in the madness." This is his story. History. Who invented a world story that goes in a straight line and will one day have a happy ending?

"When the Russians crossed the Vistula, they sent me to Buchenwald." His finger moves all the way west across the Polish border into Germany. "When the Americans crossed the Rhine, the Germans started – again! – to move us. They were *squeezed* between the Russians and the Americans." His finger moves east. The approach of the enemy only intensified the Germans' zeal to complete their mission. My father was nearly killed the last day of the war.

"*Juden eintritten!*" Hearing this demand for only the Jews to file into the *Platz*, says my father, "I knew this could mean nothing good." For months, the approach of the Allies triggered orders for last-minute wholesale slaughters. I wasn't the only person who gathered information slowly over a long time as my father added new details. The world did also. Fifteen years later, I learned that Himmler had given the order that no Jewish prisoners were to fall into the hands of the Allies.

"*Juden eintritten!*" I don't know how much my father sensed, but when the prisoners were ordered out for another transport, he judged that he would be too weak to survive it.

All through the war, they had divided sick from healthy. Today, the sick were to remain behind. All through the war, it had meant immediate death to fall among the sick; nevertheless, that day he jumped into the group of sick prisoners. This is when he looked around for my mother's brother, Feivel, and did not see him. Once they were disbanded, he hid under a bunk. The bunks were raised on pieces of wood. "I will stay here either until I die," my father hesitates for barely a blink-time, "or until they find me and kill me." A half day passed during which he did not move. From under the bunk he heard what sounded like crashes of thunder – artillery fire. It went on for hours. Then suddenly there was quiet. That afternoon, the Americans liberated the camp. The prisoners who had gone in the truck had all been taken out and shot. Some of them, like my grandfather, were marched into a river. Meanwhile, forty boxcars packed with men from Buchenwald rolled slowly on broken rail lines for three weeks before showing up in Dachau. When the boxcars were opened, the floor was half a metre deep in 50,000 corpses.

When we finally get up from the park bench and we put one foot in front of the other, he answers an implicit question. "It was an *accident* that I survived. It was not normal." My father, who early on refused to wait in line for a piece of bread and to sew for the Hitler Jugend, is the same man who offered himself as a carpenter and, judging his own vital signs, threw his swollen straw of a body under a bunk to die.

Years pass before he adds the detail that tells what that judgment cost him. "I raised my head and I did not see Feivel. I was alone."

More years pass before he adds another detail that suddenly makes the choice unbearable. "I knew that by hiding I would miss my day's ration of bread."

◆ ◆ ◆

My father was not well at the end of the war and he is not well now telling about it. A few days before his plane leaves, he complains of chest pains. I sit on the clean grass and wait while he rests.

He comes out with his perplexed frown on. He laughs at himself, oh no, it's nothing. "I thought I recharged my shaver in Israel. Maybe it was the wrong current. I will ask at the desk for a battery." In the afternoon, he walks across the lawn of the Hotel Waldberg toward me. All the lines and curves that crack into a grin are creased into a frown. "It doesn't work." He lifts his shoulders. The next day, he tries to puzzle out the enigma of the shaver once more. "I knew I was supposed to recharge the current in Israel. Maybe I forgot." I look closely at his face, at stubble barely visible to me: he is unshaven. "I will go into Zurich," I say, "and get you one of those shavers you can use and throw away. How is that?"

Even to mimic habits of grooming oneself conjured a mirage of autonomy, I had read somewhere. "I will go and buy a shaver and, yes, I will confirm your flight." I thought we could spend the morning together and I would go in the afternoon while he took a nap. But I find him in the lobby telephone booth. He can't get through to the airline and I can't drag him away from the telephone. He will be tense until he has done the correct thing. Our lives are a holding pattern of allaying nerves for a calm that never comes. In that case, it becomes all the more important to grab the smallest fraction of a moment now. In town, I confirm the flight and ask the Swissair office to provide oxygen and whatever a person with a weak heart needs to travel. I do everything above and beyond the rules. They want a doctor's order.

"I don't need a doctor, I want to go home," he says. Montreal. "It's not my heart, it's my nerves." He is catching up with his body's trick of twenty years ago. Only now it can be both. I call the internist suggested by the hotelier.

The doctor arrives, a tall dark-haired man who takes such long strides I run to keep up with him to my father's room while telling him his story. "Show me your medications," he says to my father. My father brings out the bag of pills. The doctor's jaw drops. "Lithium *and* an antidepressant?"

At supper I deposit a *Teller* (plate) of overpriced, overcooked vegetables from the hotel cafeteria on our table. My father looks at the wilted cabbage sceptically. "In Montreal you can get a whole meal for a quarter of the price." From a table across the terrace the doctor waves and comes to sit with us. My father thanks him for the nitroglycerine chest plasters: "They have the same in Canada, but not so good." My father also pays compliments to Swiss watches, Swiss chocolate, Swiss cheese, Swiss …

"He didn't feel well in that village. Perhaps the air was too thin?"

"Not really," says the doctor. "More likely it was the change of climate. Oh yes, I got your message and called the airline," he catches my eye and laughs. "And I told them the *whole* story."

"He is a nice man," I say, looking out my father's window.

My father perks up. "I don't think he is married, Lizzie. I have seen him eat dinner here alone before."

Later, my father calls me from Montreal to say he had a wonderful flight home. He didn't understand it, the entire plane was full, yet he could stretch out and rest because his row of seats was entirely empty.

The last day together. He was too weak to walk in the forest so we sat down on a bench near it. He peers into the woods with a frown as I ask him to tell me more.

No, he does not think so much of his skill with trees.

"You tried to follow the tree's balance for as high as it could go. Where one side was banged or bent by the wind, there you cut the next length. It took someone who knew something about it." He shrugs.

The bench we are sitting on leans against an old and beautiful beech tree.

This beech tree is marked out for identity, like a similar one in Buchenwald. When the forests were bulldozed to build the camp in the early thirties, there was one tree that was spared and fenced around. It was known as Goethe's tree. Legend had it that the eighteenth-century German writer, the national poet emblematic of the Enlightenment, once took his rest under its branches on a walk through this countryside, and deemed the view the epitome of civilization. "Here one feels great and free." The part of the tree where the main trunk ends at the big branches was discarded by lumber mills; on a human being, this would be the generative crotch.

While other trees were razed to build prisoners' barracks, all during the war Goethe's tree stood as men fell in the *Appell Platz*. Like that other tree, this tree that we sit under until my father's heart pain subsides also has an identity. Around its trunk I see a glinting medallion that commemorates its age: a name that I suppose means "beech tree," and the date. Although I am usually quick to recognize the family ties between words, I still don't get it. The translation comes to me syllable by unbidden syllable, quarried out of my own resistance to the territory. Yet for as long as I have known that *wald* means "forest," for so long have I also known the name Buchenwald. "Beech forest."

At night, I rescue us from the austere choice of *Salatenteller* (cold salad plates) at the hotel cafeteria. After nightfall, we are in effect trapped on that hill. I call a taxi to take us to a restaurant with wine and candles and tablecloths set with silver.

When I come out of the restaurant bathroom and head back to our table (there are actually two identical dining rooms) so that, when I round the corner, my father is not where he should be sitting. Gone, vanished, lost – until, in what takes eons, I learn to turn the other way, with the shock that I am traversing future time and space; that this is how it was; that this is how it will be; that I will look for him everywhere, from so far away, so many miles, out of millions and millions of people; they came and they came and they came from all over Europe, so that if he had made himself a carpenter, and not shared his bread, it would have sufficed; if he had shared his bread and not jumped among the sick, it would have sufficed: if he had jumped but eaten the chocolate, if he had abstained but not jumped off the train when the Gradmanns couldn't. But since he has done all this and more, he has gotten us out of Poland and started over a fourth time again in Canada. He made us as safe as he could, but still it didn't suffice; he fell ill of the whole story, his eyes emptying out many times my mother's town of Demblin, and his own family's neighbouring town Ryki of his brothers and sisters, the barracks outside the gates of Częstochowa where the children were kept, the population many times over of his block in Buchenwald, of the wagons filled with healthy ones. And watched his daughter, whom they performed miracles to save, fall ill like himself. Because he has done all this, it can only be he – who? – the expressive Slav/Jew out of whose eyes stream numberless sparks of life so that I will recognize him: my father. For whom all this did not suffice but that he should gather in his swollen body where they lay twig-angled as many as he could, his brothers and sisters anonymous as trees, and carved out of Buchenwald a forest of beech trees.

Chapter Five

IMMIGRANTS

A King has the gift of foretelling the future of his kingdom from his dreams. They inform him especially as to next year's crops. One year he foresees something very strange. "Whoever eats next year's produce will go crazy," the King said. His adviser said, "Let's not eat next year's produce, we will eat last year's." "What good is that?" said the King. "Everyone else will eat it, and they will think it is we who are crazy, not they. No, let's eat what everyone else eats, with the difference that at least we will know we are crazy."
A Chasidic story from the Talmud

In 1980, twenty-five years after we arrived in Canada, I was living in the same Montreal neighbourhood where we lived then, among the newest wave of immigrants and the Chasidim who had never left. Since the turn of the century, each wave of Jewish settlers had come off the boat to these streets within sight of the mountain on which was planted a cross. Sandwiched between the French and English "solitudes," the immigrant Jewish neighbourhood first became known to French Montrealers through its wood-fired bagels and its smoked brisket. Cured according to recipes that had preserved meat through the long Lithuanian winters, hot sliced brisket fuelled garment workers through the long Canadian winters. The affinity between the French Canadians and Jewish immigrants lay not only in their taste for food but also in their demeaned mother tongue.

So indigenous to Montreal did smoked meat become that an eventual separatist premier of Quebec would be photographed chomping on it *haymishly* at Schwartz's, while making sure that the unheard-of French translation, *viande fumée*, took up more space on the sign than "smoked meat."

Where the mountain plateaued into several city blocks of Fletcher's Field, on Sunday afternoons in the fifties my father would exchange news with other *greener* (greenhorns). After the concentration camps were opened to public view and a wartime-stimulated economy demanded skilled workers, Canada opened its doors to the remnant of refugees it had closed them to during the war. This is how Montreal became home to the greatest number of concentration-camp survivors in North America. This is how Montreal became a shard of Demblin.

In the summer of 1980, I sublet a flat in our old neighbourhood from a *heeger* (a Jew born "here") who was studying in Europe. It was my American friend Sally who found me this interim lodging on Park Avenue, where my mother and I would walk to meet my father coming home from work at Pascal's Hardware store. To move across Park Avenue used to be literally the first step up. When Mordecai Richler, the chronicler of these streets, returned to Montreal, he moved into the Anglo enclave on the other side of the mountain, Westmount. Now Leonard Cohen, who had a privileged childhood, *he* could live here. But Sally, with no such baggage, had bought a house across from my elementary school and was raising her family there. "The Plateau," with its picturesque outdoor staircases deadly in winter, was becoming, as the tourist ads would tell you, "the heart of Montreal."

The flat was right above a Greek bakery in front and a yeshiva in the back. The heat rising from the twenty-four-hour bagel factory on the side nearly knocked me out. Catching a dozen of these lean, chewy bagels as they tumbled out of the oven (six poppyseed, six sesame, boiled and baked to a resilience that hardened on the third day into a Jewish infant's teething ring) had become as *de rigueur* as climbing up to St. Joseph's Oratory to catch a glimpse of Brother André's pickled heart. We were part of the last wave of Jewish immigrants to this neighbourhood, most of whom were moving away even as we arrived; only the palette of Chasidic sects, including remnants of the rare eighteenth-century Satmar, stayed put. Men in fur hats pulled bloodless little boys across the street to *shul*.

In winter, my mother used to pull me on a sled across the street to Fairmount School. Public schools in Montreal were either English-speaking and Protestant or French-speaking and Catholic. Whether we learned English or French was our parents' last worry. But Catholic schools did not allow Jews, and Protestant schools tolerated them, so my classroom of Holocaust survivors' children grew up belting out "Onward, Christian Soldiers."

Although we learned English in school and brought it home to our parents, the *heeger* could tell us by our accent. An accent apparently specific to that Montreal generation, it was marked by our immigrant's conscientious enunciation: "I was walk*ing*," we said, instead of the casual American, "I was walk*in'*."

Meanwhile, our parents stumbled upon the assumption that immigrants who came to the New World were by definition backward. Only their Old World delicacy kept them from letting on how much in order to fit in, they had to backpedal to shibboleths they had outgrown in their youth.

As Jewish communities had always lived on the sufferance of the larger culture, it was expected that each new wave of Old World immigrants embarrassed the assimilated wave before them. The newest immigrants were embarrassing by virtue of the very enormity of what they had suffered.

Not just my mother but all immigrant groups seemed to inhabit their history longer in Canada, perhaps because there was less of a dominant culture to assimilate *into*. When, in 1947, Prime Minister William Lyon Mackenzie King said he was allowing refugees in on condition that they not change the character of the nation, it begged the question, "*What* character?"

With all due respect to Prime Minister King, only Holocaust survivors could truly appreciate Canada. Every Canadian knows that the outstanding Canadian character trait is that we don't have any. We don't *have* an over-arching identity. To these Jewish refugees, the absence of a prescribed national type was the greatest gift. The Holocaust they had survived had been grounded in the most extreme nationalist crusade. They did not miss parades or flag-waving. Any burgeoning nationalism distinguished itself by pointing its finger first at the Jews as the obvious outsiders. Decades later the larger Canadian diffidence would attenuate the raising of a Québécois coming-of-age pure laine (pure wool) ethnic standard on which we could hardly avoid being a blemish.

Nothing made me feel safer than the ice cap that stretched to the North Pole. To the south, we had a big friendly neighbour who thankfully ignored our existence. When they *did* notice us, it was to remark from the point of view of their comparatively dog-eat-dog society, that Canadians were "nice."

In this I am speaking of myself, of course, because my parents did not have ordinary fears. They had not flinched at the five angry Semitic countries surrounding Israel, nor did they lose sleep over a nuclear holocaust in which everyone would die, unselected.

Our family not only suffered the external pressures of immigration but was also torn by internal reproaches. On our way to Canada, the family stalled in Paris for six months, perhaps casting about for a means to stay in Europe while "eating up our funds," as my father put it. A Canadian embassy official in Paris remarked to my father that we seemed reluctant to emigrate. My mother's reluctance to leave Europe once put us on a train to Frankfurt, Germany, where my parents had friends. Once we crossed the border into Germany, my sister was frightened of seeing former SS men. I was frightened by the sight of my first Santa Claus. "Have you gone crazy?" my father yelled at my mother.

In March 1953, we boarded the SS *Homeland* in Le Havre bound for Canada. My mother and sister were violently sick during the entire crossing. We landed in Halifax on March 15, three days short of my sixth birthday and nine days short of our visa expiration. The ground was too frozen to kiss.

Our first years in Canada were not so good; the worst, according to my mother. My father did not have a trade. He had a friend from the *lager*, Mr. Taichman, who sat him down at a sewing machine, but "I had no talent for it."

Anxiety mounted monthly around my sister's high school fee. They had put her back a grade in order for her to learn English; within several months they promoted her by two grades. My sixteen-year-old sister was in danger of joining the proletariat that she championed.

"The nerve of the Stajnbergova saying she should quit school and go to work in a factory!" my mother said. "If they had more students like her, they wouldn't be so panicked by the Sputnik."

My father woke up every morning coughing until he retched. It was his chore to shovel heating coal up from the cellar. One day he went down and did not come up again. My mother found him in a faint at the bottom of the stairs, his body spelling out his loss of self as it did once before in the bath at Buchenwald.

Fortunately for my sister, her father was an entrepreneur. He was hardworking, self-reliant – all the virtues of the Protestant work ethic – without any sense of these being virtues in themselves. They were all by-products of something else.

In the New World, he became the oldest stereotype of the Old World Jew: a *klapper*, a "knocker" on doors. He was a peddler and worked twice as hard, but nobody told him what to do.

◆ ◆ ◆

One day, I came in while my parents were on their hands and knees scrubbing the entry where the galoshes and empty milk bottles were lined up on the step. While the North American generation of the 1930s may have been marked by the Depression with a sense of frugality, my parents were marked by the concentration camps with a sense that willed self-deprivation was a form of blasphemy. It occurred to my eight-year-old brain that I could trade in the milk bottle for a nickel's worth of candy and not ask my parents for money. Proud of my acumen I asked my mother for the milk bottle and told her why. She looked up from scrubbing the floor on all fours and laughed. She laughed so hard she sat down in the soapy water. In the ghetto, children used to barter bits of string or bottles for food. That was my first and last financial coup.

For my friends who did not grow up there, these streets were bustling, and colourful. Full of life.

When I was about eight or nine, I was walking home from school with friends and saw, from a block away, a commotion in our part of the street. Coming closer, I saw a crowd of children gathered outside our window, peering through the pulled-back curtains on the ground floor under the steps. My heart pounding, I guessed at the attraction. They were watching my family having a fight. I could hear my mother's piercing soprano. She had in her hands my sister's fine blond hair and was pulling it. My mother's screeches rent the air. "I jumped out the window! I tore through the wires! I saved you! I saved you!"

My sister rarely came home in those years. Leaving Israel had been another cruel sundering forced on her. When we arrived in Israel, she was twelve, played Chopin and Bach, read poetry and *Huckleberry Finn* in Polish, and had named her baby sister Elzbieta after a Polish queen, fortunately not Yadwiga. Within the less than twenty months that we were in Israel, she bloomed like a desert flower. She went from playing Chopin on the piano to playing Yemenite folk tunes on a wooden recorder, learned Israeli folk dancing, and exchanged Polish for Hebrew. The newborn state of Israel could have been created for her: a Holocaust survivor young enough to develop as a free Jew in the Promised Land. It had been more of a broken promise since Britain had reneged on its League of Nations–backed 1917 Balfour Declaration to secure a Jewish homeland and then prevented boats of desperate Jews from reaching it during the Second World War.

Difficult as the struggle was, with no peace in sight, for the young victims of the Nazi genocide there could be no greater contrast than the self-rebuilding demanded by the rebirth of their homeland. Their rebirth was its rebirth. Long before the Holocaust, the Zionist project had been to make over the Jewish image created by the restrictions forced on them as despised foreigners. Banned from owning land in much of Europe, Jews had not been farmers or soldiers since the last time they inhabited their homeland. The Jews were the indigenous people forced off this land and every other. The kibbutzim, those communes of ex-ghetto Jews who tilled and defended the land, lived in conditions of gender and economic equality that made them a light unto the liberation of nations everywhere. The social ideals my sister had been taught as theory in Communist Poland were a way of life here.

Dropping her Polish nickname Lusia, my sister retrieved her Yiddish name Toba, or "dove," and asked to be called by its Hebrew translation: Yonah. My parents called her a *sabra*, the cactus likened to a native Israeli, because it is prickly on the outside but sweet on the inside – only to be torn out by the roots, at the age of fifteen, to go to

Canada. "We shlepped her from country to country!" my mother said, guilt stricken.

In her short life, my sister had recapitulated modern Jewish history. Born into the Holocaust, she wore a yellow-and-black Jewish star sewn onto her back. In a reversal of the diaspora, she returned to Israel as a schoolgirl to plant a blue Jewish star in its native soil for the first time in two thousand years. And now she found herself in *galut-golus* exile again. When we arrived in Canada, she devoted herself to Hashomer Hatzair, whose Montreal *bayit*, or house, became her second home.

One afternoon, my sister's high school physics class was cancelled for an all-girl counselling session. "They're teaching us how to *trap* boys," she snorted. Her waist-long Polish braids had been cut off, and the resulting 1950s haircut was a disaster.

She came home to find her kid sister in front of the landlady's TV set, watching Dale Evans and Roy Rogers singing "Happy Trails" on their horses.

"Do you think it was fair for the white man to take advantage of the Indians?" she demanded. "How would *you* like it?"

"Not one bit," I said.

My sister was my ultimate intellectual arbiter. No elementary or high school teacher held a match to her. Although I watched television and danced to rock 'n' roll, I absorbed enough of the capitalist critique from her to give my grade-five class a lecture on the value of labour. My sister taught me according to the theory by which she was taught: you are never too young to learn anything if it is presented according to your capacities. If I was considered precocious, it was because I read Russian literature from her bookshelves a decade ahead. In return, she thought I was funny. I made her giggle just by speaking Yiddish.

Whether comic or embarrassing, the mother tongue was both. Mother-bound, kitchen-bound, ghetto-bound – the hybrid dialect of our expulsion was to her a lower form of discourse. Yiddish was the mother tongue par excellence; the linguistic mitochondria spoken by everyone but ineluctably passed on by the mother. Hebrew was the language of the Book that kept male Jews literate through the ages.

It seemed natural that I, who was never let out of my mother's sight, spoke nothing but Yiddish and my sister learned to speak all languages on our passage but that. At first my sister was an accomplished

Polish schoolgirl; in Israel she learned Hebrew, the revived language of our pride. In those early years of Israel's hard won existence, with thousands of victims pouring in from displaced persons camps, the intention was to wipe away the ghetto stain.

That's why while I could hear Yiddish under cover of American English, the last place I expected to hear a Yiddish tone was in ancient Hebrew. *If I am not for myself, who will be for me? And if I am only for myself, what am I? And if not now, when?* We sounded just the same before the stain.

As I swallowed Yiddish whole from my mother without ever learning to read it, and as I heard it mostly from her, she defined it for me. I didn't know whether anyone else, for example, had ever compared a face to a chamber pot.

When I made my sister laugh, I didn't know how funny I was being. How could Yiddish not be ironic, just from its use of ancient Hebrew words for everyday purposes – *raboine shel oylem,* king of the universe, what a fuss …

I knew only that Yiddish spoiled me for the constraints of literal English. In Yiddish you could say somebody was a donkey or a saint without being asked to produce a tail or canonization papers. The Hebraic words for "sin" and "hell" were only used to exaggerate things they really weren't. "Open the window; it's a *gehennom* in here." A Yiddish command like "Enjoy" that suddenly accompanied every plate of food, frightened nobody. "Be well." It's not the word that's Yiddish, it's the syntax. Yiddish commands presupposed intimacy and even affection and in no way resembled the root German-language marching orders.

I spoke Yiddish without thinking I knew any Hebrew. But scores of my parents' Yiddish words were Hebrew – pronounced and accented in the Ashkenazi manner with the *a* sound become an *o*, or in my parents, case, a *u*. My parents' Polish Yiddish, sometimes characterized as Galitzianer, after Galicia in what was once southern Poland, was further distinguished from the now-standardized Litvak version developed in the rabbinic scholarly city of Vilna. Apparently, we belonged to the wild and crazy Chasidic counterculture: the world of the Singer brothers, the rebbes and their courts, the sayings, the melodies, the dancing. Imagine my surprise to hear my rational secular father say, "We belonged to the Sokolow rebbe." The Hebrew word *tachat* for "bottom" or "under" became in Yiddish – *tuchis*! By the second generation of immigrants, American English preserved Yiddish tics somewhat like Yiddish had once preserved Hebrew, with nobody the wiser.

Perhaps because the people of the Book were actually the people of many books, and not One Word but many, many, words seemed to have a different weight in Yiddish, at once lighter and heavier.

During the European sojourn, Jewish boys studied the ancient texts in Hebrew and Aramaic, but they argued over them in Yiddish – the arguing that banishes us beyond the pale of Christian spirituality is our form of devotion. In our house, it replaced prayer almost completely.

As a child, I held on to Yiddish, which, like mothers, went with you everywhere. Yiddish, like the Jewish people, absorbed new elements without losing its flavour.

That flavour was all that remained, lacking even the after-school Hebrew class, to round out my English Protestant schooling. If I couldn't roll words on my tongue to test them for their Yiddish flavour, I would have ended up looking at ourselves through Christian eyes too. What Jews give to the poor is *tzedakah* justice – not charity, which undermines the radical notion that we are righting an inequality that should not have been there in the first place. Jewish history is so much older than the blip of Christian Europe from whose foreshortened view it is regarded. "An eye for an eye" begins to sound different when people around you are taking not only an eye but an arm and a leg too.

As if Jews ever took an eye for an eye, or anything else straight out of the Bible without its having first been massaged by another thousand years of oral debate. In the ancient world, the Torah was read in the marketplace on Mondays and Thursdays. The moneychangers *belonged* in the Temple.

Perhaps it is this extreme old age of our history that induces a certain collective amnesia and a double standard. For example, that Jerusalem is the birthplace of three religions is constantly repeated, but how this came to be nobody remembers. It came to be so because two of those religions were offspring of the first, Judaism, and then these two proceeded to run their parent off the face of the earth. Separating itself from its Jewish origin was especially crucial to the spread of

Christianity among the nations of the Roman Empire, and as Jesus was a Jew who addressed only his fellow Jews, the separation was served by a brutal reversed slander. Islam also converted many nations, by sword if necessary. Only the parent religion, Judaism, remained tied to no more than its original small nation, who *lived* there. And who at one time or another could not stay alive anywhere else. In 135 CE, the Romans crushed the final Jewish rebellion, executed or enslaved the population of Judaea, changed its name to Palestina, and instituted the policy continued by the Christians of the Holy Roman Empire to keep Jews from ever living in Israel again.

From then until 1948, the Jews were an exiled and persecuted people with no national homeland. In 1967, the Israelis retook Jerusalem with its Wailing Wall, the last vestige of the Temple that had been destroyed by the Romans in 70 CE, a very long time before Islam. When you think about it, which few people do, it is the most amazing homecoming in history. The Jews invite visitors to everyone's religious sites. The Muslims cordoned off the Temple Mount on pain of getting shot. The Catholics have Rome, the Muslims have Mecca, but no amount of Biblical, archaeological, historic, political or genetic evidence suffices to legitimize a Jewish Jerusalem, or for that matter, a Jewish Israel.

Having been torn away from nurturing the reborn homeland, my sister ventured forth to adopt all the cultures of the world. In her transition from high school to the downtown campus of McGill University, my sister blossomed from Greta Garbo's Iron Curtain maiden into Ninotchka the morning after she has seen Paris: her silky blond shoulder-length hair turned up in a flip; her slimmed hips glided on high heels; she swung a beloved cracked and blackened Mexican tooled-leather bag that blackened my mother's morning. On top of her glass-fronted oak bookcase, which my father had brought from our rooming house, there appeared a makeup mirror, an eyelash curler, and a bottle of Quelques Fleurs, which her kid sister took to sniffing.

A young man would come to pick her up – Nigerian, Kenyan, or Indian, fellow colonial students from the rainbow of the British Commonwealth upon which the sun never set. There is a picture of me blowing on an incense stick, a gift from one of her boyfriends' cultural range of nations – the original meaning of the word *goy* – whom my mother would be feeding a third portion of apple cake when my sister rescued him. What mattered to my parents was whether somebody was Jewish, not out of exclusion but out of having been themselves viciously excluded.

"Why would I go out with another Polish Jew?" my sister said, "It would be like committing incest."

In the late fifties, my sister, blond and square-boned, would leave the house wrapped in a turquoise sari, her deep-set blue eyes twinkling behind her glasses. My mother only raised a *grachke* when she found her chicken soup spiked with curry.

It was only when my mother got wind that my sister was making herself conspicuous by her behaviour, and that no Canadian boy would go out with her, that she came down on her like a ton of bricks. There was a Japanese-Canadian beatnik whose mispronounced Scottish name figured greatly in these quarrels. My mother, for whom the feminine ideal had been Marie Curie, was now hearing from her acclimated friends that a woman should not become *too* well educated.

Alone among immigrant survivors, my mother complained about the place we were in.

You would think it would be easier for people who have been once uprooted to move again. My mother complained each time we moved, even if it was to a better apartment. My father bringing home a new lamp dug her ever deeper in this alien territory: "I'm not staying here! I'm going back!"

She complained that there weren't *enough* people. In the new upstairs duplex, she stared fixedly out the picture window. "You could sit here the whole day and not see a mensch. It's lucky if you see a dog."

My mother complained that the food didn't taste the same as it did in Poland, although you would never guess it from the amount she ate and cooked for us. When we came to Canada my mother worked briefly in a restaurant, which made an impression she never let us forget.

As a matter of fact, the difference between the *geyle*, the "yellow" ripe assimilated Canadian Jews, and the *greener* greenhorn arrivals was nowhere more evident than in the breeziness with which the *geyle* ate out. It seemed they had lost the embedded-in-the-taste-buds wariness, the discernment of asking, "Where does this chicken come from? Who were its ancestors, its acquaintances? How did it live and how did it die? My mother furthermore wanted to know whether it walked around free in the *hoif* – courtyard – or was it chained in a cage? Are we eating the remains of what another animal has mauled or have we taken the responsibility of killing it painlessly? The blood left our faces as my sister announced she had eaten blood pudding and found it good.

Although my mother and sister maintained that religion is the opium of the people, my mother had a *Yiddishn tam* (Jewish taste). The notion that taste and distaste can carry ethical meaning had its beginnings – like all of our mental leaps induced by loss or exile – when the loss of the Temple's altar with its food offerings moved sanctifying to the kitchen. The word *keilim* referred to Talmudic or sacred vessels. But that is not the way I heard it first. In the way that Yiddish preserved ancient Hebrew words by using them for everyday purposes – which it meanwhile filled with ongoing history – my mother called her cooking pots "*kaylim.*" So that her cooking pots contained our evolution, in which the most ordinary acts and places can be sanctified.

My mother would have laughed off the idea that she was kosher (Polish ham?). Nevertheless, her taste betrayed a bias that seated the conscience squarely in the stomach. Impatient as she was, the American rib steaks we quickly assimilated rarely left the grill still pink. A chicken from the St. Lawrence market, soaked and salted, would lie on a slanted board to drip away any remaining suggestion of blood.

The aversion to blood and fetishes had something to do with the sanctity of life. I cannot say "sanctity of life" in English without sucking out the *Yiddishn tam*. Sanctity of life, but not a fetish of that sanctity, either. That animals were killed to support life was accepted in full consciousness, but it went beyond this concession to wallow in it. "It doesn't have a Jewish taste," means it is disgusting or lifeless. It is disgusting *because* it is lifeless, such as the pièce de résistance on a platter with an apple stuffed in its mouth as if it were still living.

Disgust, a visceral response that came in handy to avoid eating poison, had somehow been extended to such dishes as a baby kid boiled in its mother's milk. To avoid this at all costs, milk and meat were not to be eaten together. Neither were limbs hacked off an animal while it was still alive. In this way at least, body and mind were one. But the aversive reaction had to be cultivated like any of the senses. It took 4,000 years of the *feh* response to turn the stomach at human carnage, so that when General Patton entered Buchenwald in April 1945, he vomited.

S'iz im nisht git gevorn. It made him sick to his stomach.

Gehennom, the word my mother used for hell, came from the Valley of Hinnom, where the ancient pagans supposedly burned children as sacrifices to Moloch. Hell was a place where life was blackmailed for a horrible price.

The *milchume* (the war) and its hunger, rather than making my mother indiscriminately grateful for any morsel of food, only made her fussier. What she fed us had to have met its death without suffering, as if validating an ancient intuition against nourishing yourself on the fruits of violence.

"Fresh! It has to be fresh!" My mother was a Jewish cook. Should she crack an egg and find the fertilized thread of blood, she discarded it.

She made everything herself by memory without measure, rolling out *lokshen* noodles by hand.

"Is she still cooking chicken feet for you?" my sister giggled.

My sister laughed at the pot of manicured chicken feet my mother would have boiling on the stove when I came home. For my sister, however, my mother prepared a baking dish of quivering garlicky gelatin slowly rendered from calf's foot cartilage; a nourishing tradition that made *me* quiver. *Fees*, my mother called it simply, feet.

All of my mother's whole-earth cooking techniques, all this *Yiddishin tam* the American Jews had buried with their immigrant roots, retaining only the processed tops.

It was true that I relished the lowly chicken feet fished out of the aromatic broth by a Jewish mother as she kept "the best" for her family. Occasionally there was something simmering in a pot that I left alone. My medical student boyfriend Michael, a *geyle*, struggled to identify the more exotic organs by lifting a cover off a pot in which simmered my mother's lunch.

"What is that?"

"Put it down," I said.

"Is that *spleen*?"

My mother's one cooking implement was an axe. Vegetables went in whole with their skins, garlic cloves, fish bones that she hacked with a cleaver on a board set on her lap, *hack, hack, hack*! Chopping by hand left the *kotlety* and gefilte fish their character, resilience, and under her bad aim, their downright resistance.

The first time I tasted French fish mousse (*quenelles de poisson*), it slipped down so easily I gagged.

One day, I saw the cleaver enter my mother's arm and split her flesh from wrist to elbow. "It's nothing," she said, "This is nothing."

◆ ◆ ◆

When as a child in Canada, I walked with my sister, she held my hand and yanked me forward while she counted calories. Women didn't have bodies in the 1950s; they had "figures."

"Apple, 75; yogourt, 110…"

"Yonah," I tugged at her hand.

"Don't interrupt me!" she snapped. "Carrot, 14; Melba toast, 15." When she completed the calorie count from one end of the day, she started over from the other, "Yogourt, 110; apple, 75 …" and squeezed my hand in her annoyance that the numbers came out the same.

I was so much luckier than my sister in the time we were born. I escaped the war, I escaped the panty girdle. I didn't escape my genes, or I might have gone without a bra too. But my mother and especially my sister, a.k.a. "Daisy Mae" in summer camp skits, were classically proportioned. *So how had I*, I asked myself on my sixteenth birthday, *come by these extra rococo curvatures on my upper thighs?* Riding pants, if you want a picture. *Peau d'orange* – trust the French to have a word for the texture. They discovered cellulite. I loved reading in French, to which my missing vocabulary only added allure.

My mother's stock response to complaints of this sort was: "It won't hurt your chances with the matchmaker." It was with a heavy heart, however, that she took me to an optometrist's shop when I was twelve. Both daughters with glasses.

My mother kept ranting that I was puny, but we were on the cusp of the sixties and I couldn't wrestle a pair of jeans over my Jewish hips. My artistic friend, Saskia, one of the few European immigrant non-Jews in my high school (her only reminder that she was Christian was the Christian Girls in Training [CGIT] meetings her mother made her attend), was a foot taller than me, with long coltish legs and sharp angular bones no bump would ever dare to colonize; this despite eating half a buttery challah and a hefty portion of my mother's cheesecake at my house every Saturday morning. Meanwhile, there I was, in university at eighteen and betrayed by the current winter wear of a pair of ski pants that my father had brought me – ski pants without skiing; that was the trouble, the pants were for girls who got some exercise.

"What are those?" my medical student boyfriend asked, pointing at my *pulkes* – my thighs, as in chicken thighs. He had never seen anything like them in his anatomy books. I had another flaw, in his book. I was Jewish. It didn't matter that he was Jewish too, born in Canada. "Are you Jewish? You're beautiful," he said, running the two together too quickly. "Do the two not go together?"

It was never cool to be Jewish, except for maybe a Bob Zimmerman minute in the sixties. Traditionally, it has done nothing for your sex appeal, because the beautiful Hollywood "stars" who are Jewish, change their names. Could Betty Perske be Lauren Bacall? Now Lauren Bacall did not "look" Jewish. Although there ought to be a magazine page like the one in a women's magazine for "older" women. This is a page with a bombshell CEO that says, "This is what forty-five looks like." We needed a page of Paul Newman that said, "This is what Jewish looks like." (Okay, half-Jewish.) My Jewish boyfriends always told me they never dated Jewish girls, and I was supposed to take this as a compliment. As an Old World Yiddish-speaking Polish immigrant, I must have struck them as so different from the girls they knew that I may as well not have been Jewish at all.

To my surprise my mother didn't deny the cantaloupes cantilevered over my legs. She sighed. "What can you do, you're built like that."

"Well, it says here," I read, freely translating from the French, "massage helps to break up the trapped fat."

Like applying suction glasses to a corpse, I could see her thinking. "Lie down," she said. How different could it be from tenderizing a brisket? I lay on my stomach while she pounded my *pulkes*.

"What're you doing?" my father said alarmed through the door.

"Men," she said, and punched my thigh.

In the spring of my first year in university I woke up on a Saturday morning to my mother running the bath water and muttering under her breath what had she done to deserve this. My sister took the

Homeric ship to England in 1963, while I was in grade ten. I had the full run of her glass-covered bookcase on top of which I also kept my blush. The street where we lived still looked as naked as when we arrived, with no grown trees or spring buds. Actually, the first sign of spring in Canada was not visual but sonar; the neighbour who owned a fishing rod heard the ice cracking on the river. He left my mother a present: a fish in a pail of water. I never got out of bed earlier than she, otherwise she would feel compelled to get up to feed me, and how selfish could I be? We were both prisoners of her obsession. Saturday mornings she permitted herself to leave for downtown and walk the length of Montreal's elegant robber-baron boulevard, Sherbrooke Street, which stretched from the English west end to the French east end. The heart of the street was the tree-lined McGill University campus. The university in the same town meant I did not leave home to go away to school.

Suddenly I, who had *enjoyed* writing exams, scribbling away while the pages fell off my desk, now sat there without a thing to say. I fell facedown into the freshman pit of Dantean *accidie*, as if yielding to my mother's commanding futility. Yet school had been the only area in which my mother allowed me my autonomy. If anything, I was distracted by the real subject, the glass of fashion, the Platonic cave of flickering images, the visual triage of the girls in their expensive clothes. There was a corridor leading from the humanities to the library known as "the Gaza strip" because no girl could escape the size-up from the male snipers on the windowsills. No matter how well dressed, Jewish princesses never became Ice Carnival queens.

Being Jewish was never glamorous; from the rejection of the Greek ideal, the romantic lead, the mythic hero on horseback (Jews portrayed the Indians in westerns), certainly the Wagnerian Siegfried, and myths themselves with their blotting out of the particular, the humorous, the physically vulnerable. The beautiful and the good were not one. Moreover, kvetching, candid about the body, skeptical, demystifying – preoccupied in my youth with our recent history and at the same time the all-important desirable image, I thought, *Every Jew is an old person*.

On the other hand, for Saskia and the few Gentile classmates in my Jewish-populated high school, it was a shock to find out that the whole world was not Jewish. They missed the food and the affection. A WASP townie had trouble reading the signs. "I didn't know whether you liked me or whether you were just being warm and Jewish."

From that time I would wake up only to be felled under the hooves "of a galloping apathy," as my childhood friend Dora called it. Her parents had survived Auschwitz. We so much shared the same sensibility that she finished my sentences. "Do you realize we're the only children of immigrants who are *shorter* than their parents?" Unlike other immigrant children, we lacked drive. "Maybe born into that trauma we just don't have the same strength as everyone else," she said. "Don't make it worse by feeling guilty about it. If your friends want to choose clothes for you, let them."

If not for artistic Saskia, I might never have changed out of my favourite outfit: a pair of Michael's old pyjamas that forgave me my bumps, my bodily fluids, and embraced me without exerting any pressure on me.

That Saturday morning in spring, Saskia arrived like Primavera, wearing green stockings and tiny green flowers suspended from her new growth of hair. The straight Dutch-boy hair and bangs that she came by naturally became the iconic hairstyle of the decade. One day, sick of her dolly image, she cut it all off. She still looked pretty, so she took a buzz saw to it. Then thin as she was, her scalp in tufts, she got to me.

Whenever I went to the bathroom, I met the eye of the fish staring up at me. And I went often, in the throes of my first colitis attack.

"There's a fish in the bathtub," I warned her.

Saskia thought on her feet. "Quick, get one of your sleeping pills!" Could fish digest pills? I was sceptical but I got one of my blue Doriden capsules and stuck it in the fish's open mouth.

I wasn't at home when my mother returned. We never ate the fish. It became my mother's and sister's favourite story about me.

◆ ◆ ◆

Whenever asked about my illness, there was never any question about when it began. The attack came on suddenly when I was nineteen, after a Chinese banquet on New Year's Eve, that rare excuse to stay out all night. Michael had his own apartment in the McGill "student ghetto," his asthma making it difficult to trek to the university from his parents' house in the cold. We went to his apartment, but instead of spending the night locked in embrace I spent it locked in the toilet.

This had the advantage of making it easy to tell exactly when my medical history began. Otherwise the reason I repeated the story was so that I could dwell in the part I left out. The boy who had pointed at my bumps turned out to be also his opposite. If it wasn't cool to be Jewish or to have bumps, it was off the aesthetic scale to have the trots. I never met anyone less surprised, less squeamish, and more compassionate (especially for a horny eighteen-year-old). He visited old lonely patients in the hospital on his own time. Puffy and moon-faced, Michael was my first example of the effects of steroids two decades before I took them. "Why can't my mother cook like yours?" he asked in our hallway where I made him wait till his bronchioles opened up while I ran upstairs to fetch him a hunk of my mother's *klops*. The first time my mother invited him to sit down at the kitchen table, I was unable to explain why I stayed in the bedroom and let him eat alone.

I let him prick my finger for blood cells to study under the microscope (because I was more himself than others he jabbed in vain). Jews are not shy about talking about the body (one reason Jews make good doctors is their traditional bias toward repairing things in this world and not the next) and my boyfriend was born to be a doctor if anybody was.

I refused, however, when he asked me not to flush the toilet so he could study the symptoms. The first attack was accompanied by insomnia for which I was prescribed sleeping pills. By that time the effort to sleep had me so tense that every night after taking the pill I would talk on the telephone to Michael until my words got slurry.

My mother responded to my pallor with what else – doubling the fried *klops*. My horrified friends wrapped them up and smuggled them out of the house in their purses. My father asked the pharmacist for the name of a stomach doctor. In the sixties, BC (before colonoscopy) diagnosis depended on the art of the physician. Months went by in which the first martial gastroenterologist tried to discipline my bowel to perform every morning with prunes and enemas if need be, not to leave the house until it did, and not to go at any other time. Every month or so, he would order a set of demoralizing barium X-rays to check for the effects of this wholesome regime for which my father received a guilt-inducing bill.

Eventually my Lodz-born classmate, Mary (Mary? Safer than Miriam in postwar Poland), whose *geyle* dress-manufacturer uncle had ulcers, rescued me with the name of a Czech specialist on Sherbrooke Street. "Your symptoms are consistent with ulcerative colitis," the doctor told me. Not irritable bowel syndrome like my fellow Lodzer *kishke* complainer. Not functional but pathological; inflamed, not irritated. Why couldn't I develop TB and bleed from my other end? My youthful obsession with images had to answer to having to go to the bathroom. All prejudice was aesthetic, I concluded. First we had to be made to look ugly. It almost did not surprise me to read in Michael's medical textbook that this gut-gnawing illness of our lowliest body function – so private and shameful it went unspoken – particularly afflicted Ashkenazi Jews. Nobody else could take the embarrassment. Besides, from Job onwards, it seemed axiomatic that our guts should roil. It was not just the greater family gene pool of Ashkenazi Jews to which I belonged. My illness recalled the humiliation, the loss of control, the excremental attack against the Jews. When told about the dysentery of the camps, my guts wrenched.

At about this time a sea change occurred. I never saw another medical bill. Universal health care had been enacted in Canada. Health care was paid for at another time, in a different category, by taxation. What this did was to separate the individual's burden of illness from the burden of paying for it.

Perhaps the lifting of guilt kept the illness within bounds for another twenty years.

In the summer of 1967, when Canada turned 100, and I was 20, the most coveted job for co-eds was as an Expo 67 hostess at the breezy World's Fair site. Having pummelled my bumps down to molehills, I answered an ad for go-go dancers at Chez Gros Pierre, a downtown Montreal nightclub. I couldn't imagine getting paid for dancing. (In my jaundiced opinion, fortified by my sister's copy of *The Second Sex*, both jobs traded equally in young female flesh. If not, why didn't Expo hire fifty-five-year-old hostesses?) I couldn't imagine that I could show up every day without getting sick. We were protected by a law forbidding us from even speaking to customers. So long as we projected Brigitte

Bardot, Pierre gave us free rein to blast the street with Motown. There was nothing "go-go" about our dancing; no white boots in cages and no flapping arms. I did not feel "white" enough to frug like American frat boys did to surf music. I was in rhythm 'n' blues heaven: Wilson Pickett, Joe Tex, Booker T., James Brown; that summer every singer I danced to came to the Esquire Show Bar where we caught their last set. The lyrical Smokey Robinson songs were my cue, but I didn't think I could do justice to James Brown until I asked for some help from my only African-Canadian colleague, Louelle.

When my sister visited us that summer of 1967, she came to the club to see what her kid sister was up to. I put a word in to the bouncers, Mario and Tony. They laid out the red carpet for her.

One quiet Sunday afternoon, I was reading to "A Whiter Shade of Pale" between sets at Gros Pierre's when two plainclothes police came in and arrested me and the other dancer on the charge of disrupting traffic. (The club's picture window looked out on Montreal's main drag, St. Catherine Street, continually choked with traffic anyway.) Booked and fingerprinted, we were put in a jail cell. My new co-worker, Sadie, confessed that she was a tourist; she came from an Orthodox Jewish family in the Bronx. "You gave the police your real name?" she said. "I couldn't do that. What if it got back to my parents?"

My most pressing concern that day was hearing that Michael had been hospitalized with an asthma attack and I couldn't get to him. There must have been a dearth of local news because next day the newspaper's front page sported the story, "Dancers Disrupting Traffic," citing my name and address and that of a Sylvie Lavierge from Pointe-au-Pic. My parents knew what I was doing; this was something else. I had broadcast a Jewish name (if not for Sadie's quick thinking, it would have been *two* Jewish names) doing something louche. Although what was the point – we were not supposed to be better than everyone else, neither were we supposed to show up as no better than everyone else, either. I rushed to tell my father before he read it for himself. "You didn't do anything wrong," he said.

My father had a lot on his mind. It was also the summer of the Six Day War, in which Israel, born like me in the wake of the Holocaust, defended itself once more against its neighbours while I suddenly found myself defending the land of the left-wing kibbutz experiment to my New Left friends. My sister was shaken. She said she could not countenance a world so cynical it would countenance the destruction of Israel. My sister was a staunch leftist, and here the left had ganged up on Israel for winning a war it would have to constantly refight. From its modern rebirth in 1948, its five dictator- and monarch-led Arab neighbours vowed to destroy it, and that vow has not been recanted to this day. Instead of recognizing the Jews as their Semitic brethren, they began to practice anti-Semitism against them. On one side was the threat of annihilation, on the other was the refusal to be annihilated.

To me it seemed another bind where we could do nothing right. To lose would mean to cease to exist; but we were not supposed to win, either. We would not be forgiven for not being the underdog. Whether from the left or the right, the atheist or religious side, we could count on being wrong. Only the Jews could add to their troubles by winning a war.

We couldn't be better than everyone else, but we couldn't be like everyone else, either. It wasn't my parents who raised an alarm because I had exposed our Jewish name in the newspaper; it was the assimilated Jewish community, still frightened. The fear of reprisals, of one of us standing for all of us, that was as old as the diaspora and horrifically justified in the concentration camps, was still plaguing us in Canada. Where could I get myself arrested without the burden of besmirching my sensitive minority? Only in a place where everyone was Jewish. For all their freedom, North American Jews needed Israel. My escapade did not bother my mother either, until a neighbour reproached her. "Why do you do things that allow people to say such things to me?" What drove her nuts was my not finishing her basin of applesauce.

I moved in with Michael after he came out of the hospital into one of the streets around the university called "the student ghetto." My parents shouted (my father more than my mother, I worried more about his making himself sick), and the next day my mother sent my father over with a trunkful of food.

Chapter Six

"SEND AWAY THE MOTHER BIRD"

In the early sixties, my sister won a graduate school fellowship in philosophy and set sail for England on the SS *Homeric*, from where she was to return only on summers off from teaching when she was not touring the continent. As a glamorous hardy blonde, she clambered over Capri and got sunstroke in Greece. She made it back to Zakopane and took pictures of our apartment house in Lodz.

Just before her departure for England, her romance with the boyfriend whose name my mother mangled had been at its pitch. "Did you tell him I've lost weight?" she asked a friend after a successful trip to Italy. Once I heard her slam down the telephone, slam her bedroom door shut, and break out in sobs. The fights with my parents got so bad she spent a winter working in New York. When she went to England, he went to Yale with another Polish woman. My father felt forever guilty for causing her pain, but the romance was broken without them.

On her last visit, my father took her to Cape Cod and fed her all the lobster she could eat. My mother graciously stayed home: she said that just looking at the ocean made her seasick.

On Rosh Hashanah or Passover, my sister would call me from England: "Mother sounds desperate. Father is depressed. The least you can do is go visit them."

In the summer of 1980, after a long absence, my parents joyfully announced the news of her coming visit. Right after, my sister called me from England.

"What have I done?" she whispered. "I've been asking myself, God, what have I done, tying myself to them for a whole month? Until I remembered: why, I can stay with you! We shall talk," her British *a*'s narrowed lugubriously, "and Mother will bring us bags of food." It was my turn to panic. I *lived* here. Ever since my sister had started therapy, she was so full of our family pathology that she talked of nothing else. Besides, it was a bad time for me to be welcoming my sister. I was psyching myself up to move out of Montreal.

"No," I said, "you can't stay with me. I'm going to, err, ah, Toronto."

"I've been roaming the streets absolutely roaring – shouting – at them," she whispered. "They shall call me the Madwoman of Hampstead." My sister's voice is perfectly modulated, with a light accent moulded by our wanderings, which, while irremediably foreign, was nevertheless deemed civilized by the English. The most American slang to which she ever descended was to call me, thrillingly, her "kid sister." Although we got off the same boat in Halifax, I was an immigrant; she was an émigré.

My sister called me back.

"I understand why you don't want me to stay with you," she said. "My therapist says that you – that we – protect our privacy because we had an invasive mother."

"That's it," I said.

"I've written them a long list of things not to say, not to criticize me for, and not to do."

This list, sent ahead of her arrival, was going to help like applying cupping glasses to a corpse, to quote my mother – which my sister would never do, because she didn't speak Yiddish. As our migrations caught each of us at different learning capacities, our family did not share a common language. We sounded like the Tower of Babel, or like a concentration camp where, my father says, Jews were thrown from all over Europe.

Or so I thought.

Only years later will I learn that in response to my sister's perfect

Polish, my parents consciously chose to speak Yiddish with me so that it would not be entirely lost. "Let's at least speak in Yiddish to the little one."

My mother never learned more English than she needed to buy food. My father speaks English, even some French, but my sister won't hear it, because his Polish is perfect but his English is not.

"I'm fat." My sister swallowed a sob. "But you love me even though I'm fat, don't you?"

"What does *fat* got to do with it?" I yelled.

It's no wonder she had to be reminded that we were born of the same mother. She is nine years older; in our case, it means born on either side of a breach in history. I was born "after." She was born "before."

◆ ◆ ◆

Few small children survived the deportations. They were of no use as labour, and as seeds of the condemned race they were the first to have their heads smashed against walls in front of their mothers. This last rumour (rumour it must be, because why would people do such things?) took possession of my mother.

"You're not going to the airport to meet your sister?" my mother heaved. I don't want to wait in my mother's nerves for her daughter to land out of the air.

My mother's face is pasted against the plate-glass window, standing to be the first through the arrival gates. They arrive hours early and no matter that they are getting old, they crowd toward a clear view of their agony.

Going to the airport means going to a *wysiedlenie*.

In the first *wysiedlenie*, she pushed her child out the window; in the second, she pushed her through the space between barbed wire. But the third time, when they arrived in Częstochowa, the Germans took the children away from the parents upon arrival. For some reason, they did not shoot them immediately. Instead, they were kept in a barracks just outside the gates of the camp, out of reach, but not out of sight, of their parents. For three days and nights my mother and father pressed their faces to the holes in the barbed-wire fence.

"Are you from London?" My mother charges the first person through the gate like a red flag. Travellers arriving from anywhere in the world are accosted by a short earthbound woman bearing down on them and demanding in broken English if out of the entire planet's population they've seen her daughter.

"Ma, they're Japanese!" I pull her away.

"It's not Flight 547!" says my father. Flight, shmight, my ma takes no notice of such mediations as the order of flight numbers or the fact that different flights fly in to the same gate. Let others put their faith in numbers, procedure, announcements, and system. If she had been calmer, more reasonable, if she had hoped for the best rather than sensed the worst, if she had for a moment entrusted her child to God or man, if she were any less a nightmare-filled mother, she too might have waited like the others.

Who waited on that night of October 28, 1942. In the last two weeks of October 1942, thirty deportations left central Poland for Treblinka. When the SS man came to get the women and children at the farm and told them to get ready, my mother threw her child and herself out the window.

Much later, worn down by hunger and who knew how many more desperate feats, with the knowledge that the next time vigilance might fail them, they arrived in Częstochowa.

"They examined us," said my father, "and they said after the examination they would give us back the children."

The children were separated from the parents, but they were neither given back nor murdered. For three days and nights they are kept in a barracks on the other side of a fence "made of rough wire," says my father. "You know, with big holes so you can see through." Aimed at their heads from the watchtowers on all sides above are the rifles of Ukrainian guards.

I do not want to inhabit my mother's psyche for that drumming three-day moment. I do not want to even imagine them but those three days explode out in our lives forever after: in the clawed-open boxes, in the panicked pushing onto a bus. There was nothing more gratifying to Nazi ideology than to induce the collaboration of biology, and to have the prisoners' own bodies betray them.

"Where are you rushing?" I pull her back. The Germans *want* you to rush to your death. In arriving early, you are doing their job for them. You are *still* doing their job for them.

One would think that the hundredth time they get there early only to prolong their suffering, they would learn that most likely the event would not happen again. "We were so worried! We were so worried!"

Whether those three days blasted their learning circuits or forever overrode all further experience, they have not learned. The annihilation of inessentials at the time scoured the inessentials essential to learning. My mother's passion burned out her patience. From one day to the next, it was as if the incommensurability of this event was seared into her brain, so that if her brain could hold this, it could not hold that. Anything else became irrelevant, was swept aside, and this event remained immediate. The luxury of the cortical delay that allows deliberation was swept away as well. My parents have no distance. They crowd around the gate with the others, anxiously awaiting the word from the loudspeaker. They press their faces against the wire, straining to catch a glimpse of their child.

All my mother's intermediate learning neurons – anything less urgent than life or death, all or nothing, Tzaddik or Hitler – were razed, burned out, extinct, short-circuited once and for all as extraneous, deluded, and so nerve-fraying in their suspense as to be murderous themselves. Imagine this woman who does not wait for man or God, forced to wait.

They announce that the plane is delayed.

"What did they say? What did they say? Are you going to tell me or not?"

"Don't tell her," I beg my father who has turned white. The more staunchly we resist her panic with a facade of calm, the more we are secretly infected. What, are we crazy, planes *do* crash. She turns on us, "Sadists, SS men, your blood runs cold like Hitler's." If not for her, we would all be buried ten feet under. My father is a *shvacher*, a weakling (if it were not my sister up there in the plane, she would add that they are like two peas in a pod); I am a *shtark* character with an iron will, demonstrated by my refusal to eat all she wants to feed me, but this resemblance to her endears me to her not a whit at this moment.

"*Raboine shel'oylem! Mach nisht a grachke!*" (Head of the Universe! Don't make a fuss!) says my father. Around us I notice the ring of curious eyes, amused smiles. I am back looking in with others at my family. I break out into a sweat at the hallowed Cossack spectator sport of laughing at anxious Jews.

Stop looking at us! *You* be calm at arrivals and departures. *You* be complacent that forces will always combine to return your child or sister or husband. Even as I try to calm my parents I defend them.

"Sadists! *Kalte brieh!*" (Cold creation!) my mother mutters. My father begs me for a cigarette; I want to ask him if he can spare a Valium.

When Lusia arrives, my mother's eyes go bright and big. My father and I get out of the way. In a tearless, detached, slightly surprised voice, "Lusia" is all she says.

These are the parents Lusia is so afraid of meeting through the gate.

Chapter Seven

MY SISTER'S VISIT, MONTREAL, 1980

In the summer of 1967, my sister had come to visit when I moved out of the house. In the summer of 1980 she came to visit when I decided it was to be my last summer in Montreal. I had let my apartment go and sublet this one in our first neighbourhood, as if taking off from where we had come in. It happened to be one of the many times Quebec voted on separation, with the rhetoric that a child who has reached maturity should become independent of his parents. From the bookshelves of my borrowed apartment I pulled down one of Kafka's diaries. I opened it to a page where he complains that he will never leave Prague or his parents.

After the nervous breakdown at the airport, I called to invite my sister out. "Not this evening. I have to wash my hair," my sister whispered. I remembered the ritual of coaxing her fine blonde hair to fall in a plumb line to her jaw so that it swung as she spoke. She never left the house unless immaculately groomed, no matter how depressed she got, nor how much weight she gained from the lithium eventually prescribed (as to my father) to combat the depression.

"I know you would like to take me out for a lovely French meal," my sister confided, "but what I would really like is something *American*, like a hamburger." Just the item that our mother warned us never to eat. We were deciding upon a restaurant, as if our mother would let anyone out of her house hungry enough to need one.

"She keeps coaxing me to eat! My God," my sister giggled over the telephone, "I weigh 200 pounds!"

I took my expatriate sister to Schwartz's for something not merely American but uniquely Montreal.

"I'm seeing a new psychologist," said my sister over the pickles and *karnatzel*. "She does behaviour modification. Short term. But she has really opened my eyes."

This surprised me, because I remembered her first psychotherapist who should have obviated any further treatment. After Lusia had settled in England in the early sixties, my mother dragged me with her to England in the summer of 1965. We went by boat because she was afraid to fly, and again I didn't see her throughout the entire voyage. Only one good thing came out of this torment, my mother said, emerging two dress sizes slimmer.

At the time, my sister was in idyllic living quarters, sharing a sublet Georgian townhouse with other graduate students. Thick trees in the window, a rose garden in back, lilacs dripping from the piano in her room. My mother took in the tinned and processed goods on which my sister's roommates subsisted and ran out to the nearest butcher's shop, where she ordered five pounds each of his finest Scottish lamb and beef. She asked him to mince some of the beef that passed her inspection, and stood over him while she made him wash out his meat grinder. The butcher refused to fill my mother's order (five pounds?) until he called my sister, unwilling to take advantage of a mistake owing to her poor English.

My sister would peer out on dark English winter mornings and go back to sleep under our Polish goosedown comforter. My father mailed it to her when she complained of the damp. She never got the degree she went to study for. She used to put off writing her papers in a kind of perfectionist procrastination by which she challenged herself to do ever better in less time. Finally, she lost interest and felt guilty for having lost interest.

"Guess who my analyst is?" Lusia sprung on me one day. After a few years in England, my sister, whom I had obediently called Yonah through her Canadian years, instructed us to call her Lusia again. Lusia had been her nickname in Poland, when a Yiddish name like Toba was asking for trouble. I had called her Yonah for most of my life, so when instructions came to call her by the now continental and exotic Lusia, I had to think twice before I opened my mouth to remember which of her names was in currency. So I settled for the irrefutable "my sister." Now I blurted out the most famous psychiatric name I knew, despite my near certainty that the father of psychotherapy was no longer alive, because dead or alive I couldn't imagine anyone but the best treating my sister.

"Freud?" I hazarded. She smiled. "You are not far off." My sister was being interviewed as a candidate for analysis by the Anna Freud Clinic. The Jewish founder of psychotherapy had fled the Nazis for London in 1938, just in time for his direct descendants to cope with the full import of that exile.

"What she needs is sun! She needs *menschen*! Who can live in such darkness the whole time?" My mother began her campaign to return my sister from the insular English gloom to a merely externally besieged Israel. Being eighteen and in the same city as the Beatles did not make up for being caught between my mother and sister.

My sister's shrink advised her to evict her mother. My mother and I went to Paris.

Between my mother and my sister, who eventually joined us there, I had such a bad time in Paris then, that fifteen years later I wondered why I would contemplate returning.

At Schwartz's, Lusia was feeling expansive. Our distinctive smoked meat – as superior to pastrami as Montreal bagels were to New York's – arrived on the table. She took a hearty chomp of a jaw-stretching wad of smoked brisket flimsily flanked by slices of rye. "I was thinking that you might really like to have a flat in London one day. I am going to leave it to you in my will."

"Cut that out," I said.

She told me about the new treatment she was trying. "It's a therapy that focuses on the present and not the past. For example, I said I wanted to lose weight, the therapist said that I'm to like myself first," she said, pausing for breath. "Can you imagine? I never thought of liking myself!"

My sister and I remained virgins to therapy longer than most people. Its subjectivity bothered us. Why would we engage in therapy that dealt with suffering caused by *mistaken* perceptions that could be swiftly sorted out by a short stay in a concentration camp? My socialist sister used to regard it as another distraction from righting social inequalities. This was all before my sister's state reduced us to the single question: does it work?

In London, my sister underwent psychoanalysis. My father, already carrying antidepressants, went to London and asked her psychoanalyst, "Will this help my child?" When he saw her bedsit, "She is living in a *cellar*," he said. That was when he put a down payment on an apartment for her.

It was unfortunately impossible to know with certainty, her interviewing analyst wrote, whether there was any history of depression or suicide in the family. She did mention that her father had "a nervous breakdown" two years before, during which he had visited doctors "hypochondriacally" with vague stomach and chest pains. She was too embarrassed to say what her father did for a living.

After seven years, the analysis was pronounced a failure. "He concluded that my oral fixation was due not so much to mother-child relations as that I did not have enough to eat in the first years of my life." I waited for my sister to giggle, a lovely sound that bubbled through any ideological scrim of the moment. I waited in vain.

"Why didn't our parents pay attention like other parents and put me on a diet when I was fifteen?" She knew why. Therapy was returning her to blissful ignorance so she could be shocked afresh each time by their deviations.

"It's *normal* to be angry at your parents," she said. "My analyst said he himself was very angry at his parents for sending him away to boarding school."

I munched on my well-done chicken livers, for the iron. "There's something missing," I said.

"What?" She perked up.

"The theory is universal because everyone has parents. But universal isn't everything. Where in this theory do we get to be angry at Nazis?"

"Universal isn't everything?" she said, giggling.

We walked across Fletcher's Field where years ago I used to walk hand in hand with my father on Sundays. I ran ahead to catch the bus that she had once taken home from university assignations and nuclear disarmament rallies. I wanted to cry. My sturdy sister, the barefoot folk dancer, who could hike the hills of Montmartre without losing the thread of an argument, struggled to heave herself onto the bus.

A mother sat across from us with a baby on her lap. If we both liked holding babies, my sister was magnetized. In a few moments, the infant levitated – what mother would refuse her? – across the aisle and onto Lusia's lap.

"It's your fault. You really were an exceptionally adorable baby," Lusia said. "How good-natured she is, and not afraid of strangers."

"She doesn't kvetch," the young mother allowed with a smile.

My sister laughed. "Yiddish is so expressive."

"Nem a klayne hentele" (Take a little hand). I invite the child to grasp my finger.

"Where did you learn that word?" my sister asks. "Even if people in England knew how to speak Yiddish, they would never admit it." My sister learned languages as needed, refusing only the German prerequisite for the Idealist philosophers. But she could not bring herself to speak Yiddish, the same way she could not bring herself to touch her mother.

◆ ◆ ◆

I can see they've been fighting when I walk in the door of my parents' apartment. My sister, unlipsticked and unleashed in a bathrobe, flicks her face away from me tearfully and disappears into the bathroom. My mother is dry-eyed and desperate, clawing at the air as if she's just been deprived of a last swipe at her prey. She wanders around in a torn and spattered housedress, with a *shmata* under her arm, her eyes burning. Furious clouds from a pot boiling on the stove blast the icy conditioned air. My father looks oppressed. The only person smiling is the Eskimo Madonna above the living-room couch. This is an oil portrait of an Inuit woman in a parka holding a baby in classic European position. My mother brought her home proudly, her one original, of whose merit she needed to ask nobody's opinion. A mother.

"And you say nothing?" my mother needles my father. For many days, she said nothing, but she didn't need to say anything. Her bosom spread out on the table, her hand holding up her head, she had only to fix her unwavering blue gaze on her daughter. Was this because my sister said she wanted to visit Quebec City?

Seething all the more under self-restraint, my mother has finally flipped her lid, molten bile scorching every nerve ending in its path. My sister's list of "Things Not to Say" has been flung to the winds: (1) Don't tell me to go on a diet. (2) Don't tell me to get married. (3) Don't tell me what to wear.

"I'm a mother! I'm supposed to stand by deaf and dumb while you bury yourself alive?"

My mother has been blaming her and my sister has been throwing the blame back. Blame for what? For not being like everyone else? Our parents weren't like everyone else. We had no rules, no allowances, no curfews.

"If the war had lasted any longer, I don't know if Lusia would have survived," my mother said. "She was so thin that she had no appetite. When we were liberated and returned to Demblin, I didn't have a piece of bread to give her. One morning I woke up early and somehow got a hold of four eggs. I thought, 'Good, now we will both have food to eat.' I made an omelette and thought we would share it. Before I had a chance to turn around, she had eaten the whole thing. I was happy," says my mother, "I was happy she ate."

"Suddenly in the mountains she started to eat a lot," said my father. "She came home like this," he spreads out his arms. "The doctor told us to stop her, but we didn't have the heart."

My parents had only their uncalculated anxiety and their trust that we would not do anything bad, a trust utterly justified by our premonition that if we allowed a hair on our heads to be harmed we would have to answer to their immeasurable grief.

Because it is better to be crazy if everyone else is crazy, my parents reclaimed some of the conventions they had rebelled against in the shtetl. In that rebellion they were enacting the essential Jewish move of suspending belief in false gods. Imagine what it must have been to balk at propitiatory human sacrifices. Down the pages you could hear the prophets nagging, "Don't fall for this!"

My mother knocked on the bathroom door where Lusia had barricaded herself. "You are doomed! You are digging your own grave!"

"If she combed her hair a little *up*, instead of straight down," said my father.

So this was what they were fighting about. Once, when everyone wore beehives, Lusia's straight, jaw-length swinging hair was starkly original. Now when everyone wore their hair more or less like my sister, my mother belatedly woke up. "Who's asking you to be original? You're *burying* yourself with your originality."

On the disposition of every hair hung our fate.

"You'll be sorry when you no longer have a mother! This is the last time I'm going to ask you, do you hear? Oh, may I go to sleep and never wake up again!" My mother's voice broke.

"Do as I say or you're doomed! You're *already* doomed!"

◆　◆　◆

My mother speaks at the kitchen table in a tearless voice that, as she ages, quickens with fever:

"You want to know what a shtetl was?" my mother blazed. "A shtetl was a community of about one hundred families living in *finsterkeit*, in darkness, oppression and poverty. It was a calamity on our heads. I was the eldest of eight children; we did not always have enough to eat." One time, her mother took to her bed with no desire to do anything. The doctor said it was her nerves; she had to have absolute rest and a change of air. "I put her and the youngest children in a buggy and went with her up into the mountains. After a while she began to eat; and I knew she was better."

"We got married in 1937," says my father. "In 1938, Lusia was born. In 1939, the war broke out."

"On a bitter day the Germans drove us into a ghetto they had made out of the darkest alleys in Demblin. People got sick from hunger and from the lack of sanitation. Lusia caught diphtheria. It was forbidden for Jews to leave the ghetto. They were shot on sight. I made my way out of the ghetto and found Dr. Gelber. He agreed to come back with me and, thanks to him, Lusia got better.

"In the fall of 1942, I, my mother, Lusia, and other women with children were at work on a farm appropriated by the Germans.

"One night on the farm, it was the twenty-eighth of October," my mother continues, "I heard a horse and buggy drive up outside the farmhouse. We were all, about thirty women and children, in a loft on the second floor with a window out on the fields. I heard footsteps of military boots come up the stairs and I took hold of Lusia. I knew who was coming. It was Wagner, the SS man who had come the week before to watch us as we came in from the fields. This time he came in, and he turned on the gas lamp. The women awoke from their straw pallets. He told us to get ready. He said he was taking us to Końskovola where we would be safe. I knew he was leading us not to life but to death. One thought took hold of me. It was said they killed the children in front of the mother's eyes. We were all going to die. But I wanted to *iberkumen zayn*, be killed together with, and not a moment after, my child."

Whether cow or ewe, you shall not kill it and its young in one day.

My mother jumped out the window propelled by an aversion so basic our ancestors honoured it in animals. What had been recognized as an act of no greater cruelty to an animal, the Germans were going to inflict on her.

Send away a mother bird before capturing its young.

I don't know whether my mother had heard of the massive ghetto deportations that autumn of 1942 in Lodz and Warsaw, in which the children were taken first. Sometimes they were laid on platforms in the ghetto square crying for their mothers in order to bring home how helpless the Jews were. Or of the infants thrown out of windows and shot by soldiers on the ground like game in the air.

Nisht in mayne oigen. Not in front of my eyes.

"Outside the house there must be another soldier with a rifle.

"'Hurry up,' Wagner said to us.

"The frightened women whispered to each other. 'The men will save us.'

"'The men must be in trouble of their own,' I thought.

"'God will save us,' the women whispered.

"'Gott would save us,'" mutters my mother. "'Gott is an SS man.' I threw Lusia out the window. Then I jumped. We fell. I turned my back toward the house to receive the bullet. But no bullet came. I scooped Lusia up, and ran. I tried to kill us and we were alive. That's the only reason we are alive.

"I ran into the field and sat in the high grasses. There were other mothers with children in the house with me – *mames mit kinder*. There was my mother." Her voice cracks into a lower register that I would do anything not to hear. "I held Lusia without making a sound. Fifteen minutes later I watched the SS man drive them out of the house to the wagon. He beat them as he drove them. I watched him beat my mother.

"It was bad with me that night," my mother says in her tearless voice.

"I will tell you everything about myself, but I can't talk about those who died." Her speech lightens only to travel more quickly. "All that I am telling you is nothing," my mother said. "To say what happened as it happened keeps only to the living and for that reason does not tell the truth. As much as we don't talk about the stones and the air and the trees but they are there; so much were there the living who died."

"They wandered all night," said my father.

"You're not telling it right!" my mother bursts in. "Lusia was trembling like a leaf. Every step was a *toyt shrek*, a risked death.

"We wandered the whole night," my mother begins again, "frightened by the sounds of dogs barking. Sometimes I carried her, sometimes she walked beside me."

In my mother's blind tearless sight, this child she wanted to die with rather than watch her be killed, with whom she survived instead to watch her own mother being led away, was it that night the wrench occurred, so that this child she would rip through barbed wire to save, she would steal potatoes to keep alive, she would risk her life many times over ("May I die, but let her live") but she would never touch her again?

"Every now and then we saw the light of a farmer's cottage. But whomever we asked might denounce us. Lusia was shivering. I knocked on the door of a farmhouse. The farmer looked at us and shook his head. 'Who is it?' said his wife. '*Zhids*. Jews. Mother and child.' 'They can't stay here,' said the woman. He took a lamp and led us to the hayloft where he kept feed for the animals.

"The farmer brought us a piece of bread and a bowl of milk. I tore off some bread and gave it to Lusia. 'No, you,' she pushed it back to my mouth. 'You eat, Mama.' I should eat."

My mother got restless sitting in the hayloft. "Say that there was a time when only the worst fear could match reality," says my mother.

"Every minute was another minute. You could not think even one step ahead. What am I sitting here for? What am I waiting for? We will be found and we will be shot. I asked the farmer whether the *lager* in town still existed, were there still Jewish people? There was no place to go, having escaped one camp, but into another camp.

"He said that when his son took a wagon of vegetables into town, we could ride with him.

"When we got to town I set Lusia on the road beside the farmer's son. German soldiers patrolled the streets.

"'Why are you trembling, there is nothing to be afraid of.' She was blonde, she looked nothing like me; she has Slavic features like her father. If something happened to me, nobody would take her for a Jewish child. I put her hand in the boy's hand and asked them to walk ahead.

"Walk in front of me. And don't look back, do you hear me? Whatever you do, don't look back." My mother walked behind, making the space between herself and her child larger and larger.

"At the gates to the camp lay four dead bodies. I recognized them, I knew who they were. They had been shot trying to enter the camp while the gates were closed. But the gates to the camp were open. Yes, they were open. We had no place else to go. We walked in."

The first time she watched with her child from the bushes as they beat her mother and took her away. The second time, in July 1943 in the railroad camp, my mother was on cleaning duty in the barracks surrounded by barbed wire when they came. While an armed soldier searched the place she tore through the barbed wire with Lusia. She never again saw her sisters.

"I wasn't good to you? I'm a bad mother?" my mother thundered. "Who threw you out the window? Who pushed you through the wires? I saved you!" The bedroom door slammed shut again.

She saved her. She threw her out the window. She pushed her through the wires. You did not leave the life of a human being then to God or man, only to a mother.

"There is not a breath I draw without thinking of my little sisters." My mother's voice rocks in supplication. "Oh, what do you want from me, what have I done for this to befall me?"

"Ma, stop, please!" I run to her in a panic.

"There are nights I go to sleep and pray never to wake up again. I saved you because I'm a mother!" My mother pounds on the door: "I'm a mother!"

"Is that her fault, that you saved her?" says my father.

My father turns to me on the couch under the Eskimo Madonna.

"When the train arrived in Częstochowa, Lusia trembled at the Germans with rifles," says my father. "They took the children away. We gave her what we had for her, a little coat, in case she should need it."

"I dressed her," my mother turns back with limp hands. "She was shaking with fear. 'Mama, *Dai me do pani!*' Give me away to a Gentile lady!" she pleaded. "I said, 'Don't be afraid. There is nothing to be afraid of. Am I afraid?' I laughed. I made myself laugh."

They kept her for three days.

Then they gave the children back. "You see, I was right, her mother was always right. She believed me when I said there was nothing to be afraid of. But I was afraid for the rest of my life."

They gave her back, but my mother could no longer take her back. During those three days and nights, her soul contracted itself so tight that it pinched itself out like the flame of a candle.

My sister comes into the kitchen. "Why did you never show me any affection?" asks my sister.

"Because I did not want to get attached to you," my mother answers. Her hands fall limp by her sides. "She says I have been a bad mother, that I have shown her no warmth; that she never saw me smile. Can you understand it? Who else has done what I have done for their child? I am a force of nature," says my mother. Like the goddess searching for her daughter, she would have frozen the earth.

I wonder at the strange limpness of this force of nature, my mother. Head thrown like an axe to the wind, but the unquestioning limbs are quick to go passive, to take the rifle butt, the blow to the head, the fall on hard ground.

After the war her hands could no longer do anything small, detailed, or gentle. All gestures incommensurate with those three days fell useless and irrelevant from her. She could no longer hold a baby. The site that burned out her mother sight was a Holy Mother site. She became a wanderer in the intense cold, throwing her face into the wind until it was numb. Only then would the tears flow. "*Ich bin a meshigine mame.* I am a crazy mother."

"When your mother began to have birth pangs with Lusia," says my father, "this was in 1938, before the war – I took her to the hospital in Piliv, where she was born. Demblin didn't have a hospital. I held her by the hand the whole way; she was shaking like a leaf. Like a leaf." I don't know whether my mother had a premonition of what motherhood would demand of her, or whether her extreme courage has always been a measure of her extreme fear.

My mother never had the patience but this summer afternoon of my sister's visit she allows her well-groomed elder daughter to polish her nails. My mother's worn hands fall limp into my sister's. Mother and daughter sit at the kitchen table, the mother making the ultimate sacrifice of keeping still. The daughter's blond silken head bends over the mother's hands in concentration, as she gingerly holds the fingers one by one and carefully brushes each nail. "She likes that," Lusia says, "having me do her nails." It is sometimes as easy as pleasing a child, pleasing her mother.

Finger by finger the daughter applies a soft rose colour, her own plump white immaculate fingers curled apart as when playing the piano so as not to touch by accident her mother's blind worn hands. I have never seen a kiss or hug between them, except when my sister turns a perfunctory cheek on arrival and departure. Occasionally, with fascination my mother admires the fair hairs on her daughter's skin, but never touches it.

They gave her back, but my mother could no longer take her back. Once the goddess tore the flesh from her flesh, how should she take it back? How could she coddle, comfort, console this hacked-away piece of herself? Mother and child are frozen in profound misunderstanding: my mother froze her tears in order to show her child a tearless face. My father called her a "hot" mother. She was the deceptively frozen Inuit mother who could suspend life in order to sustain it. My mother gave her life twice over. For this she condemned herself to wander the wintry streets – the colder the better; like Demeter, she took the realm of winter for her own. Only the extreme cold could make the tears stream down her face.

"I hate to have her touch me." My sister shudders. "She is my *biological* mother."

Lusia holds each of her mother's fingers as if it would burn her. "Don't move and don't touch anything." My mother smiles shyly and lifts her eyes at this impossible request, but she kvells that her daughter knows the proper impossible requests to make.

Gingerly my sister applies a clear sealing coat, something my mother never did, because she did not have the passion. My mother is beatific, the dishrag forgotten on the table. Her child, on the other hand, knows how to do everything. This paragon of elegance and propriety, her daughter, is deigning to touch the untouchable. Where did she learn this? The mother knows she has taught her nothing and yet miraculously her daughter has learned how to do everything.

My sister releases her mother's hands with the fingers drifted apart in the air. "Don't touch anything until they are dry," commands my sister. My mother raises her hands in helpless delight. Those blind, worn, passive hands pushed her through barbed wire, pushed her out a window, and pushed her away as she made the space between herself and her child larger and larger.

I leave them together, blonde head to greying brunette. I have to parlay brittle barriers to peck my sister on the cheek. "Eat something. You look *hoishech*. Yellow like a corpse," my mother says, regally accepting my goodbye kiss.

"Wait!" My mother roused herself and started throwing food into a bag. "Wait, wait, wait."

"Leave her alone, my God," said my sister. "When she gets hungry, she'll eat."

"A lot you know!" my mother said.

I take the bag and hurry out the door. The jar of soup loosely covered with wax paper knocks over, a greasy spot spreads through the paper bag until it shreds, a *klops* falls on the carpet, I pick it up, it crumbles...

Later that night I called my sister.

"Are you all right?" I asked.

She giggled. I was relieved to hear she had recovered from this "scene." My mother had made a fresh batch of gefilte fish as a peace offering. My sister used to come home late and plough into my mother's freshly cooked pots of food so that sometimes my mother hid the pots under the bed. Not for the first time my sister gagged on a bone that had escaped the blind aim of my mother's axe. My mouth must have learned to feel for sharp objects but my sister swallowed everything whole.

"I woke them up. Father wanted to get up and take me to hospital, but Mother just sat up and laughed! Oh, she told me to eat some old bread. She couldn't stop laughing. She said the Queen Mother has been known to choke on a fishbone too. I might have *died!*"

My mother did not light Sabbath candles. The only candles that were lit in our immigrant kitchen were the thick white *yurzeit* candles in a glass left burning overnight on the anniversary of a death. She herself was a flame of memory that burned night and day.

My mother refused to sit still for our attempted seders. As soon as my father would start telling about the new suit his mother used to order for him at Passover, my mother's eyes began to glitter dangerously.

"Why don't you want to have a Passover Seder?" I asked my mother.

"People who have families celebrate," my mother said.

"But ma," I said, "You have a family."

The truth was, my mother had not only us, she had Feivel, Tzetl, and Binim. If every Seder you sit down at contains every other Seder you have ever sat down at, if every remembrance contains the remem-berers, then my mother would have had to sit through a Seder with Ester, Rivka, Pearl, Shayndel, Israel with the door thrown open in the spring of 1939.

"I used to like the hard-boiled eggs in salt the best ..." my father began. When my mother yanked the tablecloth off the Seder table, she woke up the present of which the ritual is made.

On Yom Kippur my mother threw open our house to feed the weak who were exempt from fasting. "I'm not fasting! I fasted enough in the *lager!*"

Chapter Eight

POPPYSEED CAKE

The next time I went over to my parents' house that summer, things were completely different. My mother has invited guests for *kolatzie*, a light supper. On these occasions, my mother reached into memory and brought forth a Tolstoyan banquet: cheese *nalesniki*, Russian salad, marinated herring, a palette of bread, shot glasses. Brilliantly lit, sparkling with glasses, it could have been the same table, thirty years later, as the one around which the survivors gathered in the 1946 Lodz photo. Late at night, over cups of tea and slices of poppyseed cake, the conversation veered toward the *katzet*, the *oboz*, the *lager*, and every other German or Polish name by which I know the concentration camp.

As a child in the same room or another, my stomach sank precipitously according to the turning of two Germanic prefixes: *iberkumen* I parsed as "over" and "come" so "overcome," "come through," "survive"; and its opposite *umkumen* or *umgekumen*. Heard awake in the night, the active and the passive prefix switching on and off in the conversation meant they were talking about the *milchume*. *Iberkumen*, the word that brought momentary relief, begins with the prefix *iber*– close to the German *über*–, "over," as in the Nietzschean *Übermensch*. But in my parents' friends' conversation I never heard *iberkumen* used in the Germanic sense of attacking or heroic overcoming, only in the sense of coming through an ordeal, surviving. It was in those nights that they brought up the constant sadistic background, such as

Petersen who had to have his dog kill a Jew before breakfast. There was no word for *survivor* in the triumphal sense; anyone who survived was someone who had simply come through or been rescued. For what they came through or were rescued from, they simply say the Hebrew word for war, *milchume.*

"When the final Demblin work *lager* was liquidated in July 1944, we were sent to Częstochowa in two transports. We travelled fifty people to a car, without eating and without water," said Wolf. "And upon arriving in Częstochowa they immediately shot fifteen children up to the age of thirteen. They'd prepared the graves beforehand."

Once I heard my father tell what happened in those three days in Częstochowa to save the children of the second transport.

"The wife of the German commandant was about to give birth," he said. "The commandant's wife had no doctor to attend her. Among our transport of Jewish prisoners there was a woman *gynécologue.* The commandant sent for her. And the doctor asked the commandant's wife to save the children.

"The wife was pregnant," he continued. "And, I don't know, I think she became afraid that Gott would punish her. The children were given back."

Out of my mother's nightmares surges the voice of a woman in the camp driven mad by randomness who shrieked that because her child had been killed, the other children should also be killed.

"It needn't have happened," Ben said. The Germans started transporting the Jewish Dembliners west to Częstochowa to get them out of the way of the advancing Russians who would liberate them. The Germans got themselves out of the way first, leaving only five soldiers in charge of the transports.

The Jews were not aware that the Germans were gone, but the Poles and the Polish underground nationalist army were.

"Venkart might have told us," Manya said.

"Venkart knew that we would be shot if we were set free in the countryside," Hershel responded. "A group of prisoners escaped to the River Wieprz to meet the approaching Russian army. Poles from surrounding villages and the Polish Nationalist army waited for the escaping Jews on both sides of the river. Sixty-four young Jews were murdered and the bodies thrown into the Wieprz. Six Jews managed to escape and survived. The camp commandant, Bortenschlager counted the number of prisoners at their arrival in Częnstochowa. Seventy Jews were missing."

This was why my mother took special pains to name and thank the Polish farmers who took her in those nights she wandered between camps carrying my sister. The night she tore through the wires of the railroad camp she tells of seeking shelter with the rich peasant Stachorsky, who later was informed on and hung. Or the schoolmaster Skovransky, killed by the same nationalist countrymen who were shooting Jews. There was Jan Karski, the Polish courier who brought reports from the Warsaw Ghetto of the genocide to Churchill and Roosevelt to no avail, and an underground organization that hid Jewish children in orphanages and convents.

At least the Poles fought against the Nazis. Other countries in central Europe, such as Romania and Hungary were allied with the Nazis, and evidently the Nazis considered Ukrainian nationalists the best concentration camp guards. In central Europe my parents made an exception only of the Czech people. This is forgotten because the United States quickly changed their focus to the war on communism. The only inadvertent justice meted out to these fascist states came in the form of the Soviet Army passing through on their way to Berlin.

In later years, I would hear that Poland was beautiful and should I ever revisit it, I must not miss Częnstochowa, a pilgrimage shrine for a statue of a Madonna that sheds tears. My sister forbade my parents to speak of the war in her presence. Her conscious memories begin "after," with the postwar Poland of her girlhood.

"After the war I bought Lusia a new raincoat," my father said with a chuckle, "she was so eager to wear it, she said she wished it would rain."

Two years after the war, as my father says, his family was in the best resorts. Looking at our postwar photos you would never guess anything had happened at all. In some respects, nothing had. Lusia had piano lessons, we went to resorts in the mountains, and we even had a dog that my sister carried everywhere. Although the Communist regime preached universality, she went to school in what was still a very Catholic milieu. She and her best friend Basha used to stop at a pastry store after school, where they bought puffy *ponchiks* frosted with sugar. One day Basha held the pastry still in its paper and watched my sister taking hearty bites. Suddenly Basha burst out crying.

"What's the matter?" Lusia asked.

"I don't want you to go to hell!" Basha wailed. "My parents said because you were Jewish you are going to hell!"

"Stop crying," my sister said, "I am *not* going to hell."

"She was already," my father said.

"She is *nervova*," says my mother. "It is no wonder, what she went through during the war! She used to cover one leg with the other to keep warm," my mother rocks back and forth, "no shoes, no coat."

Lusia retained a childlike self-indulgence that my parents grabbed at like a straw.

In the July heat, my father had brought home a tawny fur coat for Lusia. "One really needs a fur coat in England in the winter," my sister bubbled. My parents relaxed. "She is in a good humour." Of course, she couldn't wear it outside in ninety-degree weather.

Thanks to the air conditioning of their new apartment, she could model it for them. My father tested the sit of the shoulders, looking from one to the other with pride, and steps back. "Wait," he said, lifting the collar to frame her hair.

"Marilyn Monroe," my mother said.

"You can wear open or with belt," my father said, sitting down quickly on the couch.

"Why are you speaking so softly?" The look of exhaustion on her father's face stirred up unbearable feelings. In therapy, these feelings were called guilt. Guilt was the guilty party, and as far as she could bring herself to remember the source of this guilt was my parents. If only our persecutors had been afflicted with a fraction of the guilt we are always trying to cure ourselves of. She grew so exquisitely attuned to her own sensitivities that the slightest furrow on my father's brow sparked a temper tantrum in her. In the year that my father mistook his heartache for chest and stomach pain, Lusia brought home from a psychology course the word *hypochondriac*. Feeling bad for her father turned into his putting on a tired face expressly to make her feel guilty.

"I climbed up and down the steps," he said.

"So what, it's good exercise! I get so angry at your sad faces!"

"I am not sad. The air was so humid, it stood on my chest."

"If you are sick I shouldn't have come," she said, and flounced out of the room, her new coat flapping.

Sigmund Freud recounts how as a small boy he was walking down the street with his father when a Gentile smashed his father's hat into the gutter. The father stooped to pick it up. The son, who worshipped Hannibal, the conqueror and crosser of the Alps, didn't want to see this. He wanted his father to do something heroic.

On the other hand, if the son had not been barred from university positions because he was a Jew, he might not have stooped to treating neurotics.

"Tata?" Now that he really did have chest pains, she did not believe him. His beaten face infuriated her. "He's weak," she said, not recognizing her own face creasing into his frown. Once, he smuggled bread in for her where she was not officially alive. We only know this because he was caught. Her parents surpassed all heroic deeds in their efforts to save her. They succeeded only so long as their acts were well enough assimilated into the system that was trying to destroy them as to remain undetected.

He was proud of her. "My daughter is the best teacher," he told everyone. Proud of her? She could have been Marie Curie, Wanda Landowska, Rosa Luxembourg. He didn't know any better than to be proud of her.

She was ashamed of him, standing there with his hat in hand. "Please come and visit us when you are in Canada," he would say to her English friends, handing them his salesman's card. She could just see her mama doing away with them, with fishbones.

"But why do I feel so bad?" she asked herself. "Is it because of my parents' gross insensitivity to me? Why do I feel so bad?"

◆ ◆ ◆

A year later, I was speaking to my sister in London on the telephone from Paris. This was where I hovered precariously, gamely surviving by teaching English for a bouncy madame with an *école des langues* in the Place de la Madeleine. I stopped for a few drops of a racy men's cologne in the Cerruti store on the corner. *La convoitise.* "I don't *need* anything!" I used to say when my parents inflicted gifts on me. "A *dead* person doesn't need anything!" my mother roared back. She was right. To covet – it was a sign of life.

"Nice cities you both chose!" my mother harrumphed. But I could have told my mother that we lived in those cities not without her. I thought of the silence pressing in on my parents on Sunday afternoons. My father quietly rewashed the dishes my mother washed, because she did not have the patience to get them clean. Now they have a dishwasher, which he knows she will never learn to use.

In their new building if my father is late coming home from work, she pounds on the neighbour's door.

"You don't understand, you have family," my mother says, "I have nobody."

"Don't be so nervous," the neighbour says, "he'll be home soon."

"I have only him!" says my mother. "I have only him!"

My mother called me from Montreal:

"Your father passed through his operation yesterday." I winced at hearing "passed through": *iberkumen*.

"Why didn't you tell me when he went into the hospital?" I said.

"You don't need to know," she scoffed. "Oh, leave me alone. I have to take two buses in the snow. It's no party in the hospital. I'm not young anymore!"

I call the hospital and ask for my father. My mother would have no patience for such details as his room number. The receptionist transfers me to admitting, which transfers me to Postoperative Care, which transfers me back to admitting. "One moment, please …" None of the posts can find him. I begin to feel dizzy.

"Are you sure he's in this hospital?" asks the receptionist.

They've lost my father!

"Will you spell his name again?"

I spell it both ways: I spell it in English, which makes it easier for Canadians, and in Polish, the way it is on our legal documents. "Oh, W-A-J- Wajnberg not Weinberg. Wait a moment …"

"Hallo."

"Dad, Dad, are you okay?" Euphoric relief to hear his voice.

"Yes, yes, they just took out the pipes. You should see what a good job the surgeon did!"

My parents and sister have been meeting in Israel every Passover, and my father's surgery did not diminish my mother's drive to go.

"Why do you stay with her, Dad?" I once asked him.

"At the beginning in the *lager*, you had to wait in line for a cup of coffee. I couldn't," he said with a shrug. "She waited in line instead."

"Lusia will be disappointed if I don't go," my mother said over the telephone. As this is unlikely, as my mother has not bothered to inform Lusia of my father's operation ("We don't want to worry her!"), and as I have heard that despite appearances it was not good for either of my parents to be separated from the other, I call my sister and tell her that our father is ill.

"I'll have to reorganize my plans," she whispers. "Of course I'm not going without Father there. She shouldn't be going and leaving him alone. Why didn't anyone tell me?" she steams.

Why? As if our mother has never violated laws of disclosure before. You would think I could take some short cuts with my sister on the subject of our parents. But she reconstitutes her sense of how her family should be so that she can be freshly appalled by us each time. So I explain. I trot out motivation, character, and plot. I hear my immigrant accent vibrating in the silence on the other end of the telephone.

Finally she laughs – a squeak, but still, whew, a laugh. "I should tape your voice and play it every night so I can laugh at your jokes," she says.

My momentary relief turns into dismay. Every night? It means my sister still thinks about my mother every night.

"You should really take the opportunity while you are in France to improve your French," is the last thing she says.

The next time my parents went to Israel, my father stopped in Paris on his way home. My mother remained in Israel. Perhaps my mother thought, "If I am here, the children and husband will follow." Most likely she didn't think but was driven to keep moving with the same demonic heedlessness with which she stuffed me with food. The one time that my father was late in calling her from Paris, she was on the next plane home. On the way back, she harassed her husband to intercede for her with Lusia.

"*Matka* wants to know if she can visit you. What will I tell her?"

"Oh!" said my sister as if struck. "How dare you? Don't you know it makes me sick to see her? She practically killed Elizabeth when she was little! My hands shake so badly I can't hold the chalk!"

My sister tried to explain herself. "I wrote them twenty times," she said. Very like my calling home twenty times to tell my mother why I couldn't call her, she had written my parents over and over. "Dear Mother and Father, You cannot come to visit me this year." She wrote this various ways in Polish over and over on twenty pieces of paper.

I do not have to see them ever again unless I want to! They cannot come and stay with me even if they have paid for my apartment.

At first, she would get only as far as the first line before she started over. "You can't come visit me because –" There was no need to give a reason. Next time, she wrote several lines before the entire page ended heavily scratched out.

The next day she felt empty and sick. *Why do I feel so guilty telling them not to come?* "It is not convenient." She never sent any of the letters.

The last time they were together, my mother had made a "scene." In England, avoiding scenes was the national virtue.

"God! The first thing was, she gave away the perfume I asked her to get for me and got me the wrong one! She doesn't even realize what she's done."

"What have I done? What have I done?" my mother asked.

"Is it right to have piled all your suffering on me, to have told me these things since I was a small child? I hate you for what you did to me!" Lusia exploded.

"What have I done to you? I saved you, that's what I did to you?" my mother said with a spasm. "Oh, If only I could go to sleep and not wake up again!"

"Why don't you do it, kill yourself if you are so miserable?"

"I don't know how," said my mother.

"You know what Lusia said to me when I was leaving?" my mother would tell my father when she got home. "She said, 'Be happy. You have a husband and children, I have nobody.'"

At which my father clutched his heart.

◆ ◆ ◆

"Be nice to her, she's sick!" my mother yelled at me over the transatlantic phone. My parents were frantic. My sister had suffered a breakdown. Whenever they called her, she refused to speak to them.

"How are you?" I asked my sister.

"My life changed four months ago," she whispered. That was when physiological depression hit, the kind that made her previous use of the word *depressed* wanton. "My God, I *missed* my old depressions. I take lithium and antidepressants and a tranquilizer and still –"

Her whispering voice stops, and we are suspended in silence. I have always tiptoed around my sister not to crack her eggshell equilibrium. The quieter her voice became, the louder, I feared, the storm raged inside.

"Lusia?"

"*Wait*," she hisses. Silence. I hold my breath and wait. Through the telephone comes the sound of an industrial whistle. "I'm waiting for a train to pass," she whispers, because no way would she raise her voice over the train.

"They wanted to put me in hos –" she starts over several times. "They wanted to put me in hospital, but my friends took turns watching over me."

"You must have been terrified," I say.

"You haven't got the faintest notion!" she snaps. "Father knows how I feel. When I told him I felt bad enough to commit suicide, he said he has felt like that too."

I think of my father driving around the city, his face in spasm. "We were so worried! We were so worried!" She refused to answer their calls. "I'm not speaking to them until they admit their role in my suffering!"

She wouldn't speak to him, so he wrote her a letter. "I know your suffering," he began in Polish. He wrote her six pages of shaky handwriting telling her about the illness that befell him twenty years ago. He told her about wandering from doctor to doctor with chest and stomach pain until he met the psychiatrist who had given a name to his illness and prescribed pills. He thought of suicide on his flight to Miami, but he couldn't do it to his children. He thought of it until the drugs began to have an effect. He wrote her a second letter. He had left out something, he said. He wrote out exactly his regimen of drugs, the dosages, and how long before they took effect.

"What exactly do they say it is?" I asked.

"They don't know all that much about it. Genetic predisposition from Father, or the war and the mother we have were cause enough. They think the abandonment … when they took Father away to Buchenwald."

"Did anything special happen just before? What triggered it?" The National Health course of therapy came to a close, she said. The therapist she had told me about, the one who told her she had to love herself first, she was not to see her again. "I got attached to her," she said, with a smack of black humour that the next moment dissolved in tears.

My parents and sister saw each other in Israel, where Lusia came to spend her spring break. "Worse than I thought," my sister decided when she saw them. "Mother has aged a lot and is wearing a tragic expression on her face."

Looking at their faces revived an anguish that Lusia must at all costs flee from or vanquish. "Being with her is like being in a grave. She tells me she will tell me everything on her deathbed. But I won't be there!"

And so it was. Although our mother would not be able to tell her anything, my sister wasn't there.

At this time my sister returned to one of her former analysts, not for analysis but because he knew her the longest. He would grow old telling her it was normal to be angry with one's parents.

"But why do I feel so bad? Why do I feel so bad? Is it because these are the faces I saw in the camps?"

She's gotten so dirty, my sister thought when they stayed together. "Please make some effort for me and do not put your comb near the soap."

"I am eighty-two years old," my mother said.

"Is that my fault? I am not responsible for your age, your suffering. I am not responsible for mortality!" My sister pushed my mother out of the bathroom. She was shaking. My mother, stricken that she might have caused Lusia worry, said, "My blood pressure has gone down since Dr. Lerner gave me these blood pressure pills."

"So you lied! You blackmailed me."

"She must have realized she upset me," my sister told me. "She went away without saying anything." My mother did not used to be at a loss for words. But my sister's illness frightened my parents. And our mother was beginning to outgrow us.

"She said nothing. She went away and said nothing for hours. It was so strange. Hours later, she knocked on the door of my room. She stood in the doorway, her arms hanging down by her sides. All she said was, 'The fish is ready.'"

◆ ◆ ◆

I spoke to my sister on the telephone and saw my parents as they passed through Paris and visited me in California, but I would not see them all together again until the summer of 1993 when my mother's crisis brought us together again in Montreal.

The last time I saw my family together before then was that summer of 1980 in Montreal when we all went to the airport to see Lusia off. As soon as we arrived, my sister went off in search of infants. "Oh! I want to see the babies!" She asked to see the nursery where children about to travel were taken to be changed or to have a nap.

"Where are you going? You'll miss your plane," my mother sighed. "That's Lusia, tender beneath the prickles." Some uncharacteristic delicacy restrained her from bursting out with the obvious: if she hadn't *bagruben* herself, if she did what I told her, she would have her own babies. Would that she had never given birth rather than lived to see this. Such a fair flawless skin, such a figure, such gifts, there wasn't a thing she couldn't do once she set her mind to it. Professor Orlovski said she was his best student. "Do you have a candy?" she asks my father. "The taste in my mouth is bitter as gall."

The child she saved, grown almost beyond the age of bearing children herself, wants only to look at other children. My mother looks on the spectacle of her own daughter with something of the village superstition for the crippled or the retarded. But it's not the cripple one feels the worst for, my mother sighs, it's the cripple's mother. "Look at her," she says, "*en gantsen meshige*." My sister is in the nursery giggling, happy and self-absorbed, for all the world like a child herself.

"How could you not want children?" my mother turns on me. "A child is everything."

"I am glad I have seen Lusia again," my mother said in her tearless voice as we walked toward the gate. "She says I have been a bad mother; that I have shown her no warmth; that she never saw me smile. Can you understand it? Who else has done what I have done for their child?

"I am happy to have seen her," my mother said lightly. She says this in the same tearless voice in which she says, "I am glad I saved her. I am glad I have lived to the moment to see her alive." But when or where this moment of gladness took place nobody knows.

At the gate my mother began to tremble. We were standing together looking down the path to the exit door, where beneath us the sign at the arrival gate says, "Welcome to Canada." Looking down the runway, I see shelter after many uprooting; I see a northern land whose fierce winter protects new beginnings. Where I see a potent freshness, she sees barrenness after the conflagration, a continent bereft of mother and sisters and shtetl and the memory of everything she has known and lost, and across from our house she sees new railroad tracks strung with wire. Where I see arrival stretching toward a future that has already long begun, she sees down the runway a road to a past that will never cease to plummet toward her as the present. She trembles like a leaf. "Lusia," she says, "Lusia. When will I see you again?"

Chapter Nine

"HE WILL TURN THE CHILDREN TOWARD THE PARENTS," 1990

My parents led me to the *chuppah*, the canopy, when I was forty-three, they in their seventies and eighties – this was just in time because soon my mother became unable to lead me anywhere.

I shortened the march up the aisle to a sideswipe from the wings, because my mother had taken to falling. She fell as I welcomed her off the plane at John Wayne Airport. From the arrival gate I saw her mouth open for an instant, but her legs gave way and she crumpled to the ground. My mother was to fall countless times after that, but as if her body had memorized it a long time ago, she did not hurt herself. My fiancé mustered a wheelchair.

"Ma, this is Allan."

"Where? Oh!" she said, twisting around. "Graceful figure," she commented approvingly in Polish.

"This is Santa Ana, yes?" my father said, searching for a centre. We were in centerless southern California, where my father found me by telephone soon after I arrived, having heard on the news of an earthquake.

When I first told my father over the telephone that I was getting married in California, he was stunned.

"We'll rent a hall," he said when he found his voice. I could hear him fumbling for the happy protocol he had long since packed away in mothballs. "You'll come here and you'll get married again," he decided, and hung up.

I hung up the phone unsettled. I should have been relieved that there would be no fuss. I was still taking prednisone in the wake of a total-bowel colitis attack that for the first time and thereafter had to be stopped with steroids. But I couldn't believe that my parents would not come to my wedding.

It was true that sometimes my father surprised me, perhaps in reaction to my mother, by under-reacting. Five minutes later, the telephone rang. I heard my mother breathing down my father's neck. "We're coming," said my father.

It was Allan who had brought up the subject of a Jewish wedding. Allan was an ecologist, born in West Virginia (once; unlike his brothers who were born again). From the nose down he looked like Jimmy Dean. We took a short course in Jewish tradition.

"I guess you would like one of those canopies," he said.

"Yes, I would," I said, realizing how much. "I like even more the groom stamping on the glass."

"Great," he said, "I'll pick up four bamboo poles at Home Depot –"

"I don't know," I said, "where would they have gotten bamboo in Poland?"

"Where in the Torah does it say it can't be bamboo?" he said.

I had a headache.

Actually, the rabbi said to bring a light bulb instead of a wineglass to stamp on, it made a more satisfying popping noise and was safer.

Holding on to my arm leading me to the *chuppah* was the last fifty steps my mother walked upright. In Jewish tradition, both parents lead their child, son or daughter, to the wedding canopy. With my mother clasping my left arm and my father my right, we began the reversal to a path where I would lead them.

There was a little fracas at the head table. I asked my father to bless the bread at the beginning of the meal. My mother, who had grown a little deaf, was mystified to see my father standing up and mumbling in Hebrew. "What are you doing?" she asked him in Yiddish. From the other side of the table Allan's Bible-belt brothers clamoured to say grace.

"But that's exactly what my father is doing," I said.

"What are you doing?" my mother said louder.

"Leave him alone!" the bride yelled at her mother.

My sister did not come but sent a gift, saying she wanted: one, pictures; and two, my description of the event.

After the reception I turned back toward them to wave goodbye as Allan and I got into the car and drove to our hotel, a few yards down the beach from theirs. The next morning we found them on a bench beside the ocean. I smeared sunscreen over my parents' faces. "Mummy has something to say," said my father. My mother got up, smoothed her blouse down neatly, and turned to Allan. "We are not religious," she said, "but thank you for having a rabbi." Then she sat down.

During the ceremony, my friends had shed tears beside my mother who stood by dry-eyed. My mother once dragged my uncle Feivel and male cousins from New York to my sweet sixteen. She would have dragged every living Dembliner if she could. For that wartime generation there was no question but that everyone attend the smallest of every *landsman*'s children's birthdays, bar mitzvahs, weddings.

History fills the cup with everyone's tears. But to see my parents' friends wipe their eyes on such occasions raised goosebumps. Thank you for bringing us alive to this moment; that we have lived to see the day and the impossibility of once ever envisioning making it to this day. But neither personal nor historical pressure welled up in my mother. She excused her dry eyes to my friends: "Since the war I cannot cry."

◆ ◆ ◆

After the wedding I asked them to take their winter vacation in California. I reserved a bachelor's penthouse apartment in Laguna Beach overlooking the ocean. When they arrived I knew it was a mistake. I had put off this reunion for too long.

It wasn't only that my mother could barely walk, that her gait had tightened to a toddle. I watched the unusual delicacy with which my mother opened her purse to look for the hard-boiled eggs she'd stashed for the trip. Finally, she gave up and handed the bag to my father. "What a *moishif* – what a mess, Hela," my father quietly remonstrated as he sorted through the scraps in her bag. The extreme gentleness of his voice frightened me. He was speaking to a child.

My harried father was being run off his feet to fetch and carry, while my mother lay marooned on a couch or a chair. If she stood up at all, it was with an impatience exacerbated by the inability to stand. "*Lomir shoyn gayn*," she pleaded. "Let's go already." When I sat with my father on the beach, the sun brought out stains on the canary-yellow sweater I had given him. This was unlike him; he must be too busy tending my mother to spare any resources for himself. Yet when I invited them to California they had gamely accepted. They were at an age when a different layout of a house, an uncustomary route to the beach, let alone an entirely strange town, imposes on adaptability.

The apartment owner had not mentioned that the old-fashioned four-poster bed was a waterbed. "I'm getting seasick!" giggled my eighty-five-year-old mother, bobbing up and down. My mother was still laughing when I bandaged the bloody flesh where my father had scraped the skin from his back when he fell out of it. I was there every day, because it seemed an enormity to leave them alone without *menschen*, without neighbours or acquaintances within earshot as they would have in Montreal or Miami. What do people in California do when they get too old to drive? Move into a ghetto.

My mother, always anxious for our presence, now didn't let my father out of her sight for a minute. "Where are you going?" she called after him as he let Allan and me out. "I'm going to open the door for them!" he said. "Are you coming back?" she fretted. "What do you think?" he shouted back up the stairs.

Dishevelled personal appearance, stains on a formerly neat lady or gentleman's shirt signal a loss of attention, but how could that tell me anything about my mother, whose chaotic territory I had known all my life? She always came full tilt to meet me at the elevator in the middle of eating a whole tomato, spilling tomato seeds down her frontage.

How could I have known? She was the same as she always had been, I thought, only more so.

One afternoon I stood in the penthouse kitchen with the sun blazing in on my mother's burned pots and lipstick stains (*Too strong*, I thought, *the sun is too strong for these frail people*), and was suffocated by the aroma rising hot from the kitchen floor. "You have to do something about your mother!" said Allan and ran out onto the balcony for air. I looked at my constrained father. How long had he been living like this?

All the way in from the airport while my mother regally acknowledged, "This is the Pacific?" my husband had sniffed the air. The smell of urine was as unmistakable and as overwhelming as the ocean where my mother foundered like a sinking ship to which we would hold on and not let go. My mother had urge incontinence that caused her to dribble unconsciously and constantly like a natural spring. Her feet padding around the kitchen left footprints. No chair or sofa was left unwatered. As she toddled out of Las Brisas, I glanced nervously at the diners downwind of us.

The next day, I brought a walker and a box of adult diapers with me. "What a pearl! What a gem!" my mother kvelled as Allan mopped the kitchen floor. When gathering up all my nerve I broached the subject, my mother looked at me as if I had betrayed her. "Have you no other topic of conversation?"

I took her into the bedroom and I likened it to using sanitary pads for menstruation. To break through her embarrassment, I pulled down my own pants to demonstrate how to tape the pad. She stared straight ahead while I wrapped a diaper around her: stoic, blind, as *farnichted*, as extinguished as she could make herself.

At the sight of my mother, Allan went looking for a broom. "It is shameful to admit," he said later, "but I avoided your mother because – incontinent, unable to walk – she reminded me of my own neurological condition. I didn't used to want to go to hydrocephalus meetings: was I one of *them*?"

When my parents left, I had breakfast with them at the airport. My mother's dress kept opening to reveal her slip and I kept closing it. "Do you need to go to the bathroom?" I kept prompting over my mother's vigorous denials. The table filled with wisps of paper and wrappers as I opened the jam and butter packets, which my mother fumbled with ineffectually. I should have known something was wrong: all of her movements were tentative, whereas it used to be that only her attack had been blind. As the table filled with the proliferating mess that always quickly surrounded my mother, my father commented, "How big American coffee cups are! Everything American is big." I kept closing my mother's dress which had been fastened with a safety pin where a button had dropped off, and finally I gave up; if appearances were this hard to keep up, the hell with appearances. My children, I thought, they are my children. Until their plane was delayed and my mother insisted that I not wait with them, that I go home and eat something.

◆ ◆ ◆

In the months after they left California I tracked my parents by telephone.

"Has she seen Dr. Lerner?" I asked my father.

"Seen him?" he exploded. "Every time she sees him, she takes a bath, she gets dressed up, she thinks he's interested in her, she's twice his age! When he asks her if she can walk, she says yes."

"Why don't you tell him the truth, Dad?"

Silence. ("He's not dealing with it a hundred per cent," their GP will tell me later.)

"Didn't Dr. Lerner send her to a neurologist about her incontinence and her inability to walk?"

"The appointment time will come for her to see a specialist in arthritis," said my father, trading his maddening patience for her maddening impatience.

"What were the results of her CAT scan?"

"She didn't ask. She didn't want to go back to the neurologist." When I speak to this neurologist, and when I meet him much later, I will sympathize with my mother. But everything was fine; my father said and took over the conversation as if by heart, how he does the shopping at the supermarket, how they help him put it in his car, how he wheels it back upstairs on a pushcart.

"Who cooks?"

"Mummy cooks." Instinctively he knew if you fill up the conversation with the soothing drone of what's routine, there would be no room for what's not. The only thing he would admit to was his difficulty in helping my mother out of the bathtub. My father had angina and could have a heart attack lifting her. I called his psychiatrist, who made a request to the local social services for help in bathing my mother.

The social worker who paid them a visit called me up. "The whole apartment smells of urine." For the first time I was treated to opinions, judgments, evaluations on How Other People See Your Parents. I traced the neurologist they had seen. He looked up her file. "She was diagnosed with Alzheimer's last August," he said and hung up.

◆ ◆ ◆

I redoubled my race to make up for their lives. The reason I gave for our sudden trip to Montreal at the end of May was my mother's birthday.

My mother could not toddle from the stove to the table without holding on to the wall. Nevertheless when we arrived at their door, a huge pot of *pulkes* and *fees* was steaming on the stove to welcome me. "Put the *flomen* – the prunes – in the compote! Put the chicken in the broth!" she directed my father when she could no longer stand up.

"She wants to put everything in your mouth at once!" my father laughed.

We had lunch in the duck park at the Ritz. The hotel wheelchair was waiting for her when we arrived. "Oy, a *broch*," she said.

We barely returned home, replete from lunch, when my mother said she was going to make us supper. "Ma, we just ate," did not play. The food wars were not over. If it had at any time meant anything to her, the passage of time between meals had completely vaporized. Anyway, if she had not fed us herself, it didn't count that we had eaten. We took the opportunity to mop the kitchen and bathroom floors. "I'm going to show Allan Old Montreal."

"I'm making supper!" She rose alarmed, shuffled in little steps as fast as she could to the kitchen, and started breaking eggs.

"We'll eat out."

"What will it hurt to have something here first?" My mother propped herself up at the stove, pouring flour, eggs, and oil into a fry pan turned on high, to catch us before we could slip away. She was scorching *chemselechs*, the air-filled pancakes that a mother could conjure at a pinch from minimal resources to still hunger pangs. At the mention that we were leaving, she worked faster, the flames rising in her panic. When the smoke hit the ceiling, the smoke alarm went off.

"What are you doing?" my father came running.

"Get out the door!" I yelled at Allan.

"A minute, a minute, it'll only take a minute!" she pleaded. Through the door, she waved a spoon at me, successfully searing herself into my conscience. "One day you'll regret this!"

This was the mother on whose account I once nearly got off a plane when it made an unscheduled stop before crossing the Atlantic to avoid meeting on the other side. On my last visit to Montreal before getting married, my mother had hysterics when her forty-year-old daughter went out in the evening to have dinner with a friend. "You don't know what's happening outside!" As always, I anticipated her anticipation and told her I would be home much later than I intended. Living in her nerves in the taxi gliding through the quiet streets, I suddenly thought, *What if she is right? What if Montreal had drastically changed while I was away?* Sometimes I was so busy disproving her fears, I threw out all precautions.

With devastating effect, the thought instantly took form as a fear of the taxi driver. My heart lurched with every swerve and shadow. When I arrived, I saw from the cab the face of my eighty-three-year-old mother pressed against the plate-glass window of the apartment lobby. There stood the culprit, the destroyer of my and her own peace.

"Did you have a nice time, Lizzie?" asked my father.

"I had a nice time until I saw this crazy old woman pressed against the glass!"

"*I'm* crazy?" she blazed. "I alone jumped out the window with my child, they took thirty-eight other women and children to the gas chamber, and *I'm* the one who's crazy?"

◆ ◆ ◆

How could I have known? My mother was the same as she had always been: blindness shot through with clairvoyance. In the afternoon my father lay down on his living-room couch to rest while I sat on the sofa across from him that pulled out into my bed. Their apartment was a mess. My father was worn down, yet resisted my efforts to help. He lay down for a moment and put his head down on the couch.

"It's wet!" he said, raising his head.

"Mummy sat there," I said.

"Oy," he groaned.

I was sorry to have insisted. There were tears in his eyes.

There was no reason to push his face into the unfolding catastrophe that this time even their fullest alertness would not spare them. Throughout the entire time to come I would walk the tightrope between their autonomy and their safety. It took a *chuchem*, a sage, to choose which path would lead to the lesser suffering. The human ingenuity that had once gone into making them uncomfortable I now wanted to invert into sparing them pain.

"You are interfering in our lives!" my father protested. While they were out, I had installed safety bars in their bathroom and had a wheelchair delivered to their door. Worse than interfering, I had informed on them to a stranger. When my father had let drop over the telephone to me that it was a strain to lift my mother out of the bathtub, my telephone calls had resulted in a social worker being sent to their door. Barbara Slotkin from the local social services, whom my sister would call the Angel of Death, rode in on them with the kind of avenging fury that my mother herself was just beginning to slough off. "My God! She needs placement!"

I told my father there was as little chance of my not interfering as there had been of them not interfering in my life. "I'm sorry," he said the next day.

It was not only that their daughter was interfering in their lives. I was my mother's child whose rage to protect had brought me up virtually incompetent. It didn't matter to her that I lacked ambition, but I lacked such basic biological drives as having children. "Naive!" my mother roared. Nothing was worth doing, after what had happened to them. Nothing short of that merited a flicker of interest. But something almost like that earlier catastrophe was threatening them again.

This time, having heard she was ill, I had "broken parole" by leaving the United States to visit her while my resident-card proceedings were still going on. Half the time, I was still locked in battle with my mother. I would have to stop worrying about my own autonomy long enough to prop up hers.

At the same time, I was still so afraid of her I had allowed only two weeks for the immense task ahead.

At the Montreal airport, US Immigration stopped me. Allan had gone back the week before. I told them that I was a Canadian citizen married to an American. "Where's your resident card?" the officer asked. "I haven't got it yet," I said. I took a taxi back to the city. I was going to have to start all over at the embassy in Montreal. My parents were going to have me all summer.

"Elizabeth is staying here because of us," I heard my father berating himself to the social worker.

"No, I have no choice, Dad. They won't let me back in till I get my resident card."

"Don't try to fool him," said Barbara. "*S'iz nisht kayn aveyra*" (It's not a sin that she's staying here for you). The only time I ever heard the word used in Yiddish was as an irony on what wasn't a sin.

"She doesn't have the *kvitl*," my mother explained. It was a case of my not having the right *kvitl*, the ticket, the visa, the *laissez-passer*, the blue work paper that bought a little time, the *Bescheinigung* that justified how, through no fault of their own, they had missed the last transport; all of these twisted away from the *kvitl* on which you wrote a question that you slipped to your rebbe or through the Wailing Wall to God.

◆　◆　◆

On a Saturday morning in the car with my father, we are going to pick up some groceries when we see men dressed in suits and women in hats walking along Cavendish. "They are going to *shul*," said my father. "In Poland before the war, people used to come to my father's house to pray. We kept the *seyfer* – the Book – in the *shank*, in the cupboard." Loss and exile taught us to sanctify anywhere – a room in Poland – so long as it contained the Book. I will learn that this is how my parents met as children. "My brother-in-law was the prayer leader, what a voice he had!" His brother-in-law? Of course, his sisters were older and must have been married. And they must have had children too. He was the youngest, the *muzhikl*, as he calls me.

"My mother danced at my eldest sister's wedding while pregnant with me! My sister, Esther Hannah, came home to give birth. She hung between life and death." His mother threw herself at the doctor summoned to her daughter's childbed. "*Rateve mayn kind!*" Save my child!

Esther Hannah, one of the sisters killed by the Nazis. My genetic sharer. For whom they used to call in the local *felcher*, he says, the folk healer. She had internal intestinal sores that caused her to bleed. "Dad," I said, "I have what she had." "Maybe," he grudgingly admitted. He never allowed himself to believe that I had anything wrong with me.

My father's father, who died before the war, I know as the abundant forefather of my own father's generosity. "He gave me money.

Then, if he fell short of cash, he would ask, 'Srulec, maybe you have a few *groschen* to lend me.'" My father chuckles. His mother asked why his father entrusted such a young boy with bringing home a bag of coins. 'Why not? If he takes some, it must be because he needs it.' This is pretty well reproduced in my father and me.

"When my father married my mother, he was an unworldly scholar who did not even speak Polish. His father-in-law gave him *kest*, room and board, so he could continue to study. Then my father began to take an interest in his economic independence." He became a grain merchant and bought his youngest son, my father, a share in a mill. Which he then counselled my father to sell because the other partners were a bunch of low-lifes. My father found his place in the lumber business with his elder brother, Moishe, sledding from campfire to campfire on the forested estates.

My father and his brother would wait in the antechambers of the local counts, cap in hand, to bid for their timber. The count of the nearby Sobieszin estate ("a count is a *hraby*," my father said) the *hraby* Krashinsky married off his daughter, who apparently was considered less than stunning, to a prince. After the count died, the peasants were ruled by an absentee princess. "Sometimes the peasants were evicted from their homes just before Christmas," my father said. "Finally a law, a *ukaz*, came out that allowed the peasants to keep a part of their produce.

"A poacher on the estate shot the princess' handsome husband. His groom warned him not to ride through that part of the forest, but he didn't listen because for a nobleman *past nisht* to turn back." *Past nisht* was Yiddish for "it was not seemly," will not look good; in this case, according to the peacock code of the nobility.

"Sometimes," said Moishe, "the princess talks to me just like a normal human being, but sometimes she has to act like a princess. It is better for me when she is in her princess mood because then *past nisht* for her to bargain."

Her husband threw money back at them. "'Do not give me small change!'" Because the instant he got some cash he took the *shnelltzug* (the fast train) to Warsaw to gamble it away.

The Jewish villagers lived by a different code than the aristocrats did. The leap of abstraction that had conceived an imageless and placeless God also developed portable principles of lawmaking. What had been the law of the land became the law of the landless when the law of the land ostracized them. It was not so much of a stretch for my grandfather to go from studying Talmudic problems in trade to becoming a merchant – or a lawyer, or the most directly ethical of applications, a doctor, except that these would have required a Jew to enter a Polish university.

"Two men were once disputing a point in the street. 'Come ask the *ruv*,' my father said, 'he will look this up here and here.'

"'Oy, Mendl,' sighed the rabbi, 'if only everyone knew as much as you've forgotten.'"

I warm myself on my family, snatching the name of my grandfather – the first time I have ever heard it – out of the air.

"My family belonged to the Sokolow rebbe," my father said suddenly. There were the erudite rabbis who knew the laws, and there were the Chasidic rebbes who danced, told Talmudic parables, snatched joy out of extreme misery, and worked wonders. We were descended from those oppressed Polish Jews attached in each shtetl to a different rebbe.

"My father used to light one cigarette off the end of the other," my father says. "I was at the mill when a message came that he was dying. It was the first time I rode on a horse. When I arrived, he was still living but he no longer knew me.

"If he hadn't died then, Hitler would have killed him," he finishes my thought. "I said Kaddish for my father, and then I didn't pray again."

My father drives his Oldsmobile into the parking lot, memorizing its position in the bank of cars.

"Oh God, abandon me not when my hair is white," he hums, switching off the ignition.

◆ ◆ ◆

"Sru-lec! Sru-lec! Sru-lec!" my mother shouts louder and louder.

My father is midway from the living room to the bedroom. "I'm coming!" he puffs.

"Sru-lec!" She does not hear, and her circuits ever shorter, kills the interval by bellowing over and over nonstop, "Srulec!" I should have been glad to hear her using his name. Although married people once addressed each other in the third person out of respect, my mother's version was "*Hoch noh!*" the Yiddish equivalent of "Listen up!"

When I bring her a cup of tea, she peers under my arm into the kitchen where my father is drinking coffee with Marysia. All the time that I seek out Polish-speaking companions for my mother, I will be haunted by the profound contradiction of my parents' Polish ties. And by an accident of history, there are many Polish newcomers, whose first job – English or French not necessary– is in the homes of their long-since evicted Jewish compatriots. So this is where the Jews have gone, and must have done all right because we are looking after them.

"Why does everyone only have one thing on their minds!" my mother says in a huff. Marysia has asked my mother if she needs to go shoo-shoo, an expression I have not heard since my infancy.

If I wanted to spare my father, it has not worked. My mother has not taken to calling Marysia in his place. She would never impose on a stranger.

From my father's desk, I have been making the phone calls hooking up the social service network of the city. My tongue thick from telling my parents' story over and over, I am referred to a social worker who "works with Holocaust survivors." I am impressed by my city; I have been living outside the Pale. Here is the fact: Montreal had the largest population of Holocaust survivors anywhere outside Israel. And now they were aging. For forty years, they had trekked through the city, from St. Lawrence Boulevard across from the mountain to Outremont and Snowdon to almost suburban Côte St. Luc.

My father and I find the senior support office in the same building as the Jewish Public Library that has moved from the side of the mountain. The juxtaposition of Jewish and elderly haunts me as nearly axiomatic: weren't the categories so close that anybody old and failing might as well be Jewish? It wasn't cool to be old. It wasn't cool to be Jewish or to be anybody who has lost glamour or "dignity" or any of the apparel of image that used to obsess me when I was young.

When we meet the social worker, Judith, her slow smile reflects not so much Montreal, I realize, as the small cohort that landed in it from the same boat.

"Hello," I say, "we were in the same grade in Fairmount School."

It is my immigrant classmate in the Protestant elementary public school who has impressed me.

"How many times you've started over," she says taking notes on my father's history. "You survived by being self-reliant. Now the biggest challenge may be for you to accept help. What hobbies do you have?"

My father thinks.

Judith bursts out laughing. "Survivors don't have hobbies. They were too busy making a *parnoosah* for their children. We were so precious to them; all they could do was care for us.

"*M'darf esen moralish*. A person needs morale-building food as well as physical," she is telling my father, or else he will not be able to sustain himself to cope with my mother. While I listen to my grade-three classmate lecture my father in impeccable Yiddish, I read the newspaper clipping on her wall. A child of Auschwitz survivors, she has three children, enjoys music, and tennis, etcetera. Where previous immigrants filled the need for a soup kitchen or a library, in our generation Judith made a weekly social group for aging Holocaust survivors.

Will my father be able to leave my mother for a weekly outing with "a quiet head?" she asks him.

"Thank you," my father says, rising and shaking her hand. "We are taking up your time."

"Dad," I say, pulling him back, "Judith gets paid for talking to you." She is startled, but I have put her proposition in a way my father will not be able to refuse. One does not deprive a person of his *parnoosah*, his livelihood.

"The news," I say. "My father's hobby is the news. My father reads the newspapers and listens every hour to what is going on in the world."

We agree that every Wednesday morning a cab will pick him up for a day's lectures, lunch, and relaxation exercises.

"He's going dancing in Otvosk!" my mother blurted out on Wednesday morning. Otvosk was a pre-war Polish summer resort, which my mother had conflated with Miami, from where my father returned the first time much recovered and carrying a dance trophy.

"Ma, he's going to the Saidye Bronfman Centre," I said, ringing the bell of modern Montreal.

"He's going dancing!"

"I'm not going," my father demurred, exhausted. I pulled him out of the apartment to the waiting taxi with elderly ladies in it. All predications of helping my father depend on his free will, and my father's free will is compounded by a long ethical history. Because he will not say how he feels or what he needs, I measure it by his vital signs, his readiness to smile, the light in his eyes. Every week it was to be a battle with my father claiming he didn't want to go, and then returning home with a relaxed, smiling face. In our generation, it is incomprehensible not to lend importance to feelings of well-being. But what do we know who will not live so long in their circumstances nor see so much.

In that summer, I will yet recognize my father's quantum motion of happiness. It is a time when I will live some of the most joyful moments of my life. I will also live some of the most painful. Then I will realize they are the same moments.

Early one morning, I see my mother standing in the doorway of the bathroom, where my father is shaving, holding on to the door to keep herself steady. It is getting more and more difficult for her to walk. She must have gotten out of bed and, holding on to the walls, toddled over to the bathroom. Clinging to the door she stares at my father – for some reason she has his reading glasses on – with magnified eyes. It is so strange to see my mother waiting wordlessly. My father puts down his shaver. "Come, Hela, I will make you breakfast so you don't have to wait," he says gently. In the kitchen he pours some corn flakes into a bowl with milk and she sits down with the bowl in her lap and eats. With this compliant acceptance of corn flakes – alien nourishment – I feel I have lost her.

At noon, I find her in the kitchen standing up supported by the counter and grating onions. Deaf and engrossed in her task, she does not hear me come in. I want to surprise her; I kiss her on her neck. She jumps out of her skin: "Oh, you frightened me! Oh, you frightened me!" She doesn't stop trembling.

I hug her and say, "I'm sorry."

"Of course," she says, but for a long time she trembles, and no amount of regret suffices for my remorse.

I watched my mother reaching into the pot with a spoon, clinging to vestigial shreds of soup making. The *yoich* (broth) has been reduced to a minimum: an onion, a carrot, a shred of dill if there is one. Supported by the stove, she heaved the pot toward her to taste it with a spoon. The pot toppled a little on its edge.

"I will make lunch, Ma. You take a vacation today." She must be tired to consent to this and lies down.

"Elizabeth! Elizabeth!" She raised her voice from the bedroom, not trusting in our presence until she could see us. It has been a long time since I heard her soprano trill through the syllables of my name.

"What is it?" I yelled back because she couldn't hear.

"Peel an onion," she recited more softly from her bed, "peel a carrot, and see that the broth should cook briskly."

She let me cook. Nothing is more wonderful than the two of them sitting like leisured folk at the table, shmeezing with each other, and allowing me to serve them lunch.

"You warmed the bread in the oven?" my father shot me a smile.

I nodded.

"You turned the oven off?"

I nodded.

"Where did you learn how to do this?" my mother asked.

"From you," my father said.

"Are you saying I let her cook?" my mother glared at him. "She never cooked in my house."

For a long time I had been teaching my father the relaxation exercises that had been taught to me, but my mother would never sit still for such a thing. Now she consented to lie down on the living-room carpet with her palms open and her eyes closed. "Relax your eyes," I said, "relax your mouth." My father announced each of these directions with a tremendous effort of the body part, a flickering lip, a straining jaw. Finally, it seemed they were calm. I looked from one parent to the other lying stretched out on the carpet in the "corpse" pose and panicked. "Wiggle your toes, open your eyes." I roused them.

"Is it over?" asked my father, raising his head. "Can I go rest now?"

"How about if I give you a shower, Ma?" My mustering of aid started when I learned that my mother could not get out of the bathtub by herself. When the social services sent a woman to bathe her, she drove her away.

"Leave me alone, I don't have the *koyech*," she protested. She didn't have the strength.

"But it's me who's doing it, Ma."

Let me wash you, I wanted to beg, *or strangers will end up doing it.*

The last time, my father and I both could not get her out of the tub at all. My mother flailed like a desperate fish. I took one arm and my father heaved on the other so hard I feared for his heart. Still we couldn't pull her out, we couldn't heave her up; she kept slipping away. Finally, I asked my father to let go.

"Where are you going?" he asked.

"To call the fire department," I said.

"Don't you dare call anyone!" my mother thundered, and at the thought of being exposed naked to strangers she launched a renewed struggle, gathering all her strength for a mighty thrashing back and forth. I stood there, secretly glad of her unavailing vigour, too dumbstruck to think of draining the tub and that way at least cover her. Eventually, I hooked both her calves outside the rim of the bathtub where, with the water's leverage, and my father and I each holding an arm, we pulled her out.

It was then I installed a moveable shower and chair in her bathroom. She endures the spray with pinched eyes. I was sixteen before I could take a shower without squeezing my eyes shut against the gas that might come out of the showerhead.

"*S'iz heis, s'iz kalt.*" It's hot, it's cold. I soap a washcloth and lift each one of her breasts, which I remind myself to dry and powder.

"You used to wash us and change us," I coax her.

"But you were little."

"It doesn't matter. What difference does it make?"

I wrap her in the bath towel that I had spread over the closed toilet and I kiss her bare shoulder. She chortles. My heart leaps. I have a chance to win back my mother. Then she looks down.

"I don't like my breasts."

When I have positioned her in bed, legs resting over a rolled blanket to relieve her back, "Where did you learn how to do this?" she says. "She's doing everything like in a hospital!" my mother boasts to my father.

My newfound capability did not, however, make the world safe enough for me to leave my mother's sight.

"You don't know what's doing outside!" My mother has retained every single rape, mugging, and traffic accident of recent memory.

"But I am going to a play at the University of Montreal," I said.

"Aaaagh!" said my mother. "They killed thirteen girls!"

How could I have forgotten? A few years ago, a lunatic had let loose in a college lecture hall with a rifle and massacred his female classmates.

◆　◆　◆

As my mother began her career as an old person, my father and I took her for a "geriatric assessment" in the Jewish General Hospital. In the health-care system my mother is identified by her maiden name, just as her face is emerging after a slight weight loss to her heart-shaped maidenliness.

"What was your mother's father's name?" they ask during registration. My mother has never been in the hospital before except to visit other people. I run back to ask her.

"Israel Josef," she says, smiling. "Don't tell them how old I am."

"It's on your Medicare card, Ma," I say, fishing out of her purse the only *kvitl* she needed to access full, unconditional health care, regardless of health, wealth, illness, age or employment. I meant Canadian Medicare, which bore no resemblance to its anemic American namesake whereby a government program doled out a minimum lifeline to the elderly only because no private insurance would, assuring them a less than enthusiastic welcome from doctors. Yet this meagre government program, regarded as an entitlement, not a right, had to be constantly defended.

As I flew back and forth between the two most similar countries in the world, there was one invisible zone that refused to blend into the easy familiarity on either side of the border. And it gaped larger with each visit. Health care in the United States was a commodity like any other; the more you used, the more you paid. Doctors were "providers" and patients were "consumers." An attempt at "affordable" health care promised "a health plan for every budget!" You could buy bronze, silver, gold, or platinum coverage. This was called "freedom of choice." God help you if your bronze plan met a platinum cancer. In the United States, paying for somebody else's health care was considered an outrage. *Jeden Dann Sich.* Every Man for Himself.

In Canada, paying for somebody else's health care – through taxes, not through buying them insurance – was considered a beautiful thing. The taxes may be high, but the streets were safe. Everyone was invested in a social net. My American friends, including my husband, took for granted that the American profit-based health insurance system was the way things were. Why did it affect me like an atrocity?

If they see he is sick they will kill him. That was why my father gave his piece of bread to Gradmann's son in Buchenwald. All through the war they divided the sick and the healthy and killed the sick. As the same people who had suffered this triage once, became old and ill, it became all the more a horror lest they be threatened with even a simulacrum of it once again. It was not the same, of course it was not the same, and I hated any belittlement of the real atrocity implied by such comparisons. But I was never more grateful for Canadian Medicare. No insurance companies hedging their bets, no stigma of "pre-existing conditions," no punishment for being sick. I was relieved to know that my parents' bodies were not to be weighed or examined for parts or profit; any betting on the body according to its weaknesses, any liquidation of flesh into cash, any punishing of the sick and weak, turned my stomach.

As it turns out, Dr. Rosenberg is not only tall, dark, and handsome but he speaks Yiddish.

"*Vus machts du?*" he greets my mother, who I can tell is smitten. "Is she really eighty-seven?" he asks.

The physiotherapist asks my mother to show her how she sits down. My mother takes a blind chance on landing in a chair while smiling up at us. "It's as if she does it without looking!" says the physiotherapist. Dr. Rosenberg gives her a walker to take home with us. He wrote out orders for hearing aids, a wheelchair, a bladder-control drug that he removed when it turned out to worsen her confusion. He also signed her up for daycare at the local social services centre, "to give the family some time off."

When I take her to the bathroom, my mother supports herself on her new walker while I change her diaper.

"You're doing everything for her," the geriatric nurse tells me. "She'll become dependent on you. Just cue her."

"What are they saying?" my mother asks me.

"They're telling me not to be a *meshigine mame.*" It was how my mother referred to herself: a crazy mother.

"She doesn't like the walker," my father said.

My mother made my father send back the wheelchair I had delivered to their door. I wanted to be able to take her outside, she who used to shoo me outside to get sun and fresh air. "She will come to her own conclusion that she needs it and she will accept it then," said my reasonable father.

My mother plastered her back against the wall of the building corridor, refusing to budge. The project was to cross the street to the park where my parents used to take the breezes of a summer evening. I offered her the walker to lean on.

"I will die rather than use it," she vowed.

Her shoes pinched her, she said. I put on her slippers.

"If you don't use a cane or a walker, you'll lie in *shtib.*" I repeat her phrase back to her. *Shtib* means "room" and rhymes with *grib*, which means "grave," which was where my mother threatened you may as well be if you never got out to see people.

"So I'll lie in *shtib!*" she moans. "What do you want from me?"

"Leave the walker," my father pleads.

I motion my father to shush, and carry it in one hand while I hold my mother with the other. With her other hand my mother holds a cane, which has now become aesthetically preferable to the walker. Down the long dim carpeted corridor we go. Whenever she gets tired, I place the walker in front of her to lean on. One time, suddenly, she quietly pushes it forward on its wheels.

"That's not the way to do it," my father immediately corrects her. "You're supposed to lift and place, lift and place ..."

"Sssh," I say. From now on, I am in my mother's skin, my nerves know exactly the uproar in hers. No effort must be rattled.

I conjure the near-trance state I affect in order to learn anything physical over the fear that I imbibed from her. To my amazement my mother responds to my concentration. She takes a step, and then another. A neighbour comes out of his door and cheers her on.

On the roadway outside, with my father now coaching her effectively toward our destination, which is the park across the street, she suddenly refuses again to go on.

"As long as you're alive, you have to keep learning!" It was more than a reversal of roles. Her anxiety as I was growing up forbade me all physical activity. What I resented about the storm of interference that rose up in me whenever I tried to overcome my fears was having to tear my mother out of myself. It came to me with horror that my mother would destroy herself with her own strength. But I was no longer fighting against her; I was simply fighting with her.

"Oh well, if it means so much to you," she said with sudden noblesse oblige. It seemed hours went by while she toiled away with the self that does not waste a single complaint on the inevitable. I sent my father home to rest and we two slogged on. After a long effort we entered the park, where at the very last minute I bent back the bushes, turned her walker, and we collapsed on the nearest park bench.

She laughed. I pulled up her skirt to sun her smooth legs. "Look at these legs," she said, stretching them out. She bent her head back to receive the breeze. "Look at the sky, how blue," she mused. "Do you hear?"

"What?" I looked around, alarmed.

"I wonder who is singing that," she said softly.

"Birds," I said.

"Old melodies from a long time ago turn round and round in my head. 'Ochhe chornya.' 'Black Eyes.' Do you remember 'The Little Town of Belz'?" my mother hums. Do you remember Tarnov, Ryki, Lvov, Konin, Pulaw, Demblin? "My Little Town of Belz" was the song written before the event that allows you to substitute any and all shtetls for the lost one of Belz. My mother closed her eyes to the sun, humming. Opening her eyes again, she bent toward me confidentially.

"Tell me," she said, turning to me with the same unseeing eyes she might turn to any Jew in the Diaspora, "are there any Dembliners, Dem-blee-ner, where you live?"

We journey back. It was I who was being provincial, and not my mother, I will realize when my father's *landsman* tells me he has a cousin in Los Angeles.

"Do you have my stick?" she asks.

"All three," I say. She laughs. This ability to modulate from bitter to a lighter perspective is new. My father and I used to try to lighten her mood, and it was we who grew pale at the answering onslaught.

My father came to meet us. My mother stopped to lean on the walker and rest.

"There were very few Jewish children in Lodz when you were born," began my mother.

"On a night train to Karpacz," said my father, "you ran around the dining-car tables singing and dancing and talking to everyone. Most children cry or go to sleep at night, not you.

"'Is this your child?' a Pole asked."

My mother took up the story. "'Take care of her or someone will steal her.'"

"One night we left you alone with the maid, Leocadia. When we came home, we found she had gotten news that her son, who had been missing on the front, had died. She was crying," said my father. "You were crying louder."

My mother rested on her walker, my father stood beside her. One story enchained another in a round of remembrance; my parents were rendering me honour.

◆ ◆ ◆

"Elizabeth is coming over," my father would tell my mother every morning.

"Which Elizabeth?" responded my mother one day. "Our Elizabeth or the other Elizabeth?"

"Where is Elizabeth?" asked my mother when I arrived at the door.

"Here I am, Ma," I said. This morning, my mother had gotten it in her head that there were two Elizabeths, disturbing in that it seemed a creation rather than a forgetful omission.

"Yes, you are here, but where is the other Elizabeth?" You know who I mean, the pucker of recall in her face implied, Help me.

I racked my brain to find the rationale. Did we know another person named Elizabeth? Did she mean the entity divided by place, as the daughter who was here and the daughter who called her from California? Whether I was near or far resulted in such extremes of either vigilance or amputation I may as well be two different people.

Only later, when my husband says, "Of course she means Lusia;

'our other daughter' is 'our other Elizabeth,'" it is so apparent that I wonder at my and my father's obtuseness.

"But where is the other Elizabeth?"

"This is our daughter!" yells my father. "We have only one Elizabeth!"

Later in the afternoon when her mind clears, she will berate herself. "How could I think such a thing? What is happening to my mind?" That is more painful to me than her momentary loss of a word.

She does not know it, but in her old age she is giving birth to another Elizabeth.

◆ ◆ ◆

Before I came to Montreal, I had called my sister with my mother's diagnosis.

"My God!" she whispered. "I must go to see them."

My sister was expected on a Wednesday evening. In the morning, I packed my father off to Judith's group.

"Where is that playboy? We have to clean the house," my mother said to Marysia. "My daughter is a pedant!"

How will I get my mother to accept Marysia giving her a shower? My mother has chased away the caregivers sent by the social services. Marysia starts massaging her hair, and soon my mother is asking her, "Do you have any children? Did you get married in Poland?"

"My husband is not Polish. He is Lebanese. He came to study engineering, and somehow …" Marysia shrugs.

"If all the boys were fish in the sea," My mother teases her. With no transition my mother segues from this Polish ditty into the majestic rhythms of Adam Mickiewicz, the Polish national poet. Usually the more romantic the poetry, the more anti-Semitic the country. Without showing any recognition of the national treasure, Marysia seizes the opportunity to unbutton my mother's robe. Well into the shower, the epic stanzas my mother learned at the Polish school she endured insults to attend poured out of her. Passing the sponge to Marysia, I thought I have never learned as much to forget as my mother remembered.

My father returned smiling. His eldest daughter was coming, who spoke good Polish. *Panie* Marysia was just leaving. My father pressed on her a glass of cognac.

"Thank you very much," she said, accepting a glass and sitting down. "If my husband smells alcohol on me, I won't hear the end of it. It's against his religion. He says I go to church to get drunk on the priest's wine."

"Now I've heard everything," my mother said.

Before my sister's arrival, I brought a French press for her coffee to my parents' house. She had shouted at me over the telephone, a stage whisper of a shout, but a shout nevertheless. We never crossed my sister lest her own temper shatter her like glass. But now I became more afraid of my parents' imperious self-sacrifice.

"We will give her our bedroom," my mother announced. "Lusia needs her privacy."

My father was going to miss his weekly outing to pick her up at the international airport. When I said they were no longer capable of these things, Lusia was stung. "Elizabeth, you're a shit!"

She called me back. "I want to see you too, you know." We hadn't seen each other since my last summer in Montreal before leaving for Paris in 1980.

The night that my sister arrived, my mother asked my father to shut the blinds and lock the door so that Lusia would not be taken away.

◆ ◆ ◆

"She's very bad," Lusia said with a shudder. "She called me by her sister's name."

"She knows who you are, she's just calling you by another name," I consoled her, because it was evident my mother's attachment to us remained the same.

"She did this once before," my sister said. "Father and I left her alone for an afternoon and when we got back she called me by her sister's name. I thought, 'She's gone completely mad.' She said she had just grown anxious at our absence and blamed her 'nerves.' When I got home I found an entry in a psychiatric textbook under 'travel psychosis.' Oh, I thought, some people just become temporarily disoriented by travel, and that's what happened to her. Mother must have been sick for a long time before we knew it," Lusia concluded gloomily.

It seemed the less an object of anger my mother became, the more my sister shifted her anger on to our father. A "scene" had occurred the first night she arrived. "I left the house," she said, her voice shaking, "I ran away." She had set out to make a list, pen in hand, of my father's medications, dosages, dates. My father interrupted with the story of how he had passed out on the floor of Canadian Outfitting and frightened the saleswomen. "He fainted because he took too many pills! It was his fault! He was told that if he took one of them, he was to stop taking the other."

"He forgot," I said.

"Then why did he tell me he took only one?"

"He was more interested in telling you the story than in remembering how many pills."

"He didn't forget; he lied."

"His psychiatrist said that stress-induced depression can cause forgetfulness," I said thinking to curry some sympathy for him.

"*I'm* depressed and *my* mind works!" she snapped back.

"He's eighty," I said.

"The little saint!" she huffed at me.

I am not a saint, I wanted to say, I am an opportunist. Here is our chance, I wanted to say, here is our last chance. If you hold our parents responsible for so much of your life, then acknowledge it. This was no time to pretend we were normal children whose lives were too full and busy to think about our parents. Admit how much space they take and … give it back to them. Give them just a fraction of the attention they have commanded in your interior life and perhaps the tumult will die away.

If extreme suffering made these bonds, let them reap the benefits. History was still being made, look at our mother's eyes – they have lost their haunted look.

I am in hell, she thought, trapped with her parents in an airless place. The first night, she had fled the apartment and run out to the park across the street, where soon her eighty-year-old father came to find her. The elderly father, whom she had come to help, followed his daughter out of the house, because he had no shame, because he was weak, because he was strong, because he knew she was sick – and begged her to come back into his house.

"He must have known what he had done wrong, because he came and asked me to come in."

Once my mother was tucked in bed, I took the bus to my friend Sally's house in our old neighbourhood where I was staying while my sister was here. My parents' apartment is in an almost-suburb where the postwar immigrants ended their passage through the city. An elderly man sitting next to me on the bus, wearing a short-sleeved shirt that is the most concession to the heat that men like my father will make, is both a stranger and is not.

A woman gets on the bus. "How's your wife?" she asks him.

"We were together in the *katzet*," the elderly man says to me so I won't feel left out.

"Which one?" I ask.

"Dachau."

"My father was in Buchenwald."

He nods.

"My mother is not well," I say.

"My wife is having an operation on her heart," he says.

"How is she doing?" asks the woman. A few stops later, she gets off with a postwar abbreviation of the *Shehechayanu*, the blessing for having lived to this extraordinary occasion: "*Abi meh zeyt zich*." So long as we see each other.

Another man gets on and is thrown by the bus so the seat rail in front of us is the only hold for his arm, on which is inked a long blue number.

"How is the wife?" he asks.

◆ ◆ ◆

Sometimes it seemed as if my sister and I were on the same wavelength.

"Will you do me a favour?" she asked me a few days later. "Can you help me find a piano? I would like to play for our parents." The light way my sister said this belied its momentousness. She had returned to her first love, music.

I remembered my mother announcing with satisfaction, "Lusia has bought herself a piano."

Yes, I said, I would be happy to ask around for a piano.

When I called her back to say a friend's daughter took piano lessons and had offered us its use, she interrupted me. "There is one condition. Your friends and her daughter must leave the house while I am playing."

My heart sank. Why did she want to ruin this gesture?

"You want me to throw these people out of their own home?"

"Then never mind," she said frostily.

My sister did get to play for our parents. When we went to look at a nearby seniors' home, I noticed a piano in the lobby. We asked the director if perhaps my sister could play for my parents one afternoon. "With pleasure," he said.

I gave my sister a look. I could see her restraining herself from barring the residents from the lobby during her performance. When we walked out on the street, she waved her hand. "This is who I've been reduced to playing for!"

On the day of the concert she said, "There is no need for you to come."

I didn't.

"How did it go?" I asked the next day.

"Oh, wonderful," my sister giggled. "Only when I got up to play, Mother turned to me very graciously and said, 'Oh, you play the piano?'"

All summer my mother stepped delicately over the sliding door barrier with her walker to sit on the balcony. It was easy to tempt her outside, she who always insisted I get "fresh air."

Her every movement was slowed down by thought and by the very relaxing of the ability to grasp. She could easily slip down and out of the chair, as if she had all but given up holding herself against gravity. Every now and then she gathered herself forward as if to say something with a bemused smile, then she released back into her chair, like the movement of a wave.

As she leaned forward again, her beautiful eyes dipped into mine and gained brightness. My mother used to wither birds with a glance. Now an eternity went by while we drowned in each other's eyes.

Her gaze was more contemplatively fastened on mine than I could sustain. Should my sister approach, I would pull back as if caught in an illicit relation. Her eyelids flickered closed, as she smiled in the sun.

"What are you thinking, Mama?" My mother in her slow motion had actually been not stretching but foreshortening time; as she leaned forward from the back of her chair, she swept through a lifetime.

"I am thinking about how you imagine things will be when you are young and," there is a pause in which an age revolves, "and how differently they turn out."

The social worker from the local social service centre whom my sister called "the Angel of Death" was coming for a "home visit." My mother was on the balcony. I left her with lipstick and a mirror because she would want to put some on before company came. This simple act was to remain the bedrock measure of her capabilities. I found her a good twenty minutes later still staring into the mirror, holding the lipstick with one hand, unapplied. Who did she see in the mirror? I was frightened by the distance in time she has gone away so that the thread between lipstick in the hand and applying it to her lips has been broken.

"Mama," I pleaded quietly, "it is not hard. There is the mirror, there is the lipstick." Then she shakily passed the tube over her lips, crooked, sunken in lip cracks and still, ineffably glamorous.

The social worker, Barbara, arrived. I introduced her to my sister. "How do you find your mother?" asked Barbara.

"I find her very …" Lusia began. "She's lost weight, she walks around the house pushing the walker with knee socks on looking like a cheerleader. All I need to do is lie down next to her for her to smile and look like the cat that's swallowed the cream! She is very," my sister's face turned away from us, "very brave," she said finally with a swallow.

"She's not a kvetch," Barbara summed up.

"Yiddish is so …" my sister giggled, "expressive. I want them to come and stay with me," she said turning her head back. "Yes, yes, I've thought about it very practically. My mother has always wanted to stay with me in London. They could have my bedroom, and I would sleep in the study. They would have everything in London that they have here, except for the car."

"You think that this is now something you would like to do for them?" said Barbara.

"Yes, yes I do," my sister tossed her head and left the room before tears came.

When we sat down, my mother leaned against me on the couch. She put her head on my shoulder, and smiled at the company. Barbara had taken to talking about my mother as if she were not there. "Do you know what Alzheimer's is?" she bellowed at my father and me. "Intellectual disablement, loss of memory, loss of judgment –"

"Give her a fruit," whispered my mother.

"Inability to take care of oneself –" Barbara continued.

"Ask her if she wants something to drink," my mother nudged me in the immemorial act of *mechabid zayn*, honouring a guest. "Where are your manners?"

On my last night, I reserved a table in a Russian restaurant glinting with samovars and strolling violinists. It was their first evening out since my mother became ill. My mother emerged, resplendent in a violet dress, the colour of her eyes, that my sister had brought her. She deployed her walker, one step at a time, the shy smile, but she was not ashamed. The waiters in Cossack shirts cleared a way to the table. I ordered herring for her – that was all she would eat. The violinist and guitarist spent the longest time at our table, the violinist bending over to play nearly into my mother's ear. My sister ticked each gypsy tune off her mental list. She allowed me to photograph her and my father. My father was the only person among all the tables to reach for his wallet and deftly hand a bill to the guitarist. My mother asked the violinist if he would play the gypsy song "Ochi Chyornie" "Black Eyes."

Chapter Ten

THE OTHER ELIZABETH

"Elizabeth just called. She is coming over," my father told my mother in the morning.

"Yes, but where is the other Elizabeth?" my mother would ask. "You know who I mean, *our* Elizabeth."

"The other Elizabeth," I thought guiltily, the one who went away. The one who couldn't be at home, neither could she be at home somewhere else.

Perhaps because I was born to her two years after she watched her little sisters die of severe malnutrition, my mother did not trust my own hunger pangs to keep me nourished.

In nature (the Nazis were big on *Natur*), the mother will bite through the umbilical cord when the child is born if nobody is there to separate them.

Although I was pronounced sound (my mother terrorized "the biggest" pediatrics professor in Lodz), I must have looked *shvach* or weak to her. My mother had seen children die of hunger. I was not to be hungry.

"You ate," said my father, "but you were not passionate about it." It must have filled her with panic to see the infant turn its head away for a moment.

"She held you in an odd way," said my father and sister, baffled in later years as to how to imitate it.

My mother could not hold me in the bath at all to bathe me, so great was her fear of inadvertently letting me slip from her hands.

In nature, mothers know how to hold babies. *Natürlich*, it is innate. My father hired a nurse to bathe me, but not to feed me. Food was life.

She held me upside down, the better for her to pour food in. She couldn't wait for me to swallow or to breathe. She closed my nostrils so I would have to open my mouth.

My father protested, "If you are going to do that, I will hire a nurse to feed her."

"Don't interfere," my mother said. "It's *my* baby."

Her baby could not hold any more food and regurgitated. Nothing vindicated the Nazis more than enlisting the collaboration of nature in our destruction. A body never forgets hunger. Eventually I would learn to go hungry in order to survive the effects of my mother's hunger.

"When you were small you didn't want to eat, so I had to force you. You threw up. I taught you not to throw up," she said.

"She nearly killed Elizabeth," my sister said. When I got sick with colitis, it seemed so much a direct result of my mother's hysterical manipulation of my digestive system that I didn't understand how it happened to anybody else. My sister took it for granted. "How could you *not* be sick?"

"Failure to thrive." I saw this diagnosis usually applied to children years later in the course of my illness.

Through all the years I lived with them, I never heard my mother or my father or my sister or any Jew who had lived through the Holocaust get angry at the Germans. When my mother shuddered at what human beings are capable of, she did not mean the Nazis. She meant herself.

Not a single jot of anger or vengeance or hate is perpetuated.

Ritually, we are not a vengeful people and our joy is diminished by our enemies' suffering. During the Passover Seder, we spill a drop of wine from our cups for each of the ten plagues.

Once there was a moment of ritual anger, in which we asked God to pour out his wrath upon our tormentors unto the umpteenth generation. In my lifetime it has been cut out, because it is unbecoming of us.

The history of the Holocaust is not closed. With the freeing of new documents from former Communist countries, a previously unknown population of active Nazis was discovered: the womenfolk. Of German women, portrayed as holding down the home front with Hitler's three housewifely K's (*Kuche, Kinder, Kirche*) or else as martyrs to the Russian soldiers, half a million were on the eastern front as secretaries, nurses, or wives of the SS eager to prove they were equal to their men by shooting Jewish children. They were not following orders. This was purely extracurricular for them. It is known that most Nazis were not brought to justice but lived quiet postwar lives in West Germany shielded by their generation's countrymen, and with better health care than is even now available to the US GI. Holocaust survivors took upon themselves the job of models of tolerance. Although bringing a Nazi to justice confirmed the intolerance that motivated them. It would take the concerted effort of a Jewish state to dislodge a Holocaust maker like Eichmann out of South America and bring him to trial in Jerusalem.

When we arrived in Israel in 1950, the country subsisted on rations. My aunt Tzetl had a little girl who was a year younger than me but already bigger. "Let her eat," my mother begged. "Can't you see she's dying?"

When we were in Canada, she set up camp in a friend's house near my elementary school to prepare "lunch," the three-course European midday meal.

In high school, we lived too far for me to go home. She did her best to camouflage the full four-course meal in a "sandwich" that nobody could get their mouth around: a couple of veal chops or a pound of *klops* from which the schmaltz oozed onto my schoolbooks. That was not all that oozed.

Inside were also the breakfast scrambled eggs that I might have eaten if I were not bilious from drinking the milk that my mother had fortified with a raw egg, for insurance. I also carried with me last night's second dinner. How to dispose of soup was a problem. I threw it out the window hoping it would not fall on the downstairs neighbour's head.

I was in a Jewish mother joke. Who was I to tell this was no joke? There was an anxious mother solicitous for her child's well-being and there was her child looking unhappy, nervous and pale enough to justify her anxiety. Who started it? "Look at Sarah Kigelman! Her cheeks are red like apples!" my mother yelled, bringing some colour into one of my cheeks by smacking it.

She didn't trust me to eat on my own. So I didn't. I gave my kilo of Polish ham to a fellow immigrant classmate whose mother gave her a thin slice of baloney because her father had a hard time making a living.

Born into an eating disorder, I learned to repress hunger at, say, lunchtime, because there was a three-course dinner waiting for me at home after school. Forget about dining *en famille*. Everyone got fed when they fell in the door. Forget about eating with friends. There were no after-school activities, no ice skating that everybody did on Friday afternoons, not even the dentist who when I was seventeen and came in for a long-postponed reckoning, she ordered to unfreeze my teeth quickly because "my daughter does not eat." Not even talks with my high school English teacher, to whom she would have had no qualms saying the same thing.

Food as an instrument of abuse, who would have believed me? She became a prisoner of her own obsession. If I didn't come home right after school it would be too late for her to go and meet her Dembliner friends; she reproached me because she *had to feed me*. How could I do this to her? Eventually I cracked under the constant persecution. In grade ten I turned pale and fainted in our house. She called the doctor who made a house call and terrorized him with the few English words she knew: "Danger? No danger?" She nagged him until he gave her an answer to think about.

"I don't know," he said, "She could be hemorrhaging internally."

At the same time although it did me no good, there was another aspect to this tyranny. As soon as I came home my mother piled steaming dishes in front of me, enough to feed a numerous family. While I ate, my mother watched over me with her apron on her lap. She called me Shayndel after her mother, her private name for me. She recalled her sisters, Rivka, Estere, Perela. "They took away my little sisters, who were blooming children." Years later, I read in her town's memorial book that Pearl died in Końskovola of starvation and typhus at sixteen, while the youngest, twelve-year-old Esther, clung to her. When my mother tore through the wires with my sister to escape the railroad camp deportation, her older sister Rivka and little Esther were taken to their deaths in Poniatowa.

Should my mother find beside my place a chipped plate or bent fork, she rushed to exchange them. "This isn't good enough for you. You deserve the best. Where is there another like you?"

If I should fail to consume everything she piled before me, however, her devotion turned to fury.

"I can't bear to look at you! You look like a corpse!" Her sisters had been blooming children and I refused to bloom. It was as if by refusing food I was depriving her sisters, whom I could never feed out of the stores of my body, no matter how much I ate. Every day I threw out food that could have saved her from the obsession that was my daily oppression. I threw it away to save myself.

Because of her fears that I would not survive my mother almost guaranteed that I would not thrive.

By adolescence I had given up trying to do anything or go anywhere.

While still in elementary school I followed a Slavic classmate to a Russian ballet studio on the top floor of a building on Park Avenue, to which my mother quickly put a stop. Not before the Russian teacher had taken one look at me and bought me my first bra. My mother sent me back with a box of chocolates for the teacher. But she did not allow me to return to the after-school class, even though we never missed a performance by the Bolshoi Ballet at the Montreal Forum. "You are not going to be a balletnizza anyways," she said, "There is no point." The list of things I was not going to be, and therefore no point in doing was so long that I gave up. That was the last fight I put up. "You can do what you want when you grow up." But when you are grown, it is too late for many things.

My friend Dora's survivor parents arranged for her to learn how to drive a car as a survival skill – in case her putative future husband had a heart attack on the highway, she could in an emergency take over. My mother could not even stretch herself that far. In effect, my mother deprived me of survival tools. I was thought precocious but much of my life was spent painstakingly catching up.

"Come outside!" my friends used to call me.

"Why?" I answered. "Is the house on fire?"

Why was I so tired?

"You're not eating enough!" my mother yelled.

Eventually she began to worry that I was not getting enough fresh air.

When I was fifteen, she let me out of her sight to go to summer camp in the Laurentians. It was a no-frills Jewish community camp that was proud of its swimming record. On the first day the head of the waterfront, Yank, short for Yankel, was scouting the fresh crop for Olympic material when he spotted a teenager splashing in the shallow end with the six-year-olds. My mother had threatened us both with a watery grave if I went in over my head. The counsellors debated whether I was retarded or merely environmentally deprived.

One afternoon during "rest period" I was summoned to the lake, where the entire aquatics staff had convened to coax me into the deep end. With a lifeguard sitting on each side of me, and Yank himself treading water in front of me, I sat with my behind glued to the deck. Finally, somebody to whom I am forever grateful lost patience and gave me a nudge, so that I plopped in the lake and bobbed up again like a champagne cork. When my mother was informed on parents' day that I had dog-paddled around the lake, she shrugged. "So long as it's not in front of my eyes."

Mixed with my relief was anger that she couldn't, for my sake, squelch a *meshigas* she herself did not believe in. Other parents might be anxious about their children taking risks. But they repressed their fear for the good of the child's development. I thought of her as selfish for indulging her anxiety. I misunderstood her.

When she let me out of her sight at fifteen and was told I had been taught how to swim, she said, "If I don't see, I don't mind." Finally, I got the hint. For her not to worry, I had to go away from before her eyes.

If anyone were to ask in what way I was affected by the Holocaust, I would say by my stunted upbringing in which I was deprived of everything except food. It should not have been my mother I was angry with, but the men in dark clothes standing behind her with rifles. But I had never seen those men, and even if I had, like my sister, we are too shortsighted. Our emotions would not stretch to the cause.

In my mother the catastrophe threw off a centrifugal force that scattered us away. She was so afraid of separation that it made proximity to her living family unbearable. In Jewish mysticism, the *Shechinah*, the feminine presence of God, accompanied the children of Israel in their exile. It was as if the principle of proximity could not but be feminine. And the *Shechinah*, having tasted the bitterness of her own proximity, drove us away.

In Częstochowa, when the Germans took away the children along with the other Elizabeth, they did not hide them out of sight. They kept the children in a compound surrounded with wire where the parents could see them.

I finally got the hint. I had to go away from in front of her eyes.

◆ ◆ ◆

It is ironic that I give the impression of much wandering, because to me I have been inert. I did not leave Montreal until I was thirty-three.

When I finally left, in the fall of 1980, I couldn't tell them I was going away except on vacation. We were in a shoe store, and my father wanted to buy me a pair of suede boots. I couldn't tell him they would get ruined in the European winter rain. I was supposed to be back before winter. "Why didn't you let me get you the boots, Lizzie?"

The morning I left, my father put off work so he could drive me to the station. His metabolism burned eager on idle; the light shone in his eyes, his grin cracked his face from one side to the other, he was smoking a cigarette like he still did then. I got us some coffee, and asked if he would like a pastry. "Can you get me one of those Danish with poppyseed?" I ran through Place Ville Marie hunting for poppyseeds. They had every flavour but.

It was because of an accident that I remained in Paris.

In the shortening autumn days, I was lengthening out my "vacation" in the cheapest hotel in Montparnasse, looking for work. The days were getting shorter and rainier when, returning to my hotel room, I saw a headline. A synagogue had been bombed. It was the first time since the days when this had been no news at all.

The next day I walked up a street named after a Polish astronomer, in which the oldest synagogue in France was distinguishable only by the roses piled up against its door. Six people had been killed, two of them were innocent people, said the newspaper headlines. In the cafés around the synagogue, the Jews were being blamed in whispers for bringing on these attacks. Or so whispered the frightened neighbourhood Jewish girl I spoke to. It was raining, and we shivered. After being searched, I went inside where international camera crews and *Paris Match* fought for space with the Rothschilds. The photographers were lying in wait for the rabbi, a young red-haired Englishman who had become a hero overnight when he led his congregants out in the wake of the bomb. The French praised him for his sang-froid, the British for his stiff upper lip. He had actually saved more lives by talking. The bombers timed the explosion to go off at the moment people usually came out after services, not having reckoned with a rabbi's privilege of spieling out a particularly brilliant *midrash*.

In the crowd, I had exchanged a smile with a young American woman carrying a tape recorder. If I stayed in Paris, it was because of Naomi. She was freelancing a radio spot, she said with a sigh. We walked out in the rain and ended up in Goldenberg's, outside of which a gendarme circled the *pletzel*.

"*L'chaim*," we said, clinking our glasses of red wine.

"That's *it*," I said. "To life! Tell them we have the oldest joie de vivre!" As close to an atmosphere of the 1940s as I could get, down to the red banquettes, the whispers, and the paranoia, why was I celebrating? My return ticket was still good. Why didn't I take the first plane back to Canada? The Holocaust might also have happened in North America, I used to say, but it didn't and didn't was good enough for me. It did happen here, but here there were also people with the *awareness* of it.

Naomi took me to her apartment where her aspiring journalist friends were already patching the telephone line to transmit the next breaking story, and did not ask why Naomi had invited this stranger home with her.

I didn't have the papers to work in France, a little requirement that I had not considered. In Montreal, I had no marketable skills. In Paris I had one: I spoke English. Of course, who else but a *greener* would rise before dawn for an hour of metro and buses to the outskirts of the city where they kept their high-rise office towers? Who else would feel repaid by riding through the wet streets shining like jewel boxes in the dawn?

When my father had stopped in Paris the first time, we looked up the Mr. Gradmanns. He wanted to ask whether their son, who was in charge of an electronics company, could help me obtain a *carte de séjour*, a resident card. The Gradmanns were *landsmen* from Demblin who had settled in Paris after the war. I knew they used to put up my mother when she passed through Paris. "Once we met at a wedding in Israel," my father said laughing, "when Mr. Gradmann saw me he threw his arms around my neck! What a mensch!" my father said, knotting his tie in the hotel in the Place Dauphine. It was to illustrate Mr. Gradmann's good character that my father told me about the piece of bread he left for his son in Buchenwald.

"He was so honest that when I came back at night it was still there!"

We took the metro to the Gradmanns' modern apartment house, very much like my parents' in Montreal. They were tiny and already very old, deaf and tripping over themselves to get out a bottle of brandy. Before my father could ask if their son could help me obtain a *carte de séjour*, I pulled him out of their apartment.

"We are old," said Mr. Gradmann from the doorstep.

"May you live to be 120!" shouted my father as I pulled him away.

He and I had one evening in Paris together. An evening in Paris should be gay.

As it turned out, I got my *carte de séjour* by government fiat.

I was gamely getting by teaching English, when the new socialist government passed an amnesty to regularize illegal workers.

I took the metro to the northern end of the line to a huge warehouse for the medical exam. It was packed with groups of women dressed in an array of styles, some with blue forehead tribal markings more specific in their variety than I had ever seen before. I dwelled on these distinctions, because in some situations the reminder that we are all of one species is less of an equalizer than a reduction. We were told to undress above the waist. All of us, braless, had one after the other our chests pressed against X-ray machines.

"I should be used to this. I come from herded stock," I said to myself. From the moment I arrived at this warehouse on the outskirts of the city, I had to push back the suspicion that this was one of the collection points for the deportation of Jews. Why, after my parents' odyssey for Canadian citizenship, was I volunteering for this?

While I waited in a line to have my blood drawn I saw, ahead of us, a hall in which endless rows of women sat with their arms strapped off and stretched over white bowls. One look at this and I got dizzy. When I came to, I found I had lost my place in line and had to start over.

I had pulled my father away from the Gradmanns and that history, but history kept pulling me back. What were the chances that on my own in Paris I would bump into a person once removed from the young man to whom my father had given the piece of bread in Buchenwald? This person was my English student, Mirka, a lively married Czech woman whose kinship with me was rendered transparent through the prism of France, which makes exiles the gift of distilling and reflecting their own cultures back to them.

Ricocheting around Paris like a billiard ball, I would come to rest in her apartment off Montparnasse. It was the only home life I had so far entered in Paris. Mirka's living room had little in it except for a glass table on which a sweeping bouquet overflowed as in a pool of water. Always different, the flowers were never waxy tulips or gladioli that "lasted"; instead, they were perishable blossoms and at the slightest breeze from the windows spilled petals that Mirka, with Slavic abandon, allowed to lie strewn in that otherwise pristine room. Next week, they would be gone.

Neither did she want easy lessons. In Czechoslovakia, where only her mother still remained, she had learned French by transposing Proust's page-long sentences into another tense. To think I had thought up the same assignment in English, with Hemingway. But it didn't matter what I prepared, our conversation soon darted off on its own.

One afternoon, I arrived to an unmistakable bitter scent wafting from the kitchen. "Dill," she said, "the aroma of eastern Europe!" She was preparing dinner for her husband Pierre's boss and his wife. It was the first time Pierre respected an employer, a fair man who behaved more as his mentor than as an authority figure. Pierre's employer was of the same nationality as me, she added after a short hesitation, a Polish Jew. She was struck by how much we resembled each other, we were both so small.

I took out my address book and found the telephone number and address of a M. Gradmann. "Is this him?" I asked Mirka.

This was the boy to whom my father had given bread in Buchenwald.

My father gave me the flowers on the glass table before I was born.

◆ ◆ ◆

Some time later, I was referred to a charming Polish Jewish man for a translation job. This one was another news story. In 1984, a group of Polish Carmelite nuns moved to the Auschwitz site. The building they chose for their convent had been where the Nazis stored their Zyklon B gas. At this time there was still no mention on the site that 90 per cent of the people murdered at Auschwitz were Jews. Jewish survivor groups protested and meetings were arranged between Jewish representatives and the Polish cardinal.

My job was to meet with their representative, a Polish Jewish survivor living in Paris who had been in Auschwitz, and to translate the conversations between him and the cardinal into English for American Jews. Moshe asked me to meet him at the memorial to the deportation. It was a small building on the Seine that I had never visited. Inside I waited beside a model of a concentration camp under glass, complete with train tracks … I was fleeing the building when I bumped into Moshe, a refined middle-aged man overflowing with Polish Jewish charm.

He took me down among the archives where another man was standing on a ladder among the stacks. Moshe introduced me in Yiddish as a Canadian. "She doesn't look like. Where were you born?" The two men teased each other about Galitzianer and Litvaks.

I took the documents and said goodbye. "The next time can we meet in a café?" I asked.

When I had finished the translation, we met in a café and Moshe ordered coffee and cake for us. The report on the discussions with the cardinal said that the Jewish representative opened first with the statement that, with due respect to heroic exceptions, the stance of the Catholic Church during the Holocaust had been one of indifference.

"Why do Polish Carmelite nuns want to tack their nunnery on to the Auschwitz site?" I asked Moshe, whose brother and father died in Auschwitz.

"To get into heaven," he said with a shrug. "Take a piece of cake."

Next, I read that the cardinal tried to shame the Jews by saying it would be an interfaith centre where people of all religions – such as Hindus and Buddhists – could go and pray. I could just see Hindus hot-footing it to Auschwitz. After 2,000 years of demonizing Jews, thereby laying the groundwork for what happened at Auschwitz, the Catholic Church did not utter a peep of protest during the Holocaust, and now it wanted, in its necrophilia, to soak up our suffering. What would a Buddha have done at Auschwitz, what would a Jesus Christ? What a question. *The* Jesus, a Jew who urged rebellion against the Reich, would have been the first to be pushed into the ovens.

The only recourse the Jews had was that Auschwitz had been declared a UNESCO World Heritage Site and was not to be tampered with.

"All I know is that the Catholic Church has centuries of tricks up its sleeve that we can't begin to know," Moshe said. He thanked me and said he was leaving for Cracow again.

"Watch out for that cardinal," I said as he waved goodbye. Moshe was right. The nuns did not budge for a decade after our meeting and the affair was only resolved through the intervention of a higher power. In 1987, Catholic cardinals and Jewish representatives came to an agreement that a new Jewish-Christian Interfaith centre and convent would be built a little distance outside Auschwitz. In 1989, it was completed but the nuns refused to move. As a matter of fact, Jewish protestors came across workmen doing renovations on the Zyklon nunnery. In 1993, US vice-president Al Gore and Isreali prime minister Yitzhak Rabin met with Polish president Lech Walesa during the fiftieth anniversary of the Warsaw Ghetto Uprising. Any further Jewish protest threatened to trigger an attack by the anti-Semitic Polish group the Committee for the Protection of the Carmelite Convent. One of the Jewish representatives said, "Can you imagine the resulting headline: 'Jewish Protestors Attacked in Auschwitz'?" The upper reaches of the Catholic hierarchy must have imagined it too. This is the headline that appeared instead: "Pope Orders Nuns out of Auschwitz."

I did not hear from Moshe again until the following spring and then it was not he but his wife who telephoned me to invite me to their community's Passover Seder. Moshe was in the hospital, recovering from surgery, but he wanted me to come. I thanked her, and started to make demurring noises but she was adamant.

"We are not going to leave you alone during Passover!" This Jewish imperative was all the stronger because of its source. His wife was not Jewish, Moshe had told me. On the contrary, she had been in the opposite of Auschwitz – a camp of Aryan-looking children separated to preserve their racial purity. They met after the war. Of course she had converted to Judaism. I travelled to a suburban *shul* where a banquet was laid out.

As a child, it was my job to open the door to Elijah, the anticipated guest who would end oppression and establish justice. He would turn the parents toward the children and the children toward the parents. Opening the door of your home on a spring night when the moon is full – it seemed an expansive, almost reckless, gesture for such a vulnerable people.

It was only years later that I learned that my favourite Jewish custom of throwing the doors open on a spring night was not Jewish at all, in its inception. In the Middle Ages, Jews were ordered to keep their doors open during the Seder under suspicion of drinking Christian blood. We will open our doors, the Jews said, but we will open them to Elijah.

Children running around in this French suburb, teenage boys full of their responsibility, Moshe's beautiful wife next to the rabbi, the couple's sons offering to drive me home – I had sunk so deeply into reading about the Holocaust that the sight of a living Jewish community drove me to tears.

◆ ◆ ◆

By 1985 I had been in Paris for five years without going home.

Five years before, I had arrived into that autumnal 1980 synagogue bombing as if *bashert* destined to keep me there. I was buoyed by my good luck of finding a maid's room and supporting myself, just barely. I got my work papers, but not more work. I seemed to fulfill the medieval church's policy toward the Jews: let them survive, but not thrive.

My left foot broke in what was supposedly a classical dancer's fracture. Only I wasn't dancing: I tripped and cracked it on the cobblestones of Rue Mouffetard carrying way too much produce for one person to eat. My favourite art exhibit was the market. I had only to step out of my beamed tiny studio on Rue Mouffetard to gather the subtly changing palette of the French countryside. Every day I discovered some new species of onion or wild mushroom redolent of my mother's barley soup in which it would release the bitter aroma of the Polish earth.

Finding traces of Poland in the French earth made me so homesick that one rainy December day I bought a ticket to Montreal.

Why could everyone else go home for a visit and not me?

"When I'm dead you'll be sorry," my mother wrote, "wishing you health and happiness."

I cancelled my ticket.

Then I bought it back.

A week later, I boarded the Air Canada jet whose control panels I would have occasion to inspect that night. With a homecoming thrill I caught the French-Canadian accent of the man in the next seat. I was buckled in when out the window I saw the wing of the airplane disappearing behind billows of black smoke. We had to make an emergency landing, came the announcement. My seatmate was crossing himself. This was what all my cancelling and vacillating, my abuse of free will had got me. The powers of my subconscious, my unconscious, and my superconscious had all ganged up to knock out the flight plan. I asked the steward if I could disembark at our emergency landing. It wasn't fair that others should suffer on account of me, I explained.

"Anything you say, Madame, but you will have to decide quickly, we are about to land in London."

What would I do in London? Call my sister and ask her advice on how to approach/avoid our mother?

I stayed on the plane.

"I am sorry I am such a coward," I said, unwrapping my lunch.

"Oh, I don't know," my seatmate said, clinking his glass to mine and raising it up in a toast. "Anyone who brings their own food on a plane has plenty of guts!"

Somewhere over Chicoutimi the pilot invited me into the cockpit. The dials glowed red in the dark, and outside I could see the snow coming down. "This model may be small compared to a 747," the pilot said, "but it is my favourite airplane. I flew one like it through World War II."

When I went to visit them, my parents accompanied me to the bathtub-sized pool downstairs to make sure I wouldn't drown. My father could swim; my mother, of course, never. Somehow I coaxed my mother to lie down in the water, hold onto the edge of the pool and let her body float. As the water lifted her, to my surprise she erupted in girlish giggles.

"Kick your legs," I said. "Kick! Kick!"

"What means kick?" she asked my father, kicking.

"She never trusted me enough to do that," he said amazed.

"Will you come swim with me in Israel?" my mother asked, bobbing on the water. My mother may have been afraid of the air and the water, she was not afraid to go to Israel.

My mother and I were dressed first and waited outside the men's dressing room for my father. After a few minutes, my mother suddenly took to rattling the doorknob: "*Hoch no!*"

"Leave him alone!" I said.

"What do you mean, leave him alone?" my mother said. "He could have passed out in there!"

When my parents began to fail a few years later, I would race to close the geographical distance I had made. The airplanes could not fly me toward them fast enough.

I returned to Paris. Failing to get a job translating film subtitles from French into English put me on notice that I was losing the only language in which I was fluent. My interview was for an American film production company where LA types in sunglasses gossiped about Warren Beatty. "How would you say '*J'ai eu un empechement*'?" I was asked. This is said by the French when they can't make an appointment, literally "I had a hindrance." I had fallen into speaking English in a stilted French syntax to make it easier for my students to understand, and was losing my North American vernacular. "Something came up," was the answer.

◆ ◆ ◆

In September 1987 I got on a flight from Paris to Los Angeles to attend a fiction-writing program. The airplane stopped briefly in Labrador to refuel, where I stood at the open door wrapped in a blanket to breathe in the last blast of precious cold Arctic air.

I spent the first months in southern California running from the blazing sun that followed me from one thin-walled student apartment to another. My father called the English department because he had heard on the news of an earthquake. I moved three times only to be blasted yet again through the picture window – it faced south! In Paris south was *good*! Somebody suggested I ask permission to have an air conditioner. I had to get a note from the doctor. This brought me in contact once more with the kindly woman GP at the student health centre who had flagged me with anemia.

My professor diagnosed me with "culture shock."

True culture shock really came when I got really sick with my first serious colitis attack. I took an antibiotic for an infection and within a week I was bleeding, cramping such as I had never known before, curling up around the toilet to sleep as there was no point in going back to bed between onslaughts.

The kindly Dr. Flowers sent me to a gastroenterologist but for some reason kept denying that I had the illness. "It happened so long ago. You don't have any medical records." It was true I had not needed to see a doctor or take a drug for more than twenty years. If I had never had the illness before there was a chance I didn't have it now. But illness was not what this was about. It was about insurance companies hedging their bets on a healthy rather than a sick horse. Whether it was Cold War indoctrination that made Americans see red at the word *socialism*, or even *government program*, they preferred to put their health care in the hands of profit-making pharamaceuti-cal and insurance companies rather than their elected government. I had lived in Canada and in France without ever hearing of "pre-existing conditions." In coming to the United States from France, I had assumed North America was sufficiently homogeneous that I was coming home. I came home to the Middle Ages.

Meanwhile I was happy to have my illness denied. California had erased my history! It was Allan who picked me up from the first gastroenterology appointment. I sailed out jubilant. "He says I don't have colitis!"

"What *do* you have then?" Allan replied, studying my bloodless face. He himself had barely survived the unacknowledged failure of a shunt in his brain. He was familiar with the denial of illness, in this country greatly abetted by health insurance companies.

Dr. Flowers sent me back until the gastroenterologist, conceding a sigmoidoscopy, saw the blood spurting at him and wising up, took advantage of a teaching opportunity. "Is this normal tissue?" he asked his students.

"NO!" they chanted in unison, while I wailed. The exam had been extended into a colonoscopy, but without anaesthetic.

"Your intestines are in a terrible mess," the academic specialist informed me, and prescribed sixty milligrams of prednisone. I remembered my first boyfriend, Michael, swollen from the drug and the suspense of weaning from it. For over twenty years, I had seen no doctors nor taken any drugs. I only asked if I could start taking it that night and not wait till morning. In the month to come I stayed behind and watered Allan's plants, unable to accompany him on a trip to Hawaii. While at his apartment, suddenly hit by the ferocious appetite induced by high-dose prednisone, I opened his pantry doors and found cans of Chef Boyardee ravioli. *How can he eat this junk?* I wondered as I opened every single can and gorged on every last bite.

I discovered I couldn't write fiction. I couldn't erase my history. How could I invent stories when I had this history crying out to be told?

I should have hot-footed it back home north of the border. And I would have, except that I had an American fiancé. My wedding dress had to be let out at the waist to make room for the bloat from my first round of prednisone.

This full-blown attack was but the second long-delayed marker on a downward slope. During the next years, severe attacks alternated with sufficient remission time that I could attend to my parents.

We were married in 1990. It was a short honeymoon. Beginning with the summer of 1993 when I was left behind in Montreal without my green card, I began to spend time there with my parents.

"My relationship with my parents is unlike yours," my friend Sally in Montreal carefully prefaced our conversation.

"That's good," I said with a laugh. But I wanted none of this goodness.

I could not understand attachments where parents would never find occasion to say to their children, "I would get slaughtered for you."

My mother had said this to me one freezing midwinter day, with tears running down her face from the cold. She never praised my father. She said: "Your father would lay down his life for you."

What I could not help knowing was that the burden of their love I was privileged to bear had spoiled me for any other kind. "I hate to see you carrying," says my father when I skirt his efforts to pick up a burden.

Once I could never be light enough. I could never be sufficiently unencumbered. *Zee trugt*, she is carrying, in Yiddish means "she is pregnant." I didn't want to carry. I refused to make hostages to survival. I refused to make a family that would take precedence over the "other" family.

The first time I tasted my mother's fierce protectiveness was in protecting her. To me no action had any taste and all things fell from my hands until I took her on. The fact that she had made things fall from my hands did not affect the energy I mustered to save her. If it was she who needed my help, there was nobody to stop me. I must have realized this at the California airport when I looked at my parents over the jam and butter packets my mother had tried to open and thought, *My children*. This is what I had been saving myself from. This is what I had been saving myself for. Now I carry groceries to my father in the cold, and I push my mother's wheelchair uphill and further for the sake of fresh air, new landscapes, and *menschen*.

I will yet carry my mother. When her mobility lessens, I will hold her in an embrace that swings her to safe landing with her cheek against mine, her soprano laugh bursting in my ear. When we lose our balance, I whisper, "Fall on me," interposing my body so she can land on my lap and there we sit, laughing uproariously.

"She is heavy," my father protests at this sight.

"She is not so heavy," I say.

I had not wanted to be like her. I had not wanted to pay the price of her passion.

But my mother was no longer exactly the way she had been. She looked different. The bitterness had seeped out of her face, leaving it soft and beautiful. Her eyes lost their fixed and haunted look. For the first time, I did not avoid her gaze but gave myself up to it. She would study me for a long time, a long time I would spend drowning in her eyes. I, who had for so long been tormented by my reflection in her eyes, was being re-envisioned by her.

"If we survive," said the ghetto chronicler, "we will walk this earth like creatures from another planet."

They were hostages to what the Nazis made of them. We are all hostages to what illness and time will make of us. We will be whoever we are then. Whoever they were behind the wire. Whoever she was at the window. I had not wanted to be like my mother, I did not want to undergo the test, as if it were ever a choice I could make. But my mother was no longer exactly whoever she had been.

Whoever she was becoming, her breath rising and falling as we sit together. As her cells had once changed to make room for me in her body, they changed again. What my father and I did not know was that my mother was right. There was another, a different Elizabeth, and my mother was in the process of giving birth to her.

In order to take care of my mother, I separated from that part of myself that had been paralyzed by her. How could I take care of her if I was inadequate? Whoever I was becoming breathed with my mother; our breaths rise and fall together.

Chapter Eleven

SHEVIRAH (SHATTERING),
NOVEMBER 1993

When I returned to Montreal a few months later, on a rainy November night, my father was alone in the apartment. My mother was in the hospital. Long term. And I had put her there. The phone conversations that attended this change still rang in my ears. I had called my parents every day from California and every phone call met a crisis. My mother had fainted or been sick to her stomach for days. Three times I choreographed the calls to 911, and the much harder returns home. Each time my mother arrived in the emergency room, it had been into the hands of a different doctor who did not know her. Each time she was taken to the hospital, I called the geriatrician of last summer, Dr. Rosenberg, for somebody to keep her history in his awareness. The third time, it came over me that no matter what her hospital tests said she could not go home again into my father's care.

"Oh, Elizabeth, heh," my father said the third time, trying to laugh, "you always call at the right time." By which I knew that the ambulance would be on its way again. My mother had fallen down in a heap. It was a Sunday, they were alone. The social services nurse who came to the house said that my mother was dehydrated and should go to the hospital.

"She is lying on the plastic undersheet with no sheet on top," the nurse said with disapproval. Marysia told me they had cut her visits down to once a week. "I did not expect him to be so old," the nurse said. "He is so … *old*."

"I'm sorry, Dad."

"Why?" he asked.

"That you have to call the ambulance again."

"Yes … We have to get dressed," he said as if walking through a thick fog.

"Never mind *dressed*!" I yelled. Where did I just read that more elderly people died from dehydration than anything else?

"Don't forget to tell them dehydrated, d-e-h-y-"

"I will take a pencil," he said. "D-e." The doorbell rang.

"What is this?" I heard my mother asking. I hung up and called the hospital emergency to get out their IVs. A half hour later, they said my parents had not arrived. I called my parents at home. They were still there, my mother protesting that her husband wanted to get rid of her so he could marry a younger woman. "Take *him*," she pointed from the bed at my father.

The paramedics went away and left her at home.

On the other side of the continent, I lay down on the floor. Then I got up and called my doctor friend Michael to ask if he could read my mother's condition by symptoms. Stuck to the umbilical cord of the telephone wire, I called the hospital back to demand what they were thinking.

"We would have taken her if her condition had been critical," were the words I went to sleep on that night. The next morning I called home. My parents were gone.

◆ ◆ ◆

"When are you coming?" my mother demanded over the telephone from the hospital.

"In a few weeks," I said.

"If you come in a few weeks, don't come!" she said. "I won't be here, I'll be in *drerd*." In the ground. It was my mother in the shape I knew.

My mother was being admitted into the hospital long-term care, "indefinitely," Dr. Rosenberg decided, until such time as a place in a nursing home became available. Later he said my father looked like a man at the end of his rope.

At night I called my father. "She has a nice room," he said, and I heard no more. My father was sobbing.

It went on for a month with me in California, resisting my mother's efforts to come get her out of there. One time, I called her and a subhuman voice answered the telephone after many rings. She demanded nothing. "I would like to see you," she said. "Very much. *Zeyeh.*" She spoke with a lisp.

"I love you," I said.

"I love you more than the whole world, *di gantse velt.*" The *v* emerged slightly deformed.

"I think she had a little, little stroke," my father said.

When my plane lifted off, I saw black clouds. Clouds of smoke were billowing not from the airplane but from the landscape below that was sunny even in November. One of those hot desert winds had arisen, inflaming a seasonal brush fire into a firestorm that raced through Laguna Beach combusting houses along the way to the ocean. Later I heard from my husband that communities including ours were evacuated in the path of this maelstrom that travelled at a speed no living being could outrun, from which I was at that moment being carried ever higher away. Just before we rose over the cloud layer, I saw flames.

My father was not waiting for me downstairs; he did not even greet me at the door. Once he let me in, he went back to eating a sandwich in the kitchen, straight off the table without a plate, without saying a word more. It was the remains of something he had brought my mother – he would never buy it for himself. The mechanical behaviour disheartened me more than anything. The cup started to shake the closer he carried it to his mouth.

"Let's move to the dining-room table, Dad," I coaxed him, sweeping up the crumbs and sliding a plate under his bread.

"I don't like it in the dining room," he said, "it's black."

The night sky filled the windows through the open curtains. The light had gone out of his eyes. I closed the curtains and turned on the lamps. My father sat in the windowless kitchen. Later, he will look from his cup to me. "Did you notice that my hands are shaking?"

It wasn't her falling that had done him in, it was her silence. He found her lying face down on the carpet. "Quietly," he said. "I did not hear her." For all the times she called him, she did not call him. She was awake, but did not utter a sound. "To see her like that, it was as if somebody beat me."

At different times in the night I hear a rattle of dishes from the kitchen; it is my father who has got up to drink a cup of tea.

◆ ◆ ◆

"What can I do? They are very interdependent, like all survivor couples," said Judith, about my father's absence from the weekly outing. There were other people on the waiting list, so if he didn't show up, he would lose his place.

"I think of her all the time," my father said. "When I wake up at night, the first thing in my mind is her."

When I see my mother, I no longer try to separate them. I would not leave her for a minute. She is lying there unhappy, and when she sees me through a half-dropped lip she laughs and cries and laughs red-faced at herself crying. "Don't cry, Mama." Uncut hair, burning eyes, the bones in her face were showing. Her image would sear me night and day. I repledge myself to her. She ignites me with a desire that the list in the corridor attempted to inform: "What to do with your loved one when you come to visit."

All those activities not essential to life are cherished here, at its nether end, to spark the embers of life. I paste autumn leaves on the wall across from her hospital bed with surgical tape. From the bags of photos stuffed in a drawer at home I hurriedly collate three pocket albums. When is it worth taking the time to arrange albums of people who have passed through the moment?

The half-lifted lip smiles shyly as she flicks the pages in slow motion. "Who's this?" I tease.

"Who's this? You think I don't remember who it is?" she admonishes. "Stop taking so many pictures," she protests, because I continue.

"*Morgen?*" Her voice is fraught when we leave, "Tomorrow?" When it gets dark, she asks the nurse to call us at home.

"Ma, we were just there a few hours ago."

"Oy, count not the hours," she berates me. "That was then and now is now."

"*Zay ruig.* Be at peace," my father says. "We will see you *morgen.* Tomorrow."

"Tomorrow," my mother says, "Oh, and Lusia's coming, I will have more *tsuris.*"

"Would you rather we didn't come?" I tease her.

"It's a sickness," she says, passing her hand over her face. "This fear."

◆ ◆ ◆

"It is my fault," said my father sitting at night in the kitchen, "it is my fault." In the hospital I had caught him slipping a pink pill he had in his pocket into my mother's mouth and telling her to swallow.

"What are you doing? What are you giving her?"

"She needs her blood pressure pill! That's why she had this stroke!"

"No, Dad, since she's lost weight her blood pressure is normal! Don't you remember? Dr. Rosenberg took her off the medication. Spit it out, Ma!" I said, fishing in my mother's mouth. The nurse walked in on this family scene and remonstrated, "Only hospital meds are allowed." Without stopping she shoots the rapidfire inquisition of dementia at my mother. "What day is it? Where are we? What is your name?"

"Oy, what do you want from me?" moaned my mother. "How should I know what day it is? I don't work and I am lying here in the hospital where all the days are the same!"

"Then why did she have the stroke?" asked my father, who never cedes all of his responsibility. "They brought her to the hospital and they didn't give her the pill the first day. I should have given it to her, and for this I blame myself."

"Stop this, Daddy." He himself would suffer when the hospital would take away his pills and not restore them.

"Why don't you go out and see friends, Dad?"

"I meet friends in the hospital."

When my mother says she is in Demblin, she is not far wrong. One afternoon, I walk in and see a woman standing next to my mother, her arms crossed and her face set as if to say, "Look at what the bandit fate has done now!" She introduces herself: "We were in the *lager* together.

I am Cela, but your mother calls me Sara Pearl, the way she used to at home."

"The way it was at home was the best," says my mother. Sucking on a piece of orange, my mother looks up with orange pulp caught between her stroke-affected slightly parted lips. "We have to keep hope."

Sara Pearl has been stunned for months by her husband's coma. She is now a little extra stunned by my mother.

"What time makes of a person," she says. "She was the most beautiful girl in Demblin. The other sisters were pretty, too. Perele, Rivka, I remember Rivka was already married, and the youngest –"

"Esther," says my mother.

"The whole family was very nice. The town held them in consideration. Your mother's father was in charge of the *gemilut chesed*." The community free loan fund. *Chesed* means "loving kindness." "Your mother had a position. It was very rare for a woman in that time. We didn't have a hospital but a dispensary – she was the first woman to serve on it."

I see her in a group picture of that Demblin clinic staff. Narrow-shouldered among moustachioed officials and doctors, my mother sat with neatly crossed legs in the opaque stockings of the time, with a heart-shaped face and luminous eyes.

She sat between "might" and "right," my father told me. "This man had the brains, this man had the muscle," he said of the men on either side of her. The man with "right" was the folk doctor Veinappel who treated poor patients for free. Jews and Christians both came to him from miles around.

Born in the "fifth year" of the first revolution in Russia, amid strikes in Demblin and parents butting heads with children, my mother grew up among that generation who carried Jewish values to the street. When rumours reached home that my mother's scholarly uncle Shloime, who had been sent at great family sacrifice to study at a famous yeshiva, had forsaken his Talmudic studies for medicine, so immense was the shame that only the bubbe sneaked out to meet him. "'Your son has strayed from the path,'" my father tells me, laughing, "is what they wrote the family."

My father told me that unlike some of her sisters, who became seamstresses to gain the independence of a trade, my mother was content to stay at home. I suspect it wasn't the lack of a dowry that kept her from getting married; it was that coming home at night to her parents' house and scarfing down the pots of potatoes was the height of independence. When she finally married, she took her youngest sister to live with her. My father remembered Esther teasing my mother: "We used to sleep in the same bed at home. You're not going to abandon me just because you're married."

"When we saw your father," Sara told me, "we said a prince has come to call."

"Have some tea," my mother says.

"You are in a hospital, Chaja," Sara Pearl says, "you are not obliged to offer people tea."

Later, my parents give me to understand that while my mother's family was poor, Sara's was poorer.

"What did Sara say?" asks my mother.

"She says that you were the most beautiful girl in Demblin."

"No," says my mother, "Esther was."

◆ ◆ ◆

"Your mother was Miss Demblin," says the Popova, another Dembliner who comes to visit with her husband.

"You know my Heniek, it's always, 'Let's go visit Hela, Hela this, Hela that.' He was crazy about her. It's a good thing I'm not the jealous type," she says, straightening my mother's blanket. She checks the covered breakfast tray. "Eat! Why aren't you eating your porridge, Hela?" she berates my mother. "It's a *refiya* –a remedy – for you!"

"Leave her alone," says Heniek.

"Now we're going to see the Stajnbergova," she says in the Slavic manner that prepared me for the names in Tolstoy.

"How is the Stajnbergova?" asks my mother.

Popova's daughter who lives in Vancouver eerily echoes my mother on Demblin: my whole life feels like marking time until the day I return to Montreal. For the children of the postwar immigrants, Montreal is the origin of another diaspora. Scattered across the continent, they remember Montreal with some of the nostalgia my mother had for Demblin. They miss Montreal as a shard of Demblin.

It was rare to hear the pre-war past laid out like a banquet. At this time of their lives, my parents and their friends allow themselves to bring the time before into its own unalloyed presence. The railing medusa of my adolescence has morphed into this rueful alertness, the armour of flesh dissolved to reveal the heart-shaped face beneath, like the picture of her in the grass at twenty.

A miracle happened here: I know her as she was Before, as if she had jumped through the mirror of time. Life's transformations can restore as well as take away.

Her transformation has transformed my life story. The edge to my jokes and stories about my mother dissolves. Everything twisted untwists. As she lies there and follows me around with her beautiful eyes, I remember how I used to fear her gaze and now I meet it and return it in deepest complicity.

"It's not that you're exactly *shayn*," she says, "It's not so much that you're pretty, but you are *sympatish*. You have a sympathetic face, a special face."

I am not insulted. All through our mutual lives she has struggled with this unnatural daughter, not fulsome or healthy or beautiful enough for her fears, who in her mid-forties sits cross-legged on her bed. An old child. *Alte kop,* she used to call me. She stuffed me with food and still she could not make me into her vision of a blooming child.

"When one is young, one should live," says my mother. "Because look what becomes of one."

Part of my living is her dying. I want to be near her, even while she sleeps and her breathing blows out through her fallen lip.

The transvaluation of me: getting to speak to her on the phone and knowing she is all right makes my day. The phone rings and rings beside her hospital bed. Finally, the receiver is picked up, but with uncertain fumbling noises and my "Hello! Hello!" repeated many times before the covered-over voice, as in *Kol Nidre*, the covering over day, all vows abjured, all the past untwisted, her voice says, "Hallo."

"Star, diamond, sun, brightness," I say, "there is not another one like you in the world."

◆ ◆ ◆

No matter how much my mother dreads my absence, she vanquishes it when I ask for leave to go see Sara's husband on another floor. "Is it far?" She hoists herself up, as if ready to accompany me. "Of course you should go," she says. Sara and her son never leave him alone. It is what is behind much of Jewish ritual: you do not go out of the world alone just as you do not come into it alone. Life is with people. Urging me to marry, my mother used to repeat the saying: "Even in Paradise it's not good to be alone." Once she added, "In the last agony another person can hold your hand."

The first snow lies thick on the windows when I roll my mother into the solarium on Saturday morning. "You like this stuff," she says. The solarium has become that place that since the Babylonian captivity anyplace can become. Displacement was our tragedy and our gift. As the double-doored wooden cabinet is rolled in, I think how this portability came in especially handy for people who are too frail to go far.

"Your mother's family came to our house to pray at Simchas Torah," said my father, joining us. Simchas Torah is the celebration of the book, whose presence alone made the space sacred. "We kept the Torah in a *shank*, in a cupboard, that was the ark," he nodded at the wooden chest in front of us. "Your mother was about twelve years old …"

"Then you must have been five, Daddy."

He grinned. We were offered little cups of sweet wine and a home-baked biscuit. "*Git Shabbes.*"

The solarium is a gift from an anonymous donor. This small Jewish hospital was founded in 1930 on contributions taken up when the highest-ranking intern in the province, Sam Rabinovitch, having shown up for his first day of residency at Notre Dame Hospital, spurred a province-wide walkout by Catholic doctors.

Every day as I come in I read a little more of a frieze of inscriptions running in a circle around the ceiling of the lobby. At one end, the white letters on a blue background scrolled out a series of medieval Portuguese and Spanish names and dates. From the Iberian expulsion in 1492, the frieze gave way to French, Italian, and Ashkenazi German names. The inscription cited the town of each man's birth and the often far-flung town where he died. The frieze began with Maimonides in the twelfth century and ended with "Sigmund Freud. b. Freiburg. Died London 1939."

I came to the dedication that begins and closes the circle: "To Jewish physicians, and their historic journeys."

On my last day, I left her alone in the solarium on a sere November afternoon for my interview with the doctor. She forgot to be anxious that I left her; she forgot to ask me to take her back to her room. There were no activities going on and she was alone in the huge windowed expanse with a piano and some chairs. My mother looked out at the skyline she especially likes: this city she's claimed to despise for its barrenness is from this view of the mountain rich and new. I returned from hearing the geriatrician say, "She will deteriorate" (a downward slope of her arm marked by sudden drops caused by stroke), to sit beside her. A man standing at the piano started to play a few notes. He was barely warming up with one hand on an old familiar melody. My mother's face, for so many years slanted like an axe against the wind, now slanted up to the light from the sky while she listened to a tenuous one-handed "Aveinu Shalom Aleichem," the Jewish homecoming song. My eyes filled with tears.

Before I left, she looked at me for a long time, then pulled herself over and held on to the bar of the bed. She gave me her blessing.

"Go always where there are a lot of people," she said. "Don't stray from the crowd ... don't make yourself conspicuous."

Chapter Twelve

IT'S LIVELY IN THE SHTETL, DECEMBER 1993

A month later, my father is waiting for me in the lobby of my parents' Montreal apartment building. He's spiffy in a tweed jacket, eager to carry my bags. What a difference from last time.

When we come in to the apartment, I see the Chanukah lamp my parents brought back from Israel and never used on the dining-room table. In ancient times, when the oppressors overran the Temple, they put out the light.

"Let's light the Chanukah candles, Dad!"

My father reaches in his pocket for a yarmulke he's taken to having ready for the *minyans* in the hospital. All the lamps are turned on in the living and dining room as well. For the first time in my life, we light Chanukah candles. First, he lights the *shames*, the servant candle that serves to light all the others, the slight shake in his hands making the flame tremble.

My father picks up the servant candle and touches its flame to the first candle.

"It's *hoishech*," my mother used to shudder on dim thresholds. Darkness was one of the ten plagues, the murky chaos in which God brooded upon the waters. In her early days in the hospital, my mother was haunted by men in dark clothes who were looking for her, my father told me in a stricken voice: "The SS uniform."

Candles are burning in the already bright dining room and kitchen. My mother likes it bright, my father likes it bright; light on light that bright is Jewish light. Every day another candle will be added, and it will grow brighter.

"Wait," my father said, and the blessings tumble out all of a piece. "I have not practised it but it is so deep inside that it comes out."

"In the Jewish tradition," he smiled, "gambling is not approved of. Not because it is a sin, but because it is a waste of time. But on Chanukah," his smile widens, "it is all right to gamble."

◆ ◆ ◆

On this first day of Chanukah, the Festival of Lights, I was happy to be arriving in time to console my mother for the first surgery in her long life, not yet knowing that my anticipated arrival threw the surgery into shadow. "Cataract, shmataract! Get me my shoes and coat, please. I'm a mother."

When my father and I arrive on the long-term-care floor, my mother is sitting in the corridor with her bandaged eye and her face lights up in joyful shock. "Elizabeth, Elizabeth," she lullabies herself.

In the month since she has been admitted, my mother has taken to making a beeline on her walker to sit in the corridor. "I need the street," she says, and here there is one. Slowly the corridor fills with people hobbling out of their rooms until it takes on the aspect of Shabbes afternoon in the shtetl. "Here comes the klezmer," says my father. A ponytailed young man passes by pushing a hospital cart jingling with tambourines, bells, cymbals, the instruments of his craft. His official title is music therapist, which easily assimilates into the traditional village klezmer.

"Sing 'Oi Chanukah,'" David the klezmer prods my mother.

"She has a good voice," I say.

"Our town had a very musical rebbe," my father says to David. "The officers brought their wives to listen to the rebbe and his Chasids sing after the Sabbath meal."

To return the honour, my mother wants to sing the Russian gypsy song "Black Eyes." She speak-sings along for a few phrases and suddenly breaks off. "I cannot sing anymore," she says matter-of-factly. "I cannot sing anymore at all."

A frail man with a long white beard rolls out in a wheelchair.

"Tell me, rabbi," says the klezmer, "remind me of the story about Rabbi Akiva and a lamp."

The elderly rabbi answers very softly.

"I didn't catch that," says the klezmer. "Tell it to her in English."

I bend over his chair.

Out of the hunched-over man comes a quiet but fluent voice. "One day Rabbi Akiva met a blind man holding a lamp. 'Why are you holding a lamp, you who can't see?' asked the rabbi. 'So other people can see *me*,' answered the blind man, 'and help me if I fall.'"

Our neighbour, a tall, thin man with a mustache, has come out of his room in a bathrobe. "Do I speak Polish? Of course I speak Polish. I was in the Polish Army. I was in Auschwitz, Dachau, Belsen, all the best schools. Sam Kozovinsky." He shakes our hands. "You were born in Lodz? After the war I was on a train. A Pole looked at me and pointed outside, 'There lie buried all the Jews.' Tell me," Sam says, looking at me, "*how* were you born in Lodz?"

"After the war," I say. "My parents went to Lodz after the war."

"You are from Lodz?" says my mother. "Perhaps you knew some distant relatives of mine."

"What were their names?"

My mother thinks and shakes her head. "I forgot. Shmuel," she remembers. "Shmuel made stockings."

"Oi mamanu. I have to remember this song, it makes me so popular. Help me with this," Mr. Kosovinsky sings to David on a counterbeat.

"There is nothing more precious than a mama," Sam sings in Yiddish.

"What about a father?" somebody objects.

My mother winks at me.

"Sam knows a thousand Yiddish songs," the klezmer says.

"It's the generation to learn from," I say.

"It's the *last* generation," the klezmer says.

A nurse comes by with eye drops to put in my mother's eye. "Give her an orange," my mother says.

"Your mother has the most beautiful smile," says Hélène, the floor's secretary. "Every morning when she passes by on her walker to breakfast, she stops and gives me a big smile."

"What did she say?" my mother asks.

"She says you have a beautiful smile," I tell her. She never smiled before.

"When I walk through, I don't have the strength to say hello to everyone who greets me," my mother complains.

In the last month, without changing place my mother has imprinted the shtetl on to the hospital. My mother has "adapted" more in one month in the hospital than I had seen her for the forty years in Canada. Later I will learn that the atmosphere has been consciously cultivated by the head nurse and social worker.

"On the mountain is the solarium," my mother says as the corridorful of people starts moving, with walkers, wheelchairs and IV bottles.

"I'm not going like this."

She used to dress up to go on the mountain, and now she wants to dress up to go round the corridor to the solarium. It is the first time in her life she has worn pants. Every time I come, I bring her a new lipstick, which she presses on her lips in a still potent cue. It will come back to haunt me when I am told that she delayed a fire drill with the demand, "Give me my *shminka!*"

In the solarium, tambourines, drum brushes, and various music makers are passed around the wheelchairs encamped in a circle. The rabbi's three children scurry around on the piano bench, but no amount of coaxing will get one of them to sing.

"That we want to show off our children, and that they tell us to leave them alone is one thing we can always count on," he says with a laugh. A Filipino administrator who must have just missed the operatic stage sings "Mao Tzur." A Caribbean man, tapping his foot, sings, "Send a Light." In her new blue pantsuit accented by her scarf, my mother, one eye joyful and the other bandaged, shakes a maraca.

I wave to my mother and sit down on a bench on the side. "We have just admitted a woman with a family like yours," whispers the social worker.

A wan woman enters the circle, her IV-hung wheelchair guided by a woman of about my sister's age in a ski sweater. The father asks in an eastern European accent whether he can sit down next to me on the bench.

"My mother's there in the front," I say. "We came from Poland."

"How long has she been here?"

"Two months."

"Two months?" His face falls. "I speak Polish. What don't I speak, Polish, Russian, Lithuanian, because we lived on the border of these countries. My daughter," he covers his mouth not to embarrass her, "is a professor of linguistics. She was with us in the war, and we all three survived." Tears spring out of his eyes.

"Thank you," we say. The rabbi's young son offers us challah and a paper cup of wine so that we can join in on the *Shehechayanu*, the blessing of the moment – a baby's first tooth, the first fig of the season, the first day of a holiday, any anniversary that has completed its cycle. If all the blessings simply enunciate awareness of themselves, if every ritual such as Passover marks the time since the last Seder and remembers the rememberers, the *Shehechayanu* with its *chai* for life enunciates the ontological ground of all of them: that we are alive to say it. "Thank you for sustaining us and bringing us alive to this moment."

For bringing us to this day and for the times and circumstances when it was inconceivable that we would make it to this day. For the times I nearly saw them shot, hung, or starving in front of my eyes.

"It is *unbelievable*," my neighbour says. "We gave my daughter away to be hidden. After the war we came out of the bushes and we found her again." The tears explode down his face and splash his jacket. "My wife spoke good Polish. She went to the nuns and asked them if they would hide the children. We took the children out of the ghetto at night. I was the one chosen to bribe the German guard to look the other way."

"They take good care of my mother here," I say.

"They are supposed to put my wife in the new nursing home, here I have the address. He unfolds the paper and hands it to me to read because he is blinded by tears.

"Are you from Demblin?" my mother asks my neighbour's wife,

Rokhl, when we have introduced everyone. "No? Then are you from Piliv?" Piliv, or Pulawy in Polish, was the town where she was born.

"No." The daughter smiles. "We are real Litvaks." Rokhl's face is motionless.

"Don't they have a drug for Parkinson's?" I ask the daughter.

"Yes, but it gives her hallucinations. My mother started to speak with people who have been dead for years. My father couldn't cope."

When we have settled my mother in bed, she says, "My mother comes to my mind often now. Every night before I go to sleep she stands before my eyes.

◆ ◆ ◆

As my father and I leave the hospital, a blast of Arctic air slaps us in the lungs. Frost! I have taken into my cells my parents' pleasure of walking in a frost in Poland. And in Montreal the sky signals the weather in a way opposite from everywhere else. It is when the sky is the clearest, and the snow lies at its whitest, that the temperature has plunged the furthest.

It was on dazzling days such as these when the sun shone without heat that my mother loved to walk.

"I have to go home," she said that afternoon with a renewed urgency that frightened me.

"Why, Ma?"

She concentrated, pulling out a length of thread that has rolled up in it a story.

"I have to go home and take back the money. I'll take back the money they owe us, and you will see I will save the family. I'm not afraid."

Only by a fluke of my father's memory that dovetails with my mother's do I know what she's talking about. That night he tells me about an incident early in the war. His big shipment of wood had been stolen. The German military then appeared in Demblin, appropriating all Jewish goods including the remnants of lumber left in his shed.

"They gave us a piece of paper that documented this." A worthless piece of paper in my father's view. "We drove by in a droshky and saw the lumber piled up with their supplies." My father had invested so much in the big shipment that little cash would have remained for the days ahead, when you could still bribe the German guard to look the other way while you slipped your child to safety. "Your mother wanted to ask them to reimburse us. I told her she was crazy, but she took a horse and carriage and drove to the military outpost. The cashier was closing for the day and asked her to come back the next day. She was all excited. She went back the next day, and you know what?" He shrugs. "They paid her."

It happens before my eyes. Standing by the doorway I see her edging herself off the bed. She is so close to me and I cannot stop it. No sooner is she upright than her feet slip out from under her with a thump! Her behind lands flat on the ground. Did her head bump the bed? I come running; the small Filipino nurse, Kimi, comes running. I hold her head while Kimi checks for bruises. "Give her some grapes!" my mother hollers while still in midair. She never asks for help but if she has no choice but to receive it she must give something back in return. My mother gave a bottle of eau de cologne to a nurse for helping her; it was the wrong nurse, my father said.

There is somebody to whom my mother insists on giving neither as honour nor as blood money. Lately my mother has been moved into a room with Susan, a woman who returns from her endless walks with scratches and bruises. "We put your mother in with her, it is shameful to say," said the head nurse, "because your mother can still defend herself and the other lady cannot." When I come in the room with a bag of my mother's favourite foods, my mother motions to Susan rummaging around the dresser and says, "Give her something to eat, she hasn't eaten a thing all day."

"But Ma, they take her to breakfast just like you!"

"Not a morsel of food has passed her lips all day, I tell you!" In my mother the imperative of sustaining life has burned away tenderness and prejudice, knowing as she does the price at which life is sometimes sustained.

Usually I get my mother's tray and we sit together. Once I came too late and looked for her at a long row of tables pulled together. Lunch was delayed. Some of the patients laid their heads down on the table. One of the women was stuck repeating "What about me?"

My mother's former roommate, Shirley, said one more time and she would slap her. My stomach wrenched at finding my mother in this lineup sitting with her head held high and her hands and ankles demurely crossed. When biology has their number and they are again humiliated by their bodies, they are counted as institutional beds. It's more than the demographic of Montreal's disproportional aging Jewish population, more than that among these are more Holocaust survivors than anywhere else, that has always made me suspect that every old person is a Jew. Do not treat my parents like numbers. Once they *were* numbers. Suddenly my mother, casting around for a fellow witness, caught my eye. She laughed, I laughed. There were tears in her eyes.

◆ ◆ ◆

The head nurse, Ruth, asked if she could photograph my mother putting on her lipstick. "It is for a seminar on how to deinstitutionalize life for long-term patients," she says. *This is something my family is good at,* I think proudly and then a little uneasily when I remember the smoked turkey my father has left in the nightstand. De-institutionalizing.

I hover over my mother as she eats her lunch. Institutional food is difficult to fob off on my mother. When she came to the hospital she didn't eat, the bones jutted through her face. It gave my father a scare.

"Can you get me a piece of schmaltz herring?" my mother asks.

I wrap up a piece of herring in the fresh onion roll I brought, which I then tear in little pieces. Nothing used to be too big for my mother. Now her fork hardly manages to pierce the meat, she picks up what she can. When I arrived, anxious, I fed her. Now I exercise the patience beyond anxiety that is strange to both of us – to let her feed herself. She chews and, with wide eyes, watches the people pass by, fascinated. When she catches me watching her, she chews with added vigour.

She nudges my father and says with pride, "Look at her. It is a matter of life and death to her whether I eat or not."

Suddenly she turns slyly to me.

"What would you do if I died?"

She answers quicker than I can: "Nothing, right? What is there to do?"

"Are you planning to die?"

"Everyone dies," says my mother. "But I have lived through such hard times, two world wars. It is amazing I am still alive."

"Yes," I hurry. "Since you have lived through such hard times, you're not going to die now. *Ich hob dir leeb.* I love you," I now ritually spring this phrase on my mother. To which she ritually shakes her head.

"*Tsi feel,*" she says. "Too much."

After lunch I help my mother get ready for the Oneg Shabbat.

"Take Shirley too," my mother nudges me. "I have somebody. She has nobody."

Shirley, the woman who mocked my attentions to my mother, needs help with her bra.

When Shirley is dressed, my mother says in a formal Yiddish that echoes the *Shehechayanu,* "I am glad that you are also able to be here on this occasion."

"Thank you," Shirley replies.

Bensh licht. Every Friday the klezmer honours someone with the mitzvah of blessing the light. Lighting the candles is the feminine hallowing of home that welcomes the Sabbath bride, the Near One. "It's so nice to have a mother and daughter ..." he begins, at which point an apprehension grips me – "our time is up, we are unmasked as fakes" – and then subsides in a larger acceptance. My mother never performed the Friday night hallowing of home, and the last person she saw conjure the flame was her own mother. Will anybody understand that in no act is my mother more Jewish than her refusal after the Holocaust to bless the light?

But when he calls our names my mother flies out of her wheelchair with joy at being called, forgetting she can't walk.

"She can't walk!" I motion to the klezmer. "We will both hold her up." Forgetting, moreover, that she does not *bensh licht.* We help her to the table with the candlesticks. She stands mute, thrilled, and staggered.

"Do you remember?" the klezmer coaxes, unfolding a kerchief for her head. She looks up at him. "I've never done this," she murmurs in Yiddish that thankfully nobody but me hears. "Help her, Elizabeth." My mother has the excuse of forgetfulness, but what excuse do I have. My mother has never blessed candles in her daughter's memory. The Germans incinerated the mother who blessed the candles.

"*Baruch ata*," begins David, "Blessed be," until a miracle meets us, and my mother joins in on *oylem*, the universe. We make it back to her chair, my mother radiant.

"You see," my mother said euphoric, "he noticed that we were Jewish children and that's why he asked us." I don't remind her that practically everybody in the room is Jewish.

The woman who repeats flits by in a robe with long billowing yellow sleeves. "Look, a *malech*," my father said, joining us. "God sent down an angel." A nurse's aide invites her to dance.

My mother eyes her and says, "She'll soon give her a *patch*." A smack.

When the *shames* recruits my father for a *minyan* of ten, my mother scoffs.

"He's getting religious in his old age."

"No, you always accept," my father said. "You never know when somebody needs to say Kaddish for a parent." He's not being religious. He's being kind. It's the same thing. In requiring ten people, the tradition turns us back always to one another.

My mother tells me another version. "Soon after the war your father and I were walking together, and strangers called to us in the street," she says. "Are you Jews? Good, please come because we have had a little boy and we don't have ten people for the bris. Can you imagine what this meant to us?"

It meant, I thought, *that having survived fulfilled a mitzvah.*

◆ ◆ ◆

My parents are sitting in the hospital room in the grey light two days before my departure. Suddenly my tearless mother grimaces. "I never imagined it would be like this" and the tears are running down her face, her face a spasm, "that I wouldn't take you to the station."

"Nobody's taking me to the station, Ma." I kissed her face, her eyes.

"The only bad thing you ever did was to move so far away from me," she sobs. "But it's not too late," she looks up "you can sell the house and buy one in Montreal."

I hold my mother. "I will stay for a while. Dad, you go home."

"*Nayn!*" they both object at my going home alone, she tearstained and louder. Finally, I wheel her to the elevator we will take and ask the nurse to wheel her back.

When the elevator stalls, I step out again and peek around the corner. She has asked to be parked in the corridor, *tsvishen menschen*, among people.

I kissed her eyes and her wet face, I wanted never to waste a single drop; her tears water the earth. Because if the tearless goddess has again become vulnerable like the weeping forsaken bride, if my mother sheds tears now, it means there must also be times now when she is truly no longer crying.

Vi nemt men a bisele mazl?

Vi nemt men a bisele glick?

Where does one find a little luck? Why, then I've left it in Montreal. Why did I ever leave this place? Why did I ever leave them? I ask myself on the way to the airport. The answer taunts me with the queasy-making tautology of the life cycle: "You left to get away from them."

At the airport I take out the resident alien card the lack of which had kept me in Montreal the summer before, and show it to the US immigration officer. "Going home?" she says.

Chapter Thirteen

MAME–LOSHEN
(MOTHER-TONGUE), 1995

Jokes are a way of kashering, of making kosher. They do this not by separating but by putting everything on the same table.

My sister liked this joke: "Two Jews are being led to the gallows. One asks if he can have a last cigarette. The other one turns to him and says, 'Spiegelman, don't make trouble.'"

"*Lach nisht*," my mother said, "Don't laugh. You don't know whether he was worrying not for nothing."

◆ ◆ ◆

After my mother spent a year in the hospital's long-term care ward, I got a call saying that a place had become available for her in a nursing home. My mother had spent a year in an acute-care hospital, a privilege unheard of anywhere else. She had been surrounded by hospital-level staff and people of all ages. I was one of the few relatives not looking forward to her move to a permanent nursing home.

The move was announced suddenly when I was far away. I called my father. Yes, he had packed her suitcase. He would accompany her in the handicapped transport.

Like all medical facilities, the nursing home was publicly funded, the Canadian government having shouldered the mitzvah of caring for the elderly. Residents paid a monthly fee if they could. A spanking-new facility in a country proud of its universal health care, with a human rights charter inspired like all those after 1945 by their recent transgression on the bodies of such as my parents, of an ethnic group known for its care of its elders – it had a good, if recent reputation. My sister had been on a visit when the nursing-home request was filled out.

"The big one was just miles and miles of old people. I told the social worker she would like the small one better. It seems more intimate and less like," my sister exhaled into a giggle, "a concentration camp."

But it was not intimate. Unlike the acute-care hospital's conscious efforts to deinstitutionalize, the nursing home's fondest hope was to live up to the image of an institution. Girded by rules, its facade was maintained by turning a blind eye to the actual failings on the floor. My mother was moved from a public hospital to a public nursing home within the same city, but she might as well have been sent to another planet. It was no worse than any other nursing home in Quebec and probably better, much better than the common run in the United States, but it was a rude change. We went from a place whose credo was to make people as well as they could be to a limbo of lowest common denominator calculation. It seemed to function according to a set of laws separate from the rest of the society.

"If you don't take me out of here, I will commit suicide," my mother threatened over the telephone. *Ibergein selbst mort.* German words.

"When you come here you won't have a mother."

I called the nursing home's social worker. "But your mother is doing very well," the social worker, Tiffany, said.

"*Ich hob kaynem du!*" (I have nobody here!) my mother said.

At that time I still had a hope that what I told the social worker would somehow be translated into action. Nadia, the companion my mother liked, had found my mother soiled and ashamed. I called the director, a former social worker, to tell him that my mother would not ask for help, but she needed it.

"You are trying to overprotect your mother," he said, sight unseen. "It is good for her to struggle." For all his authority the director seemed unable or unwilling to organize or increase his staff. So social science was instead practised on the weak link, the patients and their families.

Whenever a patient or his family had a complaint, they were sent to the twenty-six-year-old Tiffany, to be talked out of it.

The management seemed compelled to maintain the delusion that it could totally fulfill the needs of the patients. Many of the patients had outside companions paid for by the family – most crucially to feed stroke victims. The director snorted at these "babysitters," but nobody would leave a child this helpless without a babysitter. At the end of life, we needed as much help as at the beginning. Except that at the end, for Darwinian reasons, we skimped on it. Even without budget restrictions, there would never be enough help.

However I tried to help my mother, there was a rule forbidding it. Without accepting it, I gradually realized that I was racing against the clock to make things better for my parents while the institution was merely waiting for the time to run out.

When we arrived in Canada, my mother heard of a barbaric practice in this new country; that when parents got old, the children would put them in a place on the outskirts of the city. "You would never send me to the Hospital Hop, would you?" was the promise she extracted from me, who was eight years old at the time. "Hop" was how she pronounced it. The Hospital of Hope had moved to just around the corner.

It was snowing when I landed in Montreal. When I arrived at my parents' apartment, my father rang me in from upstairs. He stood peering at me down the corridor from the doorway of the apartment, his shoulders narrowed ("How straight he stands for a man his age!" people would say). He waited for me there. Remembering my mother's blind eager toddle, I can measure my parents' frailty by how far down the corridor they managed to come and greet me.

The first morning I found my mother tied into her chair in a circle of wheelchairs.

"How did you like your breakfast?" a visitor jovially asked her.

"Since the Nazis took away my home, I don't like it anywhere," my mother blurted out as I wheeled her past the stunned bystanders.

The nursing home had a rule: my father was not allowed to join my mother in the dining room for lunch. I saw the director, a strapping, moustachioed, well-dressed man bouncing up and down at the lobby desk on his toes.

I asked whether my father could be allowed to eat with my mother in the dining hall. "They have eaten together for sixty years. My father comes every day, and my mother used to do their cooking. I can't be sure what he eats by himself. My father can pay for his lunch and carry his own tray to my mother's table. It would give them some semblance of home and normalcy."

"Absolutely not!" he barked so summarily that I giggled in surprise.

A few days later, I read on the bulletin board that Judith, my grade-three classmate who led my father's weekly outings, was scheduled to give a talk to the staff called "The Aging Survivor." My hopes went up.

At the meeting Judith explained that when Holocaust survivors age and are institutionalized, they become vulnerable to reminders of their previous internment.

"Holocaust survivors were given little understanding after the war," she said. "Let's make it up to them now."

"Now I understand why some patients hoard bread," a nurse said in the audience.

"*Hoard* is a negative word," Judith said. "Bread means security. Bread is the staff of life."

If my parents and their friends were any indication, this sounded more likely of *heegers* who had experienced the Great Depression. My parents couldn't hoard food. I couldn't imagine my parents leaving a restaurant with a doggy bag, like my American husband did. For my parents the implication of having to save a piece of bread for tomorrow was worse than the chance of not having any.

Nevertheless, I was grateful.

"The couples who survived together are very strongly bonded," Judith said. "They should be allowed to eat together." I looked around the room. The director was not there.

Nonetheless my request was submitted to a panel, which I never heard about again, that allowed my father to eat lunch with my mother in the dining room.

◆ ◆ ◆

The new sensation of being a devoted daughter soon foundered in the criticism that I was *too* devoted. I was put behind the glass too.

"It's nice for your parents to have you visit so much, but isn't it undermining your marriage?" said the social worker.

I preferred the way my mother put it.

"How long are you here for?" my mother asked when I arrived.

"A month," I said.

"What a calamity!" my mother said delighted. "Just like that you leave your husband? But someone will steal him away!"

Allan encouraged me to go, at first. He knew I was all they had.

I found it annoying when I sought advice about my mother and people replied with, "What about you?"

Ruth, the head nurse at the hospital, had once called me in to say she was more concerned about me than about my mother. I looked tired. I'd been tired all my life. Taking care of my parents was the first time I managed to sustain energy.

"You should be the nursing home's biggest problem," Dr. Lerner said. "I have many geriatric patients and my problem with them is the opposite." Eventually he also said, "So you're putting your life on hold while you take care of your parents?"

What could I tell him: what life? After the price my parents had paid, I had made nothing to sacrifice. Except now I had a husband, whom I overlooked as I did everything that did not occupy my tunnel vision. It was this that my mother had prepared me to do best. In my lifetime energy curve, taking care of my parents was a high point.

My grade-school friend Dora came the closest to sharing my feelings. Years ago she had confessed to a similar sense to mine of surviving without entirely thriving. "Accept that maybe, born into this trauma, we just aren't as strong as everyone else. We are not like our parents," she said. "We don't have their strength. Who could be a shoemaker in Auschwitz and then come to Canada and open a shoe factory?"

She still kept track of our difference from our cohort of normals. "They say we can't cope because we have no model for dying. Nobody we know has ever died a natural death."

Her mother was no way as crazy as mine. So Dora had gone skiing, she went to Europe with friends during college. Her parents had taken the long view and arranged for driving lessons. She drove every weekend from Toronto to see them.

Like me, she had also married a WASP, with a last name like Smith or Jones that she said came in handy when travelling in Anglo-Saxon countries. It wasn't until speaking to her father much later that I remembered Allan's joke about our fathers' putting their Gentile sons-in-law to the test. That is, my father pulled his fine cognac out of the liquor cabinet at eleven o'clock in the morning and offered Allan a drink.

"I don't drink this early in the day," Allan said.

"Neither do I!" my father said, joyously shelving the bottle.

Dora's fiancée had inauspiciously polished off a bottle of wine. If our fathers were worried, they had reason to be.

Whenever she came to Montreal, we visited St. Lawrence Boulevard, "the Main" street of our childhood arrival in Canada. To this day it remained our source of sustenance. It was not only the original market street where our mothers bought produce, fish, kosher meat, and challah. Up to very recently, my father would drive my mother to shop there once a week, while Dora's father foraged for the juiciest plums or the sweetest grapes on his way home. It was also the street where our fathers worked. My father's depot store was some blocks away from Dora's father's shoe factory.

After stopping at Old Europe for Dora to restock her supply of her favourite coffee beans, we dropped in on her father in his shoe factory. Besides custom making fashionable winter boots for her size-5 feet, Mr. Finkelman shod the most glamorous Québécois TV *vedettes* (stars). He always had a pair of Little Dora ballet slippers waiting for me. Mr. Finkelman came out in his inimitable bow tie, his big smile, and his big ears that his little girl liked to bite when he came in from the cold.

"How is your mother?" he asked.

When we said goodbye, we walked east from St. Lawrence, to L'Express on St. Denis. St. Lawrence used to be the great divide between the English-speaking west and the French-speaking east. But English and French were not the languages at issue when she spoke of the students she taught at a private WASPy girls' school.

"When the girls grow up," she said, "they'll all talk like *this*, so people won't be able to tell who's who!"

As we walked, I rehearsed my speeches on my mother's behalf. "Even though my mother may appear demented in a medical interview ..." I started.

"... we still like to have her around," she finished for me.

On her last visit, her mother was ill in the hospital. We always went out to eat; the worse our parents' health, the better the restaurant.

"I have to make a will," she said, suddenly stopping in her tracks. "Because if something happened to me, who would take care of my parents?"

"If something happened to you," I said, "they would fall away the next moment."

◆ ◆ ◆

Devoted as I was, having lunch together was the sole fruit of my efforts to make things better. Even this would be constantly withdrawn, my father's place at my mother's side taken away and restored only with such a great fuss that it would embarrass him to insist. The straight-forward *goyish* assumption of insisting on a promise was not in his repertoire. It was not in my repertoire either. But this was shaping up to be the single pitched battle of my life.

On cold afternoons when nobody else her age went outside, I asked, "Do you want to go out, Mama?"

"*Yo.*" I steadied her on the walker to slip her down coat on around her back; then the gloves, each finger of which we pull on separately, the infantilism of which made my mother break out in laughter.

Next I wrapped a shawl around her head. "I look like a bubbe," she complained, still laughing. And finally we pushed out in the diamond-brilliant snow.

"Are you cold, Ma?" All this dressing was worth the fifteen minutes we would be outside in the tonifying air. Winter kept her alive. I bent over to her red face, the tears trickling down.

"*Nayn,*" she said.

When she took a nap I joined her, climbing over the bars of the narrow bed that were up so we wouldn't fall out. Once I was beside her, she released the bar and curled her hand around mine. *Lonchechka.* Little hand. Legend had it that she used to hold my hand through the night when I was a child in Poland, reaching through the bars of my crib that was placed next to their bed so she could calm my fears. "*Malutka.* Little one ..." she used to rattle off a string of Polish diminutives, if she left one out I reminded her. She held on to my curled-up fist and every now and then pressed it. Sometimes I was the one who fell asleep, half conscious of the periodic lifting of her head to check on me.

When I took off my mother's coat, I noticed it was wet with vomit.

"It's because your father brings her food!" the night nurse bellowed when I asked her about it.

"I cannot not bring her food," my father said when I asked him, his eyes reddening, "I cannot. In the *lager* she used to give me her piece of bread. What if she is hungry?"

The nursing home doctor put her stethoscope to my mother's stomach and said since she hadn't felt any masses, there was nothing to worry about. But my mother kept vomiting. So I took her to her beloved GP, Dr. Lerner.

"You've lost so much hair I nearly didn't recognize you," she said when we came into his office.

"You're very observant," he said, laughing.

"Why didn't you tell me we were coming here?" she whispered, "I would have gotten *dressed*."

"Sounds like acid reflux," Dr. Lerner said.

"I am healthy like a horse," my mother said, and kept reassuring me of this to assuage my worry even when she could say nothing else.

When I brought back his prescription to the nursing home to fill, the assistant head nurse emitted a slow burn as if I had transgressed some boundary in helping my mother. My mother was given the medication and stopped vomiting.

She no longer belonged to herself nor to us; she belonged to the nursing home. But in entrusting her to their care we had not given her away. The tactful thing would have been to always wait for them, but I could not watch my mother suffer in her short time left, especially when they did not justify our trust.

◆ ◆ ◆

During my mother's first stroke in the nursing home in the hot summer of 1995, she suddenly stopped speaking Yiddish. My father, Nadia, and my sister each called for a doctor and no doctor came.

"*Słucham*." My mother answered the telephone in Polish, unable to switch back to Yiddish when she spoke to me. "I have lost my *loshen*," she said when I saw her. "I have lost my tongue." Badgering her to speak, she finally burst out with the teenage phrase I used to throw at her: "*Loz mech oop!*" (Leave me alone!) This made me happy.

"Who told you she had a stroke?" the nurse asked. They will deny it until I speak to the current floor physician, Dr. Kallen.

"I am so ticked off!" the doctor said. "Your mother shows signs of an ischemic attack. It should have been in the notes! Much of the third-floor staff is incompetent. If there is any consolation, there is not much we could have done. But it should have been in the notes!"

When I changed planes in Chicago I read that 700 people had died of the heat, mostly elderly. Only the administrative offices had air conditioning. My mother was sitting downstairs and started crying when she saw me. My mother was soft, softer than I ever wanted her to be.

"*Hayb shoyn oyf tsi kishen mech*" (Stop kissing me already), she managed to say in Yiddish again. That I should live to see the day I welcomed a slam from my mother: But so softly that I had to bend my head next to her face to hear. "Where is, where is, where is ... oy," she broke off frustrated.

"Tata is at home," I answered. "What a *shayn* necklace you are wearing."

"These beads, I got them in, in, in ... "

"Where?"

"In Poland." She finished her phrase with a slight smile, as if pleased with such a good outcome. "I have lost my *loshen*," she said frustrated, of her stuttering flying starts. "I have lost my tongue."

My father was at home because he was exhausted. One of the few pleasures left to my parents was to sit outside under the trees with *menschen*. By early evening my mother had spent ten hours upright in a wheelchair and needed to lie down. When nobody came to help them, my father carried her to bed himself. When I complained, rather than organize the staff to put my mother to bed, the director asked them to note down each time my father helped my mother.

They didn't help my mother, but they cranked the bed up high to make it harder for my father to do it. When I called I heard the shrieks of a nurse's aide berating him.

"Mr. Wajnberg became verbally abusive and compared the nursing home to a concentration camp."

At the meeting with the regional health board representative that I request, the director called my father "compulsively helpful." "If he continues to help your mother," he said, "he will be banned from the building."

I had badly wanted to convince my father not to fear reprisals. Now I turned to the health board representative Mme Corbin and said, "Who was right, me or my father, about fearing reprisals?"

By complaining to the government I was making trouble. Making waves has never been big among the Jewish people.

When my mother called someone a *chuchem* it was with such great awe that I took that word to mean "a saint," whereas *tzidaikis* means "a just person," "a good person," "a saint." A *chacham* in Hebrew is a sage or a wise person. But in my mother tongue it was if goodness had been irradiated by intelligence. Goodness was not enough. A hero is someone who is smart enough to act without anybody knowing he is one.

When I told my father of the director's insistence on having him at the meeting, he took it in in silence. Then he answered from so deep inside it came out as near an articulation as I had heard of what it means to be a Jew. "A good person cannot fight against a bad," he said, "they cannot." If this was weakness it had survived the fiercest aggression.

The kitchen manager had taken away my father's seat from the table with my mother, claiming he didn't want to eat with her. "He is an independent person and is just as happy eating in the other room with the staff. Every time I meet him with his tray we have a conversation."

"Does that mean he doesn't want to sit with his wife? He's eaten with my mother for sixty years and he'd rather eat with you?" I blurted out.

"If you are going to raise your voice, I will have to call security," she said.

"Daddy, do you want to eat lunch with Mummy?" I asked him later that night.

"Of course, I do!"

"Then you will have to tell them," I said, exasperated. I knew I was giving him a task deeply foreign to his history: Be straightforward, be an Anglo-Saxon, be a *goy* who has no reason to believe that if he asks for his rights straight out he will not get them. Disregard the pressures used on all people who have not made the rules by those who have.

"But we are in a democratic country," I said to the official, "the residents should be able to complain without fear of reprisals."

"My people were afraid of complaining too," she said, "because of their religion." I was taken aback and grateful for this moment of solidarity. Her people were the French-Canadian majority in Quebec who did not call themselves Québécois until they threw off the clutches of the Roman Catholic Church in what was called the Quiet Revolution of the 1960s. This is what made Mme Corbin possible: an educated secular female Québécoise representing the provincial government.

In all this I was behaving like a *groyser nar,* a big fool. Not because I was putting my parents in danger but because there was a point where their extreme history ran into the normal politics of living. Besides, in complaining to the health board, I knew I had asked the provincial government to judge a portion of itself, and that ultimately the policy regarding care for patients in nursing homes came from the government. Mme Corbin had started the meeting off by congratulating the director on how well he had absorbed the cuts in budget, to which he nodded gloomily. Everyone had to manage their power relationships.

At the meeting, my father's right to eat with my mother was reaffirmed, and she would be changed to a different floor (leaving the present floor unchanged). The best reward was my sister telling me that my father was proud of my gumption.

I took my mother to the original diagnosing neurologist to ask about anti-stroke treatment. Could she be given one of the new anti-platelet drugs Michael said was the current alternative for patients who had "failed aspirin"? He gave her the dementia inquisition and said it wasn't worth it, he didn't see the point.

"She saved the family," I said, at a loss how to introduce her.

"Yes, I know, this happens to the most productive people, community leaders, business owners, CEOs." The doctor rattled off a list of these other mighty who have fallen, such as the dress manufacturer who terrorized the second unit or the ophthalmologist who pooped on Hilda's floor, to show that my mother was in good company.

"Who is the prime minister of Canada?"

My mother lost interest after Trudeau, but my parents took their citizenship seriously. When my mother mispronounced Mulroney as Monroe, he wrote down, "She said Monroe."

"Ask her your name," he asked me.

"What am I called, Mama?"

"Regina," my mother answered faintly. My heart sank. Her substitution of a sister's name did not mean she did not know me.

"Does not know her daughter," he wrote. I would find out this is the kiss of death – the non-recognition of a family member. But yesterday she recognized Dr. Rosenberg.

On the way back, her beautiful eyes swept up to mine.

"Don't worry," she said suddenly. "There's nothing wrong with me. I just need to go home. *Ahaym gayn.*"

I took my mother away still unsure about the reasons for his nixing the medication. It would not cure her, but if it diminished her suffering, it was worth it. My mother's body would pose the same question again the year after, when she suffered another stroke.

Somewhere the decision must have been made, one doctor told me – perhaps back in the hospital – not to treat her with blood thinners or these drugs. Was anyone doing the complex weighing that at every turn would spare her the most suffering? Because the decision not to treat aggressively, if such a decision had been made, could turn out to be a long assault of passive aggression.

It was not true that my mother had not been examined by a doctor, my father told me. With the resourcefulness that this institution frowns on he had arranged a medical checkup for her himself.

Usually my parents sat outside with Dr. Kunstler, a retired GP who came every day to visit his wife.

"So long as her eyes light up when I come, it's worth it." His wife's arm was wound through his and her head was resting on his shoulder.

Slowed down by his own self-diagnosed incipient Parkinson's, Dr. Kunstler had arrived the day after my mother's stroke to examine her with a blood pressure kit and a stethoscope. Having ascertained that nothing more could be done, my father could afford to be diplomatic with the head nurse. He had gone around the rules that we never made.

While the couples sat outside I brought out a bowl of cherries and set the bowl on my mother's lap. She held it out to her guests. Dr. Kunstler did not allow his wife to take any because she might swallow the pits. I was glad my mother still knew how to spit out the pits.

My parents were sitting outside when Dr. Kallen passed by. My father introduced himself.

Dr. Kallen said, "Taking the shade?" and nodded at them. She was about to turn away when my mother put her hand out with a dazzling smile to shake the doctor's.

Dr. Kallen had been angry to find my mother's stroke unreported. But by the time I arrived, a rearrangement according to institutional loyalty had taken place.

"Your parents are the nicest people," Dr. Kallen said, "but after all, what do you expect from the nursing home? The people here have used up all of society's resources."

Dr. Kallen is all in pink and slightly pregnant. I don't answer that my parents' and everyone else's taxes here have paid for her medical education. I am stunned into silence. The economic argument always sounds so reasonable. Hitler said, "Why should the state spend 20,000 marks on a useless cripple when it can give the money to a healthy farmer?" Who would not agree with him today? The Zyklon B gas used in the gas chambers was first tried out in German hospitals on their own mentally ill patients. The final solution got its start in Nazi medicine.

And then what comes next out of this young Jewish woman's mouth so spontaneously and so heedlessly she does not hear the echoes of what she was saying from fifty years back, is the rationale by which it was made possible: "Don't worry," she consoles me. "When they don't ask to go home anymore, when they get – excuse me for using the word – *decrepit*, it's easier to treat them clinically."

◆ ◆ ◆

When I searched for my parents, I found them neither outside, nor in the café. I peeked into the lounge. I had forgotten it was Friday afternoon.

The other day I'd seen Leni Riefenstahl interviewed on television. Going strong at ninety-two, she had taken to photographing an African tribe of wrestlers who were admired more for their strength than their grace. At least she confined herself to photographing those who exemplified this ideal. Was it her fault, she said, that she found weakness ugly? Was it her fault that the old and ill hid themselves from sight in the huts? Certainly not, when nature in so many instances collaborated with the Nazis, so that it was the victims who bore the shame of the aggression that marked their bodies. In the spring of 1945 prisoners in Germany waited at the barbed wire to welcome their liberators, young American soldiers, who one by one, vomited at the sight of them. "We are disgusting," they realized, and turned away.

I thought of some of the things the ancient Hebrews found disgusting: Killing birds in front of their mothers. Eating hunted prey. Old age and illness were not on the list. What did we bring into the world? We forbade the sacrifice of the weak. We overrode the selection of nature. We put aesthetics and ethics on the same table. Preoccupied in my youth with prejudice as image, I used to think, *Every Jew is an old person*. Now I thought, *Every old person is a Jew*.

That we are made in God's image was constantly countered by the admonition that we must make no images – whether of youth, health, or beauty – of God.

I find my parents, the two of them in *kapales*, sitting side by side at the Oneg Shabbat.

There were a surprising number of babies born to the newly liberated. Whenever my mother told the story of my birth she never left out the doctor's order: "All my healthy ones in the new wing!"

I see my mother's eyes light up. Her gaze finds mine. "I know whom I have to thank for this," she says, as with her where-have-I-gone-wrong expression, I wheel her up to the candles on the table.

Chapter Fourteen

APRIL 1996

"Mummy is leaning to the left," my father said, "when I saw her it was like a knife in my heart."

Is it any accident we fall sick in April? As if we have taken it into our genes that if spring is here, the rampaging horsemen cannot be far behind. From the Crusades to the seventeenth-century Ukrainian massacres to the cyclical pogroms of eastern Europe, Jewish slaughter took the place of fertilizing pagan bloodletting.

I have always dreaded spring. No sooner does the ice up north crack and dust begin to rise in the air than my father's mental pressure drops, while a worm of worry gnawing at my entrails signals an inflammatory attack.

Winter is a cocoon, the blanket of snow, a layer of safety. In the 1930s and '40s, St. Lawrence Boulevard was not safe for Jews on Good Friday. Easter gives me the creeps: the tortured icon, the portentous chanting, the peasants running out of church having heard that we screamed for Jesus' blood and screaming for ours. And as the Gospels have not been rewritten, as the Word is eternal, we are eternally held guilty.

April is the cruellest month. The poet didn't know how true he spoke; it has been particularly cruel for us because of the likes of him, with Easter rubbing its blood fetish off on Passover.

◆ ◆ ◆

"I went to the Seder in the nursing home, and your mother smiled at me, but she didn't recognize me," said Nadia when I called from California.

"Mummy is leaning to the left," my father said. Leaning to the left does not sound so bad. When I saw her I understood. She wasn't just leaning to the left; an axe had hacked the stem of her neck so that the head she always carried high fell like a flower cut at the stalk. When she caught sight of me from her felled tilted angle, a sidelong brilliant smile suddenly lifted half her mouth. I pressed my cheek to her left cheek and gently pushed her straight. I am a force of nature, she used to say.

As Mother Nature and my mother squared off – once it was never clear where they were separate – now with each stroke Mother Nature turned on her magnificent emissary, clawing, batting, and stunning my mother until she fell to her knees.

I kept my head pressed next to hers, propping her head up like a flower on its stalk for a long time, cheek to cheek.

"Mama, you're not sitting straight," I said.

"I know," she said. With her head bowed over and her eyes closed, infinitely wounded at what has been done to her, tears roll down her cheek. I cursed the inertia that kept me from turning right around and finding another neurologist the year before. I thought how doctors referred to a stroke as an "insult." I pressed my cheek next to hers so that my mother could hold her head up again. My father hovered beside us with a heartbroken face. He began to pick at the crumbs on my mother's clothes.

"Go home," I suddenly begged him. "Leave me alone with my mother. There is some food in the fridge ..."

"Don't worry about me!" he said.

I am holding a stalk of orchids. I resent having to put them in water because I have to turn away from her for a moment.

"Mama, you had a stroke." She nods. "I am going to take you to the doctor. He will give you a *refiya* so you won't have any more." Nods. "Who loves you, Mama?"

Faint smile. "You do." I pile up her left side with cushions and show her the flowers.

"*Zeyeh shayn.* Where is the tate?"

At lunch the table is set for the Sabbath with tablecloth and flowers. "*Shayn,*" she says. Beautiful. I sit with her and feed her little bits in her slanted mouth. I can stand it by myself; I could not bear my father's pain on observing her.

"Ohhh. What happened? Ohhh." The kitchen workers come running when they see her.

"After lunch we will put on our coats and go outside," I say to her.

"Put on our coats and go outside," she affirms.

Gerda beckons me from the next table. "Have you heard what is happening here?"

"You mean in the nursing home?" I respond with my own paranoia.

"No, in Quebec."

"Don't worry about it," I say.

"But we are Jewish," says Gerda. "It is no good for the Jewish people."

Nationalism is no good for the Jewish people, because we are the first to be pointed out like a sore thumb as not of the nation. We can never be "100 per cent pure wool," a label of the new *terroir* that repeated often enough was giving me hives. This Passover, matzoh boxes (manufactured in New Jersey) were pulled off the shelves in Quebec because matzoh is not a French word. Neither is it an English word, but that is beside the point.

The health board representative Mme. Corbin had conducted our meeting in English, excusing herself for possible misunderstanding because "English is not my mother tongue."

"English is not my mother tongue either," I said. Everybody laughed.

Mother tongue are fighting words in Quebec. Quebec, like Gaul, is divided into three parts: francophone, anglophone, and allophones (*allo* means "other" in Latin). The "others" were lumped together as "ethnics," proving that ethnic groups are always somebody else. In a world where the appeal of French culture rests on a voluntary appreciation of its quality of life, the Quebec language police remove the word *pasta* from the menus of Italian restaurants. This nationalism without a foe made Quebec regress to the narrowness and xenophobia of the Roman Catholic Church. On October 30, 1995, when the referendum on Quebec's separation from Canada was narrowly defeated, Parti Québécois premier Jacques Parizeau ranted about being stabbed in the back by "money and the ethnic vote." As it also happened to be my father's birthday, I called him.

"Don't worry," I said as we were hanging up.

"I'm not worrying," he said, summing up with a perspective that escaped the local chauvinists. "This is not Poland or Germany."

Around the corner from the nursing home where I take my mother out in the wet wind there is a gaggle of kosher, halal, Thai, Vietnamese shops and restaurants. For many years the Jewish immigrants lived between the English and French as the only significant other nationality. Like the California campus, the multiplicity that makes it a pleasure to walk around Montreal also provides the dissolution of a fixed subject from which to be "other."

The world is becoming such a diverse place, say some people, that we should cease dividing ourselves into nations. Tell that to the Québécois who go to such absurd and offensive lengths to preserve their minority culture in an indulgent Canada. The suggestion, of course, was aimed at Israel, who was among the last to become a nation and is the first to be asked to dissolve itself. It is because we are the first to be picked on as foreigners that of all the nations the Jews need a nation the most.

Besides, we are woolly enough. On Easter my friend Sally's mother, who is a French teacher in Oregon, came to visit her in Montreal. Quebec French preserves the sixteenth-century pronunciation spoken before Louis XIV in much the same way Yiddish preserved medieval German spoken before Luther. Sally and her mother were in a store when they overheard a lively exchange in an exotic language.

"Is that Yiddish?" she asked her daughter with excitement.

"No, Mother, that is French."

"*Drei di tuchus*," the devoted rehabilitation worker Nicole says, "Turn your behind." It was she who flagged my mother's stroke. "She only really makes an effort when you or your sister are here," Nicole says. I am so moved by her effort to speak Yiddish that I deluge her with Yiddish language tapes. "How do you say *ceiling*?" she asks with a sigh. "Everyone speaks Yiddish with a different pronunciation."

"It depends on the region the people come from," I say. "Like French."

◆ ◆ ◆

This time I took my mother outside the small Jewish circle to the head neurologist at the WASP metropolitan hospital. I was glad for the smallest move she made; taking a Styrofoam cup of tea.

"Oh, that's a good move. Does she still know how to put on lipstick?" Dr. MacGregor said. Later I will see, with joy, her take the proffered mirror in one hand and the lipstick in the other. I was learning with each of my mother's losses how much there was still to lose.

"You are a dutiful daughter," he said as we were leaving.

"No," I said. I was not being modest. Doing your duty at the expense of your desire is the highest Protestant virtue. But it is the same for us. I want to be with her. I cannot separate the two.

Dr. MacGregor said that after testing her carotid artery he would recommend appropriate treatment. But I feared it was too late.

When my father and I arrived for lunch with my mother, she was sprawled almost out of her wheelchair with eyes half-closed and one eye leaking rheum like an old cat.

"They didn't seat her right," said my father trying to lift her.

"No, no, Dad, don't pick her up."

My father looks at my mother slumped in her chair and the strength leaves his body. He lies down in my mother's bed while I take her to lunch.

My mother's eyes are closed when I try to feed her. Afterwards I put her to bed, exchanging places with my father. My father watches her falling into a deep sleep with her mouth open to push out the air. He wipes his eyes. I know what he is thinking. She has not smiled to see him or acknowledged him in any way.

"Dad, she's all right, she's sleeping," I protest. "She will be hungry when she awakes. She didn't eat lunch. I will go and get her something to eat. Yes?"

When I return, my father is standing over her bed, watching her breathe, one hand on her pulse.

"She's dying, Elizabeth. Call a doctor."

"She's sleeping."

"She never slept like this. My father looked like that when he was dying." The nursing home has no emergency facilities. I am on the telephone trying to call 911 and find I cannot.

My father goes into the bathroom. I hear him sobbing. We are trapped. I dare not tell my father that we are not allowed to react to an emergency on our own. We have to depend on the nurse who never sees anything wrong with my mother. I call Dr. Lanchek at his home, a central European immigrant with my father's manners who is bewildered by nursing-home rules that come between physician and patient. Adhering simply to the physicians' code, he has given me his telephone number at home to call if I need him. He has the blood pressure around her arm when she opens her eyes and smiles serenely at us. My mother accepts a sip of tea, she accepts a grape or two then she drinks. I give the sandwich to my father, which he at first offers to everyone else in the room and then eats hungrily.

A hue and cry goes up in the nursing home. "Who called the doctor? It's against the rules!" Whose rules? My parents once broke the rules by surviving.

◆ ◆ ◆

The only mercy of my mother's stroke was that it spared her the full force of reaction to my father's death. Of such intricacy was their bond that I cannot untangle whose affliction smote the other first.

I got an idea of what my mother's full reaction might have been when my father's chest pain landed him in the hospital last winter. At this late date, I was discovering something about my parents. They loved each other. Not that I am thick, but my mother never betrayed the slightest hint of harbouring any such sentiment toward my father. "Never a good word," was the only reproach he made. It was true that at times she still expressed jealous worry about a "younger woman." When I laughed and told my father, he said, "But if she suffers from this, it is not funny," which was kinder than I had ever heard from any male.

That same winter of 1995, on a day I was supposed to fly home, my father's unremitting chest pain made me call the hospital instead. Despite his pain my father dove out of the sweatpants I thought I got him used to wearing into proper pants and a belt.

He had an angiogram, not without some arm-twisting from Michael and the wunderkind cardiologist who was approaching us. Several beds away I heard him shouting in Yiddish to a deaf patient.

"*Ost mishpucha du?* Do you have family here? Whom are you going home to?"

"My father's cardiologist thinks he's going to have a heart attack," I said when the doctor read his chart, "He doesn't want an angiogram."

"It's not my heart, it's my nerves," my father said.

"If you need one, you're going to have one," he said to my father, "and if I say you're going to have one it's because you need one!"

My father chuckled at this.

"Dr. Gezuntharz," I said, reading his nametag. "That's a good name for a cardiologist."

"Thank you."

"Gezuntharz, I knew a family in Poland by that name," said my father.

"Which town?"

"Demblin."

"That's my family!" said the doctor. "My father came here in 1927 when he was one year old, but I've often wondered whether anybody else survived. Were there many people left?"

"No," my father said. "In May 1942, they took out the first half ..."

"I would like to hear more, but I don't want to upset you now." He went away telling the resident, "That's my family! What a small world!"

"Elizabeth." My father beckoned me to come near. "I knew his uncle," he said with a nod. "He was the biggest *ganif* in Demblin." I grew up with the legend of Shloimele the thief.

"Dad," I said, looking behind me, "Ssh! Keep this under your hat."

"Of course," my father said, ever tactful. "A thief, but a smart thief. The other gangsters called him 'the rebbe.' But smart as he was, Shloimele spoiled his own prospects by assuming that other people would behave exactly like him, a thief. And they didn't."

"What happened to him?"

"He was with me in the *lager*. We were sent to Buchenwald. Shloimele died on a death march."

Dr. Gezuntharz was pleased that only a secondary artery was blocked – my father could go home on medication. His chest pain however did not abate.

◆ ◆ ◆

"You are not having a good time, Lizzie," my father said from his hospital bed.

My sister called, "Why wasn't I informed?"

"Because you always say he is faking."

"Don't tell me what I say! I want to speak to the cardiologist. I have read a book about it."

During this time I went from nursing home to hospital – mother to father – and back again, nearly choked by my mother who did not want to let go of my scarf until I had brought her to him.

"Is he alive?" she asked. He was *umgekumen*, she told people, the wartime term.

"Oh, may you live a thousand years!" she burst out when she saw me. "Tell me the truth. Is he alive?"

"Yes, yes, yes, but Mama, you speak to him on the telephone every day!"

"Oh, the telephone." She waved her hand as if how can you trust a machine.

Those winter afternoons when it got dark so early, my mother's patience was cut short to fit. "Come! *Hotch! Kim!*" My mother was still trilingual.

"Where, Ma, where do you want to go?"

"*Haym!* Home! *Kim!* Come!" This twilight unease is a phenomenon of dementia, they tell me. But her restlessness is but the avatar of the one she used to express at home when it was getting dark and my father had not yet returned.

"Give him an orange!" The first time the orderly helped me get her ready for bed, she hesitated. "I am ashamed," she said.

"I have a wife and two daughters, Mrs. Wajnberg," Tom said.

"I haven't given him anything!" she remembers now in a panic.

When I return from getting some towels, her eyes are shiny with desperation, her face is red, and she is gripping the bedrails.

"What's the matter?"

"Oh, leave me alone!" Teeth bared in stroke-lifted lips. "Get dressed! Go away!" I lie down next to her. She will not be soothed. She looks at the falling snow. "It's getting dark. Go away! You're not going to sleep here anyway." This was her secret desire.

"What will it hurt," she shakes her arm at me in what was once threat and is now supplication, "to sleep with me for one night?"

"But I lay down with you after lunch."

"It's getting dark," she says now. "Go, go. Close the window!"

"It's closed!"

"Close the curtain! Close the cupboard!" She has always sent me home when it got dark. "Go … go… it's dark, close the windows, shut the door and go …"

Sometimes I think she pulls out the past by a string of language. In my life she always liked the windows and curtains open "Close the windows, close the curtains, shut the door." She must have said it once before. Where? In the Demblin ghetto after nightfall, the streets were empty and all the windows, doors and curtains shut tight not to let any ray of light penetrate to the outside.

"Go away!" she insists. "Go home before it gets dark. Get dressed, go. Go."

"Why are you pushing me away?"

"Because … because," she struggled furiously in a grimace to bring it out, "because I want you to stay!"

It made perfect sense. She has always made perfect sense. I closed everything I could – cupboards, drawers, curtains, light – and went away.

My mother's first real smile was when I told her my father was at home. I was riveted by my mother's beauty, the heart-shaped face touched with the violet of her eyes that were no longer haunted.

"Your mother was like a wild animal," Nadia said, "insisting I take her to see your father in the hospital."

First thing when my father came home I put him in a taxi and brought him to her. When she caught sight of him from the row of wheelchairs, her eyes blazed and her finger rose in exclamation. "Oy." He bent over to kiss her. She held her heart. In her room he held one hand, the other hand rubbing her back as she came to herself. I left them alone together.

Chapter Fifteen

"HONOUR THY FATHER AND MOTHER," JUNE 1996

———

The day my father died he called me early in the morning and said, "I think Mummy had another stroke. Yesterday I came home late because she held my hand the whole day. How could I leave her? I didn't sleep the whole night."

Another stroke. This would make it merely a month and a half after the last one.

I called the nursing home where nobody would give me information until they reached Nurse Hilda. I called Nadia to look in on my mother. By the time I called my father back – a little surprised he hadn't yet arrived at the nursing home – he said he had a stomachache so bad he had to get out of the car and come back upstairs. "It's probably constipation."

What kind of pain would prevent my father from going to see my mother, when his angina attacks hadn't? I called back every half-hour. It was a Sunday in early June, a few days before I was going to join my parents for the summer. My sister had been there two weeks before and said my father was looking forward to seeing me again. I had a Father's Day present packed. I called the social service nurse, and then I called the neighbour to fetch him some milk of magnesia.

"You are spending the whole day obsessing about your parents," my husband said. I went swimming. Swimming cleared my head all right. I got out of the water to call home.

"Tell my father to call an ambulance."

At the hospital they didn't know what was wrong with him. Chest pain means the noble heart is in danger and triggers a high stakes alert but *kishkes* are a lowly Jewish organ and gut pain probably means gas. "He kept saying he must have eaten some bad meat," the ER physician recalled later with a smile. He wished that the surgeon had looked at him earlier.

"Tell him my mother is all right" is the last message I relayed.

It wasn't my mother who had had a stroke; it was my father. A blood clot can choke off an intestinal artery as easily as a coronary artery. My father had "a heart attack of the gut." The pain he had been feeling for hours came from his dying bowel. In the small hours the ER physician called to say they were wheeling him into surgery. I got on a plane. The next time I saw my father he was pulled out of a drawer in the basement of the hospital.

◆ ◆ ◆

"The position of the administration is that you tell your mother!" Nurse Hilda boomed at me.

Dr. Himmel, the doctor on the new floor, surprised me by intervening. "Halachically, I can tell you what it says." Halachically, according to Jewish law. A small man with a long beard, *tzitzit* spilling out of his pockets, except for his Birkenstocks Dr. Himmel was the spitting image of my mother's zeyde, whose portrait my sister had hung up to scare her English friends. My mother just took him in without responding. How could he be a doctor, when an Orthodox Jew was not allowed to touch women?

"If telling is going to endanger the health of someone who is critically ill," he said, "then you do not have to tell them." All laws in Judaism bow before saving a life.

◆ ◆ ◆

The next day my mother held her head up straight and proud. Her expression was tragic. Jewish teaching also suggests that you take your cue from the person to be told. I wheeled her to the park.

"Who loves you?" I said.

"You do."

"And Daddy? *Deh tate?*"

"Daddy also," she nodded sagely. For which I sighed. It hadn't always been evident that she believed this.

"Daddy loves you. But he wasn't well and – he didn't suffer. I'm not going to leave you now. Do you hear?" I took her hand. "You're going to *zay gezint* for me now, won't you?" She gave a barely perceptible nod.

This was all beside the point. She will never again ask, "*Eyeh lebt?* Tell me the truth, is he among the living?" She will never again raise a clamour to be reassured that she is crazy. "Show me proof," she used to say, clinging to my arm whenever he did not show up. "Take me to him."

She expected her anxiety to protect him, like I expect mine will protect her. After all these years of resenting her hysteria, I discover it contained not a shred of self-indulgence; once the worst has happened not a whimper comes from her.

Nicole said, "Last week when your father was here you know what he said? 'Look at her,' he said, caressing her cheek. 'Ninety years old and there is not a wrinkle on her face. When we met she was poor and older than me, but I didn't care. I could marry her because I was economically independent.'"

Although my mother can still say a few words, she will never again ask about my father. There was nobody more appropriate than my mother. She knows not to ask. She knows.

◆ ◆ ◆

The night I got in from the hospital morgue to my father's empty apartment, the telephone rung.

"My poor little sister," she whispered.

"It's not so bad," I heard myself saying, because nothing that happened, not even the grave, could be as bad as my sister's whisper from the grave.

"Did he look … peaceful?" she asked.

"He looked the way he always looked," I said. "Cute."

"Cute," she repeated vaguely and hung up.

We drove up the flank of the mountain to a Jewish cemetery as close as I could make it to the park my parents used to visit. Alighting from the limousine in which we had taken our neighbour Noemi, my sister chirped for all the world like a British tourist, "Oh! I have never been to a Jewish funeral before!"

Not more than ten minutes later, as we were sitting beside our father's coffin, she described the funeral of a classmate in Israel in the early 1950s. A teenage Holocaust survivor like herself, wrapped in a shroud, whose mother said, "I saved her for this."

It is my sister who knew the Hebrew when we are asked to say: *Dayan Emet*. Let the truth be the judge.

◆ ◆ ◆

When I had been led into the room filled with coffins to choose one for my father, a kind of hysterical euphoria overcame me. I looked around at the different grains and the rich deep colours of cherry, mahogany, oak … "Wood! My father loves wood!" I said to the astonished director, who left the room and shut the door behind him. My father was in the room with me, telling me about the special qualities of the different grains of wood. I wanted to stay there all day. Sensing my father, I nearly chose the most magnificent oak one, but remembering him saying that Jews bury their dead to return to the earth as quickly as possible, I gravitated back to the simplest pine coffin.

The only way you can tell the mourners' Kaddish from the study Kaddish is that it is murmured in a barely inflected monotone through which the Aramaic vowels roll the phrases relentlessly to the end. With only a gasp for breath at the O of "Oseh Shalom," "Oh, may He bring peace on earth, and soon." Whose fierce balm can't be approximated in its rough translation as the Lord's Prayer, but only phonemically the way my father used to pray, meaning bound to sound, grief to praise. In words that mean not what they individually say but what they have come to mean, phrase and phonemes, to the people who say them. The meta-language of the Jewish people.

"I said Kaddish for my father, and then I didn't pray again," my father told me. My mouth opened to praise and grief responds to the murmuring swell of voices and on that wave where he rocked his father, I rock mine.

"What is this 'see-va' note in the elevator?" my sister asks when we return from the funeral. "Are people going to be coming here?" She shudders.

"It's a Jewish mourning custom," I say, thrown for a moment because of her pronunciation "Siva" by thoughts of Indian deities. At the end of the week of visitors she agrees that shiva, or "seven" for the seven days of mourning, has therapeutic value.

I spend the mornings with my mother, and then go home to continue the seven-day period of receiving comforters. My sister changes places with me in the afternoon.

As we change guard, my sister asks, "How did you know so quickly about Father? I also spoke to him that Sunday. He said he had a stomach ache, it was probably constipation, and ..." she shrugged, "I believed him. Father *was* a hypochondriac, you know."

I keep my eyes down to hide the shame of what I am swallowing. So long as she has a clinical name for it, and so long as she is right.

She had been the last to see him, in the aftermath of a bout of pneumonia that felled him to the ground. As I feared, my sister's discovery of his relatively healthy arteries had not endeared him to her.

"He's probably got heartburn! *I've* got heartburn and I know it can cause chest pain," she said when she called me. She did not seem to take in that he had caught pneumonia. "He keeps taking his temperature, he's driving me mad!"

"Why do you keep taking your temperature?" I heard myself asking him later, and then got angry with myself.

"Is he eating? Is he taking his vitamins?" I asked

"Vitamins, oh no," she laughed. "He's got too many pills as it is."

I would never see my father alive again. When I came into his bedroom, the carpet around his bed was white with the crumbs of pills.

"She's your sister," people say. "In your father's memory you should get along with her." But it was exactly in remembering my father that I am disgusted with her. I will not forgive her because I will not forgive myself for having colluded with her even for a minute in slighting my father's pain.

One afternoon I found my mother crumpled up, juice dribbling down a corner of her mouth. "Do you want to lie down?"

Silent nod.

The first time it happened, my father held her pulse and said she was dying. Five days after my father's death, I am lying next to my mother when I hear the same struggle to breathe. I pick up my head.

"*Juz pójdę śmierć,*" she says in Polish, "I am going to die."

Again I call the immigrant doctor who answers calls for help because he is too old to learn rules that say he shouldn't. This time Dr. Lanchek gives her oxygen and prescribes a diuretic.

"Who called the doctor?" the cry went up in the nursing home. We should have waited for Dr. Himmel, but he only comes on Thursdays. My mother was having the attack now. Dr. Lanchek said if she did not improve, he would send her to the hospital. He counselled me to take her to a cardiologist, as this was the second such episode he had witnessed.

Dr. Lanchek was too afraid to refer her himself, as he was already in trouble for responding to my call for help. I thought grimly of the Demblin memorial book, and how much of my mother's short written account of the war was devoted to the doctors who took the risk of treating Jews in the ghetto.

I called Dr. Lerner for the referral and by the next day a cardiologist had prescribed medication for her. It wasn't death but pain and suffering I was trying to spare her.

◆ ◆ ◆

At my father's desk, his cardigan behind me, all the things he used to take care of – that first I sweep off to remove all that does not help my mother to survive another day – and then I must sweep in, loving him for all he kept on doing against such tremendous odds. "Maybe I didn't tell you, Lizzie …" my father would say in his Talmudic mode of accretive repetition, in which an important detail would suddenly emerge in the retelling of overlapping versions. Each one is different. I cannot throw them out. It will be my task, endlessly put off, to go through my father's filing cabinet: his Canadian work life, decades' worth of neatly bound customer cards, "Losses" according to the year

1976, 1977; documents he has tied up crossways to make a "parcel." What makes me finally do it is the same as why we bury our parents ourselves; because if it must be done, it is mine to do rather than a stranger's.

The Wiedergutmachung under *W*, vacations under *V*, in which I find a receipt for mineral baths in Saratoga Springs. "The patient was about to be hospitalized for depression, but he ran away to Saratoga Springs."

There is a sheet of instructions from my classmate Judith's survivor group titled "How to Get a Good Night's Sleep."

"He is forgetful, tense, anxious, insomniac, he has somatization of psychic pain in the form of chest pain," I read in the file under *W* for Wiedergutmachung of thirty years ago. I was struck by how early he had filed a claim for his stolen shipment of wood.

After years of correspondence with witnesses, the Hamburg court acknowledged the quality of the wood and the fact that it had been stolen from a Jewish business and sent to Germany. But there was no absolute proof, the court said, that the wood *arrived* in Hamburg. With this, after thirty years, the court judged that the case was not within its jurisdiction; it would have to be tried all over again, by a Berlin court.

◆ ◆ ◆

There are no cars in the parking lot of the Jewish General Hospital today. In my parents' neighbourhood it is truly a holiday, on an ordinary Monday made different. I fast. I sit lulled by the September sun in the nearby packed Spanish and Portuguese synagogue that we have joined so that I can bury my parents in their small cemetery on the side of the mountain. Sephardic synagogues are the oldest in the New World, dating from the Iberian Expulsion in the same year that Columbus discovered America. The synagogue has been refilled, however, with the fresh wave of Jewish refugees from Arab lands who had lived there from before there was an Islam. This synagogue contains many rooms all carrying on simultaneous services; each room dedicated to varying liturgies according to the Arabic country from which these francophone Sephardic Jews have been expelled – Egypt,

Iraq, Syria, Morocco, Tunisia, Algeria. These expulsions are never mentioned in the Middle East debate, because after all we are used to being displaced.

I am as relieved today as the time in France when I found myself with a living Jewish community. And by the conviction that here is a place I would find my father.

When I was growing up, my father kissed us and wished us a sweet New Year before going to *shul*. On Yom Kippur according to tradition he asked my mother for forgiveness. In living we are forced to make decisions which may turn out to wrong others. Such were his sins. In responsibility lies guilt. It has taken me a lifetime to grow into them.

Shehechayanu. That we have lived to see this day.

The difficulty of saying this binds the people together. One day I will say it because my father said it and it was harder for him.

I knew I would find my father. I find him very specifically in the text of the Yom Kippur liturgy: "Shma Koleinu," Hear our voices. I have heard this before. This is what my father hummed in the parking lot that first summer at the beginning of their frailty.

"Hear our voices. Oh God, abandon me not when my strength leaves me. Do not cast me aside when my hair is white."

I read the report of his last night in emergency. They tell me that ischemic bowel causes great pain, but at the time they didn't know what was wrong with him. After a while he no longer complained of the pain, but that he couldn't sleep. He kept getting up to look for his pills. Elavil. The antidepressant that in one or other form he had taken for thirty years helped him to sleep. On his last trip to the emergency room they had also taken away his pills and forgotten to return this one. They had done it again. He couldn't sleep. They wrote down the word *agitated* then listened no more. He needed me to explain for him. An hour before he turned so white that the doctors decided to wheel him into surgery, he tried to get up to look for his pills. The nurses tied his hands to the bedposts. They tied his hands.

Do not cast us aside in our old age. When our strength ebbs, do not abandon us.

◆　◆　◆

I stayed with my mother that summer after my father's death. She was beginning to need help to eat breakfast. Hilda got upset because I came early to see my mother. No matter how early I came, my mother was sitting strapped in her wheelchair. That's when I learned the night shift woke the patients up before dawn. Red with rage, Hilda called the nurse coordinator to throw me out.

"Don't even try," I said, sitting beside my mother on her bed. "Don't even try to separate me from my mother." I was trembling.

Before going on vacation, Hilda had printed out a set of a dozen new rules I was to follow. I was not to call a doctor on my own. I was to leave the room when the staff was changing my mother.

"I don't know, I was raised religious," Dr. Kallen said, "and I was taught you were not supposed to uncover the nakedness of a parent."

"But I was the first person to put a diaper on my mother!"

For a moment I fulfilled my mother's unconscious intention and became a Talmudic scholar. Of course you did not uncover your parents as sexual beings, but if I had any taste for what was Jewish, then a tradition which had just bid me pick up the shovel to bury my father would not forbid me from dressing or cleaning my mother if necessary. I looked up the examples for the fifth commandment. To my surprise, the Talmud devoted the commandment "Honour thy father and mother" not to rebellious youth, but almost wholly to adult children of disempowered parents. To honour father and mother was "to cover them, to give them to eat and drink and to lead them in and out."

In ancient times when the parent became aged, the children were to take the place of the parents' personal servants.

It was decided that I had to ask the staff if they minded having me there. They didn't.

"The rules were changed while I wasn't here!" Hilda said, breaking tongue depressor sticks in half.

It was hot until Rosh Hashanah. We sat outside with the Kunstlers, Gerda, and other patients with their family members. There was a huge gap between our declining loved ones' being alive and dead. And this gap, rather than shrinking for us, yawned larger every day.

My mother no longer lit up with joy at seeing me, but there was a slow dawning of recognition like the different stages of a sunrise illuminating her face like a landscape. I watched my mother munch on a cherry with uncomplaining eyes. She forgot the pit in her mouth to smile at a well-wisher. The birds twitter around us.

"*S'hot dich ungekakt a foygehl*" (A bird dropped a dropping on you, Ma).

She laughs out loud, a miracle.

"*Shling*, Mama, *shling*. Swallow." I swallow for her to imitate. I even eat for her to imitate. No greater food truce between us. "And from this you're going to live?" the surprising phrase exactly echoes hers.

I am also exaggerating. But she chews and chews and it does not get chewed up. Finally I bid farewell to my chicken-bone mentor, and ask for pureed food. Before I leave, I hire a gentle giant who can lift her and feed her.

In Canada, the Jewish New Year falls at a time when the leaves are brilliant and the snap in the air makes the tart apples just barely sweet enough to eat. The freshness in the air seems to revive her. On the days that we settle into a rhythm, with her accepting the food I give her with trusting eyes, it is I who am taking and she who is giving.

What do I owe you, Ma?

I owe you the sweet whitefish with carrots it was worth carrying to the airport. Now I carry it myself so that if separated from home I still have the food my body craves.

"*Est zayn gezint?*" (Will you be well?)

And this time, as if to put away all thought that I am speaking only to myself, she answered, "*Yo.*"

"*A git yur*" (A good year), said the rabbi, gazing down at her. He stopped me before I helped her.

"*A git yur*," said my mother her eyes sweeping up.

"*A git un gezint yur*" (A good and healthy year), he said.

"*A git yur*," my mother repeated, her eyes bright.

"Amen," he said.

◆ ◆ ◆

When I called to wish my father's *landsman*, Mr. Taichman, a Happy New Year, I thanked him for telling me another version of the way my sister was saved in Częstochowa. On the day Mr. Taichman came to the house to sit shiva, he had looked youthful and lithe in a cap and windbreaker. "I've had three heart attacks," he said with a shrug.

"In our first years in Canada, your father tried to make a peddler out of me," he said ruefully. "Once I bought some goods from a man who gave me a receipt for the amount. Afterwards he claimed I still owed him half of the money. I was sure I paid it all back, but I didn't know what became of the piece of paper. I couldn't find it anywhere. At that time the fifty dollars was for us a fortune. I asked Srulec, 'What should I do?' Srulec said I was to ask the seller for a week during which I should look everywhere for the receipt. At the end of that week if I couldn't find it, I was to pay him half.

"I met your father a few days later. 'Srulec!' I said. 'My wife washed my pants with the *kvitl* inside the pocket! Here it is!' Your father smiled from ear to ear.

"I knew your grandfather. 'Mendel Buleker,' we used to call him, Mendel from Bialki. What a *balebatish* household! Whoever passed through it knew he would find hospitality with Mendel Buleker. And of course your uncle Moishe had a house in Ryki."

I got goosebumps hearing "your grandfather," "your uncle," as if Mr. Taichman had just given me my grandparents.

"The Germans marched the Jews of Ryki to the Demblin train station," Mr. Taichman said. "When we were packed into the train and it started to move, my sister pushed me off it. I ran. At that time when we ran to save ourselves, we didn't know where we were running. I ran and ran." Then he let himself in to the Demblin *lager*. "In the *lager* I met your father. He was always in a rush. Did you ever see Srulec not in a rush? He kept an eye out for your mother and sister."

Luckily Demblin's airport camp was run by a communist sympathizer who kept the labour going. When the Jews came into the camp, their portable valuables – jewellery, cash, candlesticks – were taken away. The SS wanted them sent to Germany, but the communist commandant kept the valuables there. "When they sent us to Częstochowa, the commandant returned the valuables to our Jewish leader, telling him to put them to a good purpose.

"We left in two groups. As soon as the first group arrived, the children were immediately shot. We put big shoes on the second group of children to make them look older. It didn't work. The Jewish representative negotiated with the commandant Bortenschlager to return the children to us. With these valuables, they paid Bortenschlager off."

"I didn't know that this was how they were saved."

"Your father didn't tell you?"

"My father told me that the commandant's wife was pregnant, that a Jewish doctor begged her to save the children."

"Dr. Kestenbaum!" said Mr. Taichman.

"He said it was a woman gynecologist, an *accoucherka*, a midwife."

"You know, there are a thousand stories that happened in one night."

We remained silent for a moment.

"Itchik," Mr. Taichman said. "I saw your father's cousin die in the Demblin *lager*. The Germans used to throw bread out of the windows, to make us jump for it like animals. Sometimes they would throw instead a chair leg or a tabletop or an iron bedstead. I saw Itchik run and jump." Mr. Taichman got up and lunged forward like a football player. "He caught it in the chest. I thought it was bread but it must have been something else. He fell down and died. Itchele," he said.

"Did your father still have his number?" He took out a small tin plate with the Częstochowa number that he carries in his pocket.

"My father was sent to Buchenwald after," I reminded him, "where they took everything. I found the Buchenwald identity card issued by the Allies."

"When the Germans rounded us up in Częstochowa to send us to Buchenwald, I hid," he said. "I was liberated the next day with your mother. I went back to Ryki. The Polish right-wing partisans were shooting us, and then," Mr. Taichman shakes his head, "and then it started."

Like my mother, he keeps overturning the sense of false finality. When I call him later I ask whether he would like to take down my US telephone number.

"I can't," he said. "My arm is in a cast. I fell the other night and broke it. I was asleep and I dreamed that the Germans were chasing me. I got out of bed and ran in my sleep. I ran and ran without knowing where I was."

On the afternoon of his shiva visit, he looked at his watch and picked up his cap. "*Oyf simchas,*" he said leaving. "May we meet only on happy occasions."

Chapter Sixteen

BLINDSIGHT, 2000

My sister did not outlive my parents by long. She died suddenly a few years later, alone in her London apartment, of an undiagnosed ulcer that had suddenly hemorrhaged. Friends found her when they came round with groceries and she didn't open the door.

"A tummy ache," said the coroner over the telephone.

"Terrible pain for years," said her friends. They were shocked. She'd gone to so many doctors. She'd complained of abdominal pain for months, even years, and no doctor could find the cause. Her kid sister veteran of the alimentary canal had been no help either.

We had not been talking before she died, apart from her hurling insults and my not contradicting her. From my father's death to my mother's a year later, she had no idea of what went on in the nursing home. For that I was grateful. I let her bang on about me. She was incensed that our father had made me executor decades ago and left me the Montreal apartment. I wanted to keep our inheritance intact for my mother's use. She misunderstood me, I was busy with my mother, and I did not intend to burden her with the nursing home.

Her last communication was a letter saying that applications were being taken for the slave labour in Nazi concentration camps. Would I fill one out on her behalf? She was not up to it, she said, for various reasons. I was glad that the other part of her knew to trust me.

The other part of her. She was so volatile I didn't know which part was bedrock. I remembered the time she arrived in the nursing home carrying a tape recorder.

"Why don't you and Mother speak in, you know," she burst out in a giggle, "you know, *that language*." She was too embarrassed to say Yiddish. One part of her wanted to tape her mother and sister speaking Yiddish, another part of her was so embarrassed by it, she claimed not to understand it. One part of her had never been to a Jewish funeral before; the other remembered her schoolmate's burial in Israel and probably many, many others.

On the telephone from California late at night, I began arrangements to bury my sister. The lady at the Golders Green cemetery said, "Excuse me, but did she have any Jewish affiliations?" They needed proof that my sister was Jewish. In the middle of the night on another continent I racked my brain. So distant was the Hashomer Hatzair pioneer who canvassed door to door in Montreal, the teacher of Israeli folk music.

"A Child Holocaust Survivors' Association!" I blurted. Luckily, I remembered her disclosing a survivors' group she joined in London when I told her about our father's group in Montreal.

"Go to sleep because you're tired," said the lady in England.

My heart failed a few days later when I entered her apartment that had been sealed since the officers had taken her body. I saw the towels on the lavatory floor, the black liquid in the toilet, the bedroom normal except when I rounded her bed and saw the dried black flood of blood – the scene of her final suffering. The piles of dirty clothes, the grey walls, the overflowing kitchen that her friends avoided to spare her embarrassment. I understood how she had left our father in his pill-seamed bedroom. In the bog and damp, there was her music, her books, her piano, her bottles of perfume. Just as my sister had said, rising up from outside her tree-filled window were the voices of schoolchildren. The mother and child theme covered her walls. Her kitchen walls were plastered with pictures of her friends' children and grandchildren. Everywhere Russian icons, Italian paintings repeated the curve of maternal body embracing child. Pride of place was given to the beautiful pre-war picture of our mother hung like a landscape on the living-room wall. Not vertically cropped like a portrait but allowed to continue horizontally so that our mother with her parted black Mediterranean hair sat buoyed in waves of grass endless as the sea. Before leaving my mother, my sister said, "I feel terrible about leaving Mother. It is like leaving a small child who does not understand why she is being abandoned." The last time I saw them together, it was soon after my father's death. Our mother had ceased to speak or to react. I found them in the nursing home, my sister playfully waving our mother's limp wrist and speaking to her in singsong as if to a baby.

"What's my name?" Lusia asked her. "What's my name?" she repeated.

Our mother looked nauseated and said nothing. Finally, she managed to emit a name. "Tobcha," she said. "Little Toba."

"Oh!" my sister jumped up in shock. "She hasn't called me that since I was an infant!"

My sister's date book was marked for that Friday night in the local synagogue where the children's choir of Minsk would be performing. During the Second World War no bullets were wasted on the Jewish children of Minsk. They were buried alive.

◆ ◆ ◆

"I know what you must feel like when you have a colitis attack," she said during one of her visits. "I always assumed that you were ill because of the way Mother fed you as a baby. I've been having bouts of stomach pain. Irritable bowel syndrome," she said with an ironic lift to her eyebrows. "There I was, how often do I go, doubled over at the opera!"

It was I who had the horrible digestive disease, not her, I told her friends. If she was going to be angry with me, the least she could be was happy, I thought illogically.

Why had her ulcer gone undiagnosed and her pain untreated?

She kept meticulous notes and diaries from which I reconstituted her recent life.

"She has read three books on irritable bowel syndrome and therefore is the expert," wrote a resident in gastroenterology she asked for a second opinion two years before. "Her gastrointestinal symptoms have been extensively investigated by Dr. Hepford."

When I asked her gastroenterologist, Dr. Hepford, why he hadn't caught her ulcer, he said, "Chronic for an ulcer means six months, not years. The pain did not come from beneath the breastbone where a duodenal ulcer is felt. She probably did not have an ulcer when I examined her."

In her search for clues to the cause of her pain, she had recently looked at my father's letters to her, especially those he wrote to her at the time of her first serious depression in 1982. "I know your suffering." I could make out the sentence in Polish. He told her of his own first crisis twenty years before in 1962. He had gone from doctor to doctor with various pains, not knowing depression can manifest itself in physical pain. My sister had underlined, "I had chest and stomach pain." If my father's pain had once been a somatization of his depression, then, by her reasoning, so was hers.

My sister needed her digestive tract examined again with an open mind and without her pain over-determined by history. Of course, there was her psychiatric history and her own suggestion that perhaps she was imagining it. They found my sister's esophagus scarred with ulcers. In exchanging symptoms with our father, she gave her own unsuspected clue:

"Perhaps he has heartburn. *I* have heartburn, and *I* have chest pain." Scattered around her apartment I found empty paper wrappers of Aspro-brand aspirin. Heartburn, ulcer, aspirin, bleeding.

If nobody else would apply their mind to her problem, she applied hers. I followed it now. From her journals I saw that my sister ran controlled tests on herself, leaving off one or the other of her medications to see if eliminating it made any difference. I knew how desperate she must have been when I saw the *Guide to Meditation* tapes borrowed from the library.

"She was a bit over the top, wasn't she?" said her GP. "I mean, keeping all these drug diaries. She was very intense."

Every few hours that she was awakened, she noted the pain, using a number code from one to five to measure its severity. She kept recording and noting until the last day, like the chronicles stuffed into the holes of the Warsaw ghetto when there was no hope. She wrote it down for herself, for the human community we address even when we are writing for ourselves, and, as it happened, for me to live in that indefatigable strong mind of hers. I followed her underlining pen in a drug reference book where it just skipped the warning to avoid aspirin if ulcer. Once an interim psychiatrist had prescribed antacids for her and she had felt better. There lay the clue. If only she had taken an antibiotic too. She went out and celebrated every night for a week! And then the pain had returned. Five!

Her friends said she made dates to see concerts and operas with the proviso that she might have to bow out at the last minute because of pain.

"I saw her looking happy at the opera," the dour young Scottish hospital psychiatrist took care to tell me, for which I thanked him. He had caught sight of her at intermission, he said. She had not seen him. "She was dressed up, among friends, laughing," he said. "She was *enjoying* herself."

A week after her funeral, I was sitting in her apartment when the telephone rang. It was a friend of my sister's who had been out of town calling to remind her of their opera date that night. I broke the news.

"Was it …" the friend hesitated. "Was it drugs?"

"In a way," I said. "It was aspirin. She bled to death."

"She had a theory," said her friend, "that depression amplified pain and made what was tolerable for somebody else …"

"Who needs a theory to know that if you feel lousy every twinge is going to hurt more?" I said, as demonstrated by my entire whingeing existence. "Who doesn't know that?" My barefoot sturdy *chalutz* of a folk-dancing sister, that was who. Who was not a complainer, and who would not allow stomach cramps to get in the way of a night at the opera.

I met her friends – discreet, sensitive, tactful – all the qualities lacking in my mother. One of her gentleman friends, Jonathan, drove me around to the council registries and coroner's offices where for the first time he heard my sister's first name Toba.

Between us, Jonathan and I shared her eulogy. I would fill in her early life and he would talk about her life in London. He had grown up in South Africa, the son of Russian Jewish immigrants who worked with Nelson Mandela and the anti-apartheid African National Congress movement in the 1950s while my sister was banning the bomb and working for Israel.

Jonathan asked to see my notes beforehand so that we would not overlap.

"You're not going to talk about the Holocaust! Isn't that sensitive material?" Good English taste, I gathered, unlike Yiddish taste, dictated that if a topic could not be discussed in good taste it was not to be discussed at all. British Jews had become so sensitive to sensitivity that they effectively screened the Holocaust out of their repertoire. Neither was it going to go down well to say that Lusia had been an ardent Zionist.

The same breach opened when her English friends questioned whether she would have wanted a Jewish funeral; after all, she wasn't religious. Not being religious meant putting up Christmas trees but balking at the prospect of saying a few words in Hebrew. Nevertheless, they understood why I did not want my sister to be fashionably cremated.

Later I learned Jonathan had been protecting the sensibility of his Polish wife, who had lost her father in the war. They met when Jonathan visited Poland and was struck by a familiarity of cuisine and culture – his own.

The other friend, thanks to whom I organized a memorial gathering, was not ashamed of his bond with Israel; neither was he shy about discussing the Holocaust. Martin, a hearty ex-kibbutznik a few years older than my sister, was born in Germany and as a child was sent to England as one of the *Kindertransport*.

"In the summer of 1939, my parents made arrangements for me to leave Germany."

"Germany let you out?"

"Yes, other countries were not letting us *in*. After Kristallnacht, there could be no doubt the Jews were in danger. A conference was held at Evian about it, but in the end no country would commit itself to admitting Jews. In 1938, Britain issued a white paper sealing Jews off from Palestine. In exchange, Jewish charities prevailed upon it to accept 10,000 Jewish children."

"Do you think your parents realized what was happening?" I asked.

"The process was so gradual it was hard to put it together. You have to understand that German Jews were as, or even more, assimilated then than American Jews are now. They identified completely with

Germany. It was the *depth* of that German rejection that they could not understand ... Still every child on the train, although we never discussed it among ourselves, knew they would never see their families again – not because we were told, but because the adults knew it, and transmitted it to us."

When my sister was asked whether she could describe Częstochowa, she said she could not remember it or any of the war. But asking for a pen and paper, she managed to draw an accurate map of it. Like my mother, my sister possessed a kind of blindsight. People with blindsight can see but because another part of the brain is not aware of it, it is as if they don't see. Without awareness the information is sealed off. The two have no connection, the same way one Jewish funeral had no connection with another for her. Between the persecution for being Jewish and the shame for being Jewish no intelligible links survived.

In the Demblin memorial book, there was a report by a Jewish schoolteacher of the second transport's arrival in Częstochowa:

In Czenstachov (1944) we arrived in a gigantic camp surrounded by barbed wire. We laboured to take the older children with the adults, but later, thirty-eight children remained outside of the fence, separated from the mothers and fathers. Ukrainian bandits, armed with revolvers and axes, guarded the children. They drove us into filthy barracks. In the camp we found thousands of slave labourers who worked in the enormous German ammunition factory. They put us to work, but I asked to stay with the children, knowing the fate that awaited them. I wanted to be able to comfort them and soothe them in their last hours. But it seems that it was fated that they live a little bit longer, because these children were not immediately executed like those in the first group. When they brought them a little container of food to eat, not one of the children made a move to the soup, although their hunger was great. They were afraid that they would be poisoned. And so I was the first one to take something from the big bowl of soup, and then the children took a little bit of soup for themselves without fear.

The mothers and fathers saw from the side of the fence what was happening to the children, and they strained to be able to see and be able to pick out their own child. They went through unbelievable suffering, feeling sure that their sons and daughters were just waiting to die. It went on that way for days. I was the only adult among the children. From time to time, a Jewish camp policeman would show up and seeing the agony of the parents, I was able to talk two of the Jewish policemen into allowing the children, one by one, to say good-bye to their parents. Although this was an activity that could have meant death for all three of us, the policemen organized it so that each mother separately was able to come to the gate, and I sent her child there and they fell into each other's arms, hugged and kissed, and then the child had to come back immediately. Even the littlest swallow knew how to act. It was well known to them what they had to do.

They understood exactly what was going to happen and they sat there trembling with the fear of death.

There was a little boy among the frightened children who reminded the teacher as he sat with his arms folded around himself, of a bird shielding himself with his wings. That near-death made his death almost wholesome. On another page of the Yizkor book, there is a picture of him as a handsome young officer. It read that he died as a pilot in the Six Day War of 1967, known as "the Eagle" for his bravery.

On May 14, 1948, the day that Israel "by virtue of its natural and historic right," was voted into statehood by the United Nations, Israeli Jews danced in the streets. The next day all five Arab nations fell upon it. Given that the Palestinian leaders had in 1947 refused the offer of a separate state in favour of "driving the Jews into the sea," this attack came as no surprise. What kind of people dance one day knowing they will have to fight the next? It is said that Israel has nothing to do with the Holocaust. It has everything to do with it.

I looked at pictures of my sister in the 1960s, blond and smiling in Israel, Greece, and Italy. "If not for Yonah's curiosity and outgoingness, we would never have met all the interesting people we did," said an American friend of their travels. "She would put up with the most primitive conditions so long as she had a place in which to wash her beautiful hair. I always thought her life began in Israel."

My sister's last teaching position had been at a vocational college for young adults, most of them immigrants. She was especially good, I was told, with overseas students who were hungry to learn. Of course she was also "difficult," and prone to absence. When the Thatcherite axe fell and budgets were cut, so was she and her high standards. At Christmas I would collect cards from former students with news of their fledgling physician practices: "Just an annual note to let you know we have not forgotten you or the influence you have had on our lives."

There were pictures of field trips with her students in Wales. Pictures of the annual parties she gave for her students. As I looked at the young Pakistani, Sikh, Zimbabwean, Malaysian, and Chinese students in her new apartment, splendid in an array of saris, caftans, djellabas, turbans, Turkish tunics, and African robes, it was evident that they had each responded to her invitation to wear their national dress. I knew that this had been her idea, to encourage in each a pride in their ethnic identity.

Two young academic German women asked me, during the height of the identity-politics era, in what way I identify as a Jew. I have heard all manner of qualified Jewish identity, like my first boyfriend saying he was "hardly a Jew," "a secular Jew," "a cultural Jew," or "not very Jewish."

"Hitler was sure he knew what a Jew was." I told them, "He didn't care whether you were half or one-quarter or hardly a Jew at all. He didn't care if you had yourself baptized right out of the community. I accept Hitler's definition." The king of Denmark wore a Jewish star during the Nazi regime. The least we can do, after Hitler, is to wear the badge proudly.

My sister's friends needn't have worried about the funeral being too Jewish. The synagogue in Golders Green called its cantor a reverend, but none of this mattered when he brought out the first Middle Eastern notes of "El Malei Rachamim."

A group of people showed up whom none of her friends knew, members of the Child Holocaust Survivor Centre. When I had signed my father to the Tikvah group, my sister confessed to a similar contact in London. "It's a place where you can have a coffee and nobody bothers you." The Survivors' Centre donated opera tickets to her. If anyone was going to be sensitive to the history of my sister's early years, I thought it would be this group of people. After the service the oldest man who could scarcely breathe for wheezing shook my hand. "Thank you."

The next summer I put up a stone for her, and remained cleaning up her apartment into the fall, so it was from her TV I watched airplanes hijacked by Muslim fanatics fly into the World Trade Center towers in New York. Shortly afterwards on Yom Kippur, I asked the cantor who had officiated at my sister's funeral, permission to hear him sing "Kol Nidre." I made my way to the basement of an administrative building, where a sprinkling of similarly stranded Americans had ventured forth in the rain. A choir and organ soon drowned out the cantor, however, in a version so Reform that it had reformed out any visible signs of Jewish tradition – why the organ? Where were the blue-and-white prayer shawls, the yarmulkes? The Reform movement originated in the nineteenth century among assimilated Jews in Germany who wanted to blend in with their compatriots, even replacing bar mitzvahs with communion. The rabbi was a fair-haired woman whose small turnout did not reflect her influence, as she frequently ornamented the BBC. On Yom Kippur, Jews traditionally beat their breasts, and she did not fail them. "The most urgent Jewish duty," she exhorted her captive audience, "was to lobby for more Muslim schools."

The sexton ended the evening with a reminder of the need for increased security.

In the end it was my sister's back that hurt. ("Did not the fact that the pain migrated prove that it was imaginary?") An ulcer in its extreme stage can perforate to the back. Cortisone injections into her vertebra were no help. "And you know your sister – she was so academic – as soon as she heard it was arthritis of the spine she ran off to the library and read all the books on it and convinced herself and everybody else that that's what she had. She was happy, in a way, to know what it was," said a close friend. She was told that arthritis could cause severe pain. And that it was okay to take aspirin with lithium.

A note to Lusia from this friend had been slipped under the door. "How are you? One is worried about you but one doesn't want to be intrusive."

Finally, there was my sister's simple importuning to relieve her pain. "But I spent an hour with you at home," the doctor replied.

"I feel guilty for having pain," my sister wrote in her diary two days before she died. "Desperate pain!" She woke up at 3 and 5 and 6:30 a.m. to swallow more aspirin, codeine, and an antidepressant to ease her distress. "Slept, listened to radio, did not go out or eat for two days."

The friend who came the morning of her last day with bottles of mineral water (she was nauseous now too) suggested she go to the hospital. She didn't want to spend all night on a trolley in the corridor, my sister said. Her friends did not insist. The reason she had always liked England was that people did not behave like her mother.

"Somebody must help me," my sister wrote. Only our mother could have helped her. Only our intrusive mother would have torn down the door and dragged Lusia by the hair to an emergency room.

Only my mother could have saved my sister. And my mother died first.

Chapter Seventeen

SPRING 1997

———

"I am fifty years old, Mama." I catch myself telling my mother's story of my birth back to her. We are sitting outside the nursing home, though there is still snow on the ground. Her arms are in the sleeves of her down coat pulled on backward like a blanket, her face turned up to the first rays of the spring sun. Like the picture of us wrapped in furs on a sled in Zakopane. "It was early spring, *wiosna*, everything coming into bloom, I came on so fast I was nearly born in the droshky."

My mother keeps her eyes closed in the sun. "It was *wiosna*. In Poland, the birds and buds were out. You took me in the carriage to the park in Lodz."

Here in Canada the only way you can tell it's spring is that the sun is warm enough to melt the icicles dripping from the snowy branches, and there is a heady hint of liquid in the air as the ice cracks along the St. Lawrence River. The ship that brought us to Canada, the SS *Homeland*, docked on March 15 just as the ice was breaking. I have found the landing *kvitls*, the letters from the Jewish relief agency, the Canadian immigration letter saying that we had to be of good health and character. My father carried with him extracts of Polish birth and marriage certificates dated 1950 that he collected from town halls as we were about to leave Poland. The oldest original document I find is a Buchenwald identity card issued upon liberation in April 1945. It is almost April.

Yesterday I walked along the human-sized warren of streets east of St. Lawrence (Marianne, de Bullion, St. Dominique, Henri Julien) that run straight into the mountain like a Carpathian village. The late afternoon spring sun turned the snowy mountain a rosy ice cream. I used to search for the world of forests and mountains my father had lost. But here is where he used to turn into Canadian Outfitting, which is now a sleek restaurant, and here is where he walked up Mount Royal with the cross on top.

As late as the winter before he died, he dropped me at a produce store on St. Lawrence while he stopped at the bank. He drove back to pick me up at another store two blocks down by mistake and was frantic when he couldn't find me. When I finally got into his car he vowed: "I am never letting you out of my sight again."

Not long after, it would not be possible to shop for food on St. Lawrence the way my father and Dora's father had, selecting the best grapes on their way home from work. With our parents went their workplaces and the stores they frequented; Warshaw's supermarket, Waldman's fish market that supplied the whole city, the kosher butcher's, the St. Lawrence Bakery – all closed. Through cultural and demographic attrition, Jewish St. Lawrence died. The rest of the street did not look too healthy either. On the side streets Montreal's famous bagel factories were still alive, the word *bagel* having evidently fallen through the cracks of the French language police dragnet. La Vieille Europe remained, and Schwartz's famous smoked meat had people lined up in the street, but it was no longer owned by a Schwartz. Our homegrown international star Céline Dion Inc. had bought them out and packaged the brand name for supermarket consumption. Thankfully, the health department did not approve of the packaged product and the desecration was withdrawn.

My mother had been looking forward to my arrival, Nadia said. When I didn't arrive, she fell asleep.

The night before, a spring snowstorm had cancelled the Montreal-bound flight from Detroit. My mind immediately flew to anticipate my parents' worry, but it no longer mattered how late at night I arrived. My father would not be waiting for me. And neither would my mother, in her old way. I no longer had the "*ol*" – the burden – of allaying their worry. I missed the yoke of their love that I would no longer be privileged to bear.

Separated from my suitcase and coat, when I got to their apartment I put on my father's coat. I staggered under the heaviness I used to want to lighten. When I reached inside the pockets, I found the well-worn sheepskin gloves I bought him when I was twenty. He worried that he had lost them. Ever since the *milchume*, his fingers had been prone to frostbite; with the earnings from my go-go-dancing job I bought him the best gloves I could find. "You shouldn't have," my mother said.

The tense I lived in with my father was the future perfect. I should have. Because I had a notion of the past that haunted him, I wanted to make some bits of another past that the future would also include. The man who tormented himself for losing things held on to these gloves for thirty years. "You gave me these gloves," he would say. "Everything nice I have from you."

It was from him that I learned the appreciation of humanly worked quality. The gloves are softened and moulded to his hand. Recently he had shown me a tear in a finger seam that needed darning. "I have to give it to a seamstress; you need special thread and needle." But when I look there is no tear in the seam; I can see from the darker stitches that he must have sewn it up himself.

"I can't find them!" I put my hands in the gloves moulded by his hands. "Here they are, Daddy. You haven't lost them at all."

◆　◆　◆

These are the generations of the nursing home: Mrs. Meyer, who usually sits mute and alone in a housedress holding her dentures, has received visitors. A middle-aged daughter and son-in-law, who are themselves parents and perhaps grandparents, tell her the news: "Phyllis and Barbara's kids are fine, and Barbara is expecting again." The matriarch of all these Phyllises and Barbaras and offspring, without whom none of them would exist, sits abandoned by her progeny who are busy making babies, who themselves will one day sit forgotten in nursing homes.

"Don't be naive!" my mother scolded me when I turned my head away from a necklace she said would be mine. This was the lifecycle, and it was *narish* of me to fetishize her moment or mine in it. This is where I ran headlong against the Jewish tradition of everything in moderation, the human ties that were to be human and no more. Even the ethical commands are the measure of what is humanly possible and must not outdo and must not ask more than that. This is where Jewish history rammed me against normal life.

Mrs. Meyer's son-in-law is making motions that he wants to leave. When the couple gets up, Mrs. Meyer, who has so far not uttered a word, suddenly clasps her daughter's hand. "Thank you," she says. "Thank you for coming."

"It's a pleasure! We'll come again!" says the son-in-law with relief. "Soon!"

One day she is called to the telephone at the nurses' station. A niece, daughter, or granddaughter has given birth, and suddenly a flow of congratulations and questions pour out of her as fluidly as a stream. "Yes, yes," she adds, "and how are *you*? Don't forget to take care of *you*!"

It's what life owes to life. At the end of life perhaps there is no sense but its cycle.

If I had children, would the consciousness of this lifecycle attenuate the loss of my parents? I do not want the blow attenuated

"*Ich hob dich leeb*," I say to my mother. I love you.

"*Tsi feel*," she shakes her head. Too much.

For mine is the generation of the *milchume*. We will turn the love of the children back to the parents.

I was so afraid of stroke, but it was not of a stroke she died.

My mother and I embarked on the most precise reversal of those roles that plagued me through my childhood, adolescence, and well into my adulthood and her old age. Now as she made efforts to swallow, I in my turn grew tense on the days the contents of the spoon dribble out. An apprehension gripped me so enmeshed with Jewish history that I assumed I was exaggerating. We feed our terror so that by its exaggeration we ensure the thing we fear will never match it.

My father said: "Eat more because when something will happen, you won't have any reserves to live from!"

The slack muscle pulled away from her hipbone that jutted out like a knob. I rubbed vitamin E on the bone. I mixed vitamins into her soup while she stared. In my adolescence, she used to break an egg into my milk for insurance. I could trust her body neither to feed itself nor to signal hunger to me.

Entangled with Jewish history was my suspicion about her puffiness. At the same time that she was shrinking, she is swollen. They told me her circulation was slowed from immobility. When I left a message asking Dr. Himmel if therefore we should send her to a cardiologist, he did not respond. Her swelling increased, sometimes a hand, sometimes a foot, with skin so tight that Hilda sawed off her wedding ring. My father said: "When we came out of the camps, we were skin and bone. We were swollen."

I remembered my mother's cravings for eggs, meat, and herring. I went to a health food store and asked for protein that would be easily digestible by an elderly person.

I picked the one day a week Dr. Himmel closeted himself with Hilda to get his stamp of authority for protein powder I had bought to add to my mother's food. Otherwise Hilda would confiscate it like she did the vitamins.

"How do you find your mother?" Hilda asked. "I think she looks fantastic!" She did not wait for me to answer. "And I think you should thank me for looking after her so well."

"Yes," chimed in Dr. Himmel. "I haven't heard you thank Hilda for looking after her."

A blind person could see my mother was dying.

◆ ◆ ◆

"Did nobody tell you about dementia, its different stages, did nobody prepare you by telling you what you were to expect?" I was asked later. No. Nobody spoke to me about anything medical. I never had the sense of an illness being followed. If they knew anything, they did not tell me.

At the last moment, I hired Nadia's friend, a former physician from eastern Europe to feed my mother. Valentin will spend an hour feeding her spoonfuls of tea if necessary and elicit her swallowing reflex by tapping the spoon against her mouth. Hilda declared herself horrified at the sight. My mother will gain five pounds.

Whereas I used to run errands during my mother's nap, now I curled around her for the pleasure of falling asleep to her breathing. I am acutely aware that she could not be sleeping by my side. When she awakes she accepts a biscuit and soaks it in her tea.

"Do you feel well?"

The barest nod and blink. Then she closed her eyes again.

"Does something hurt you?"

"*Nayn.*"

I will learn to be happy with radically less when, a few days later, she closes her eyes and keeps them closed for most of the day.

I said experimentally to Hilda, "My mother no longer opens her eyes. Perhaps we should ask the doctor what is wrong?"

"Oh no, not unless the symptoms become more serious," Hilda answers briskly.

I had already made appointments with Dr. MacGregor and the cardiologist. Dr. Himmel refused the request for handicapped transportation, because there was nothing in her chart, he said, to justify such appointments.

The specialists ordered blood tests.

"Mama," I pleaded. "Open your beautiful eyes."

She munched with her eyes closed. My mother, who had recently been speaking exclusively with her eyes that before wandered blind with grief, now shut them.

"Mama! Mama!" I call.

No answer, either by voice or eyes, by sound or look.

At the end of the day when she was in bed and I was about to leave her, I persisted: "Mama, do you feel well?"

"*Yo.* Yes."

"Does something hurt you?"

"*Nayn.* No."

"Then why don't you open your eyes?" I beg. "You have such beautiful eyes." No answer.

"*Di host mich leeb?*" I test her. "Do you love me?"

She struggles to respond, her eyes still shut. "*Zeyeh shtark*" (Very strong).

Joy and anguish at the knowledge that she is awake behind those closed eyes. I give a child's cry. "Then why don't you open your beautiful eyes?"

When I got back to California, I called to ask about the results of the blood tests.

"She's not co-operating in eating, she's very hard to feed," Dr. Himmel informed me, as if this was new and as if this was her fault.

"What do the blood tests say?" I asked.

"She's a little anemic. I might prescribe iron."

"Why don't you prescribe it now?"

"Why don't you take your mother to California?"

"The daughter called three times today," it said in the notes. The doctor would "reassess" the situation next week. The next week my mother was in the hospital.

Chapter Eighteen

RACHAMIM (COMPASSION), 1997

The nursing home called to say they were sending my mother to the hospital. "Why don't you wait and see?" my husband said. I had flown so many times. I had barely gotten back. It was Passover eve. I could no more sit here thinking about her than she could sit still at any Seder. "Why do you want to watch her die?"

I do what she couldn't do for her mother. I spend Passover in flight. I hope that we will pass through *iberkumen* this time. That the Angel of Death will pass over our habitation.

I found her asleep curled on her side in an open emergency ward. I found the large curves of my mother as she used to be, because she was swollen to her former size.

"Perhaps she is always like this," the WASPY resident said.

"No, she's not," I said. Nadia said that my mother was alert when they arrived and squeezed the ER doctor's hand when he asked her to in Yiddish. She followed Nadia around with her eyes.

"How is she usually different?"

"She's different. She looks around, she's curious, she answers me with her eyes." I can see that for him this is not a life.

"I'm sorry," he replied with a shrug, "we may have nothing to offer."

"But she came in with a kidney infection!" He was ready to send her back to the nursing home.

The next test showed that my mother had a kidney infection.

When I arrived at my parents' apartment, Dora called me. She came to visit her parents for Passover and asked to sleep over to avoid giving her mother her cold. Her mother had not recovered from her illness since we saw each other last.

"Remember only last Rosh Hashanah we were bringing them fall cherries?"

The next morning I found my mother with her cheeks dark pink, one eye swollen shut, feverish.

"Do you know how to feed her?" Valentin asked, Nadia's immigrant European physician friend whom I had hired too late. Ignoring Nurse Hilda's disapproval, Valentin would sit with my mother for an hour until she imbibed a glass of juice. He elicited her swallowing reflex by first tapping the spoon lightly against my mother's lips.

"No," I admitted to Valentin. "You will feed her." I said. Feeding my mother has become the life-and-death struggle she once made of feeding me. To feed her is to take her life in my hands.

Despite her flushed, puffy, nauseated-with-the-world face she swallows a crushed Tylenol with a spasm of effort. When people speak about a person "battling" a disease, this must be the self they mean that battles. With my mother this self has always been close to the surface. As soon as she opens her eyes she begins to scan the passers-by.

"She must have been frightened on the day we came in," said Nadia. "Her eyes never left me."

I rediscover the world of piled-up sheets, bedpans, tubes, towels, and the men in hospital gowns dragging their IV poles out to the corridors to *shmeeze* like Roman senators in togas.

"Miss, miss, the clean towels are over there!" an elderly man shouts from the corner bed. "Take a clean one!"

The nurse says of his urine test, "The doctor says it's not a lot of blood you're losing."

"What does *he* know?" the man ripostes to his grandson. "I know that when I go home it starts again. *Efsheh hot es tsi teeyen mit die hemoroydn,*" he conjectures with my father's sceptical curiosity. "Maybe it has to do with my hemorrhoids."

My mother is admitted to a medical ward and hooked up to intravenous antibiotics and fluids. Her face is shiny from swollenness; her eyes nearly slit shut from it. Her arms are raw from blood tests.

When I saw the swollenness this morning I felt weak-kneed. A kidney infection usually clears within a few days with intravenous antibiotics. The internist, Dr. Trudeau, says her kidney infection is coming under control, but there is something wrong with her chemistry. My mother is in metabolic acidosis, he says. She is grunting, forcing out the breaths in an effort to throw off toxins, the first of her breathing rhythms that will inhabit me. They are giving her fluids, but she's not holding them in her tissues where they belong. The fluids are spilling into her intracellular spaces because her cells do not have enough protein to hold them. Early this morning when he had pronounced her better, she had opened her eyes and said good morning. "What beautiful eyes."

The minute she opens her eyes, I yell "*Shaynheit!*" and Yiddish endearments. I am overheard through the curtain that separates us from the adjoining patient. An entire family has moved into the next bed. Rather it is the patriarch of a family, a vigorous older man who speaks in Hungarian to his wife and Yiddish to his children and grand-children and an entire community of Chasidim.

"*Noch di milchume* ..." I catch the familiar phrase, "After the war," he went back to Hungary.

My mother opens her eyes. "Beautiful eyes," said the speech therapist they sent in late on Friday to evaluate my mother's swallow reflex. While Valentin fed my mother, the therapist held her finger on my mother's throat and said, "She hasn't swallowed since I came in. She should take nothing in by mouth all weekend and we'll see again when she has recovered from her infection."

"No supper in case she chokes," the nurse reminds me. My mother is to subsist on intravenous fluids and have nothing to eat all weekend. In the next bed, a five-course feast is in progress. An adolescent grand-daughter has brought Pesach dinner to the patient, and she announces each course as she unwraps it.

"Zeyde, here is the soup with *kneidlach*, here is the *flanken*, and this is the compote. Without sugar," she adds, "because you're a diabetic."

"Without sugar!" the zeyde wags his head at such ingenuity.

"We left the *machzor* on the window, zeyde."

"Now I can make Shabbes," he sighs.

Dr. Trudeau enters with the zeyde's glucose count and is offered a plateful of *flanken.*

"How come whenever I see you you're eating?" the doctor teases.

"Doctor, are you married?" his wife asks.

"Yes, I have two little girls."

"May you have joy from them. Can I offer you something?" she asks me.

"I told you she speaks Yiddish," says her husband.

"Tell me, what is wrong with your mother," she asks.

"*Zee ken nisht essen*," I say. "She can't eat."

The weekend our neighbour's family brings meals redolent of all that my mother used to cook is the last weekend she will eat anything.

She has fought off the kidney infection, but without the osmotic pressure of protein her fluids are seeping out of her cells. Dr. Trudeau shows me a chart of albumin-protein values.

"Normal albumin is 40. Your mother's albumin level is 23. Twenty-one is fatal."

Even Jewish history must have a limit to its irony. The joke was on me. In the nursing home they said she was puffy from immobility. My suspicion about her puffiness was too farfetched to be true. ("When we came out of the camps," my father said, "we were skin and bone. We were swollen.") My wildest fear that I put to Dr. Himmel when my mother's hands swelled so much they had to rest on a cushion was true. "Could she be swollen from protein deficiency?"

I called him now in the nursing home: "What were her protein levels?" They hadn't let me see her chart in the nursing home although I was her legal guardian. The blood tests taken last summer as part of the tyclid follow-up showed low albumin – albumin is part of an egg, which is protein. It takes three weeks of low-albumin levels to throw the body into protein deficiency. And swollen as she was, her monthly weight chart recorded a constant drop.

Even after I asked whether her swelling could be caused by protein deficiency, Dr. Himmel had not requested protein levels.

"They are a little low. Thirty," he answers.

"Now they are 23," I say. "In a few days they have sunk so low?"

"You could interpret it like that."

Dr. Trudeau will explain that because she had been somewhat dehydrated, her protein levels would have been concentrated and appeared deceptively higher. Now she has been given fluids, they have been slightly over diluted to their critically low levels.

"Once she weighed 150 pounds," Dr. Himmel answers, "that was too much." He evades what she weighs now.

In the single month of November, she lost twenty pounds.

My mother opens her eyes. She needs food. At the same time, to feed her is to risk her choking. Mealtimes come and go. She hasn't eaten since yesterday. Dr. Trudeau says she needs a feeding tube. I think of my mother never eating again. I think maybe if she could take in some food, she would regain the strength to swallow again. I want to turn back the clock to the time before the lack of attention carried her away. Was this what Dr. Himmel meant when he said she was "critically ill" more than a year ago? The label might justify doing nothing, which then could *put* her in critical condition.

Valentin maintains that my mother needs to eat and that her choking on food is a smaller risk than made out. Dr. Rosenberg said that feeding tubes had problems and that it would be best if my mother could be brought around to swallow blended food. I close the curtains and Valentin starts mashing fruit in yogurt. Not wanting to shout, I put my mouth next to her ear, "*Shling arup*, Mama," I beg. "Swallow." Valentin taps her mouth with the spoon, he spoons some yogourt in, some dribbles out, he spoons it back with a little more and, after a long time with my lips against her ear and my heart pounding, her throat contracts and she swallows. It was my turn to taste the bitterness of proximity.

"Many people stop eating when they want to die," I will be told. "Perhaps your mother refused to eat."

"My mother did not refuse to eat." This is my mother, this is the self she could not help but be. The law protects "the integrity of the person." If it can be found, this accepting of food was my mother's integrity. For six or nine months this particular mind/body tried to eat.

My mother had once before been subjected to slow starvation. A body never forgets the experience of hunger. She knew that hunger was a force of preservation that too long unsatisfied can desert you. The way people who have known extreme cold fight to keep awake when the temperature drops, perhaps her body remembered that this was above all the time to make an effort to eat.

Now she does so well on the yogourt, I run out and bring back the perfect puréed iron and protein compound: chopped liver!

But in the evening she is too tired exhaling the toxins from the metabolic breakdown to make the effort. When I hear a rattle in her throat, I stop. She coughs. Her eyes, barely open in her distended face, look quizzically at me; her chest works like a bellows. I aspirate her throat with the suction tube and my hands are shaking so badly that I am jabbing her more than doing her good. At that moment, trembling while I hold her in my arms at the other end of her life, I understand why she was afraid to hold me at the beginning of mine. Why, having seen children die of hunger, feeding me took on a frantic brutality; when the life in your hands becomes a world, so does the terror of holding this life, a world, in your hands. The more fragile the life, the more it seemed a breath would extinguish it. The universe of chance and causation that I had wooed to favour my mother – *Chaja*, life – trembled in my fingers.

I understood also why doctors do not treat their own families. They don't have the distance. At close range, we cannot hold life in our hands. The Talmudic discussion on honouring parents says that a doctor may not treat his parents unless there is no other physician available, lest he inadvertently hurt them. This is with the understanding that hurting his parents will be worse for him than for them. I call the nurse, who berates me while she aspirates my mother's throat.

"You were not supposed to feed her, and if tonight she develops pneumonia from food having entered her lungs, it will be your fault!"

I am sick. If my mother had once nearly killed me with food, I was going to succeed in killing her.

"*Git Shabbes. Git Shabbes.*" The next morning I am awakened beside my mother, her calm swollen face asleep on the pillow, by high heels clicking on the corridor floor. Wreaths of young girls spill into the room: granddaughters.

"*Ich bin dir mekaneh.* I envy you," I hear a male voice teasing the zeyde.

"*Di kenst mir nisht farginen.* You cannot stop begrudging me that I am surrounded by pretty girls."

On Shabbes, crowds of Chasidic men performing the mitzvah of visiting the sick, pour in to see the zeyde. They gather around our neighbour's bed, telling *maysehs* and *moshels*, stories and parables, with the questioning lilt of why-is-this-night-different-from-all-other-nights that cradles all Talmudic study.

"Why did the rebbe? …" The answer to the question turns out to be another story. "*Refua shelema.* Speedy remedy."

Each visitor takes his leave with a flourish of blessings, wishes, and proverbs as elegant as French court obeisances.

"*Mameleh,* get me the fruit please," the zeyde says to his grand-daughter.

"Bubbe put a piece of chicken away in the fridge."

"If I want it, I can get it myself now. They took away the IV pole."

"Yes, but it's always better when someone gets it for you," the *maydele* ripostes in a voice that sounds surprisingly like the self-recording coming out of my answering machine.

"Zeyde, I peeled the pear and I left it on your table. And you didn't want to come to the hospital," she teases him.

"It was *Yontov,*" he explains. He tells in exactly what part of the Seder he couldn't stand the pain anymore. "The sea was parting … 'Tate,' Yankel said, 'you have 103 fever. We have to take you to the hospital.' Till what time did the Seder go at your house?"

"Till three."

"*Kayn eyne horeh,*" he says, warding off reprisals for the pride he is about to express. "Your father is a *gantser* professor."

"When do you go home?"

"Tomorrow, *Baruch ha Shem.* Thank God."

When his extended family leaves for the night, there is another round of blessings to us. "*Refua shleyma.* Speedy remedy."

I knew the word for remedy from my mother. "Seeing you is the best *refiya,*" she used to say.

"How many children and grandchildren do you have?" I ask.

"Eighteen, *kayn eyne horeh.* That I have lived to see them." He shakes his head. "Such a nice Yiddish you speak," he says.

"Thank you."

"Do you have children? Are you alone?" asks his wife. "The way you watch over your mother, all children should learn from you."

In the early morning I face Dr. Trudeau miserably. He smiles at me. "Her lungs are clear," he says, "so you're off the hook."

"When can you put in the PEG?" I ask. (PEG stands for percutaneous endoscopic gastrostomy, a procedure for inserting a feeding tube into the stomach.) It makes no difference how much she could eat by mouth now; it would not make up her deficiencies.

"I will give up my mother's bed in the nursing home for one here," I offered as soon as my mother had been readmitted to the hospital.

They smiled but it is done. Dr. Rosenberg says he has arranged a swap with the nursing home.

"It's a long time since I've seen her this sick," he said when he came by. Now he looked at her chart in silence. "I've spoken to Dr. Trudeau," he said. "She needs the feeding tube."

During the interval that I still have hope she will recover, I almost think the episode will be worth it if she can stay in the hospital.

"There is a new anti-stroke medication," Dr. Trudeau mentions. It is a shock to arrive again in an environment that shows solidarity in the common cause of getting people as well as they can be.

My mother is moved to a private room on the fourth floor due to the staph-resistant bacteria she's carrying from the nursing home.

"All my mother needs is to see her daughter in a mask," I say, refusing it and promising not to approach other patients. The internist who is leaving the rotation examines my mother.

"How did a person in the care of a medical facility come to be so malnourished?" she asks.

"The doctor in the nursing home claimed she wasn't emaciated," I said. "He put everything down to her age."

"Some doctors make assumptions about what is normal for ninety-year-olds which are not appropriate!" she snapped. I felt both validated and berated by her anger. Nobody had informed her that the nursing home operated on different standards from the hospital.

The internist asks me for permission to use my mother as an example for students of the classic signs of protein deficiency. I will see her pressing my mother's skin down in front of medical students, and showing the way the skin does not bounce back.

My mother, sedated, has a tube inserted into her stomach in the gastroenterology lab while I wait. It takes less than twenty minutes.

Although the procedure itself was minor, the gastroenterologist informed me, patients usually die of the underlying ailment so that some families choose not to implant it.

"I cannot let my mother starve to death," I say. I cannot, but she has been allowed to starve anyway. On the referral sheet I catch a glimpse of the diagnosis: malnutrition.

She passes through the installation well. The night before, our neighbour had asked how my mother is. "She can't swallow so we are going to insert a feeding tube," I said.

"Of course," she nodded, "to save a life." *Pikuach Nefesh.*

That night, Nadia who has taken my place in the hospital, calls me at the apartment so that I can talk to my mother. Nadia had opened the window, and a breeze entered. My mother opened her eyes, alert.

"Is it cold?" Nadia asked her.

"Yes," my mother replied.

"Ma!" I yelled with all my might into the telephone. "*Ich hob dich leeb!*"

My mother's eyes showed that she heard, said Nadia.

"Nice jacket," she had said to Nadia recovering from last Passover's stroke. "Beautiful," she said at the Chanukah lights. If you gave her a biscuit and tea she would begin to dip it and put it in her mouth. In these tiny recuperations I felt my mother fanning back at me the breath of life.

That night was the last in which Chaja flickered back at us. After the first feeding, Nadia said her abdomen was swollen. "Perhaps she is no longer accustomed to having so much in her stomach," she remarked.

When I arrive and feel my mother's abdomen, I call the resident.

"Let me look at the urine bag," he glances. Almost empty. Her kidneys were failing. Suddenly, as if by a prearranged signal which no doubt it is, the room is a cyclone of activity. Nurses roll in an EKG machine. I see my mother's frightened eyes as she is thrown around and it happens too fast for me to protest.

"I want to talk with you," says the resident, heading out to the corridor. I am hyperventilating.

"You must know already what I am going to say. Your mother is dying. It won't take long. Her kidneys are not working, but the underlying cause of her death is malnutrition."

I lie in bed with her the whole time she is dying. "You have made yourself a nest," Nadia says. My mother's arms are raw from blood taking. I get up to call Dr. Himmel again.

"If you want to know about her feeding, ask the staff," he says irritably. "I wasn't here."

"You weren't there for the protein levels?" I say. "For the swelling and the weight chart?"

"I'm busy," he cuts me off. "I have people to see."

In the time to come, another Quebec nursing-home GP will surmise that the nursing home must have known my mother was malnourished, but it was becoming accepted practice in nursing homes to allow demented people to starve. It was not cruel not to nourish demented people (my lawyer will prefer I not use the word *starve*), went this rationale, because they do not feel hunger or thirst. According to this doctor, not installing a feeding tube earlier allowed the demented person to maintain "life with dignity."

I look at my mother whose breaths are beginning to be torn out of her.

"Was she hungry in the nursing home?" I asked the resident.

"She may have been," said the resident. "We don't know."

I stood by and watched it happen. Like my mother, I had cried out warnings louder to make sure the reality could never match my hindsight-primed foresight. I had been deafened by my own shouting.

When I protest, I will find that if it was what most nursing homes ordinarily did, standard practice, then it was right to do it. Contrary to our prophets' nagging to refuse to do something merely because others did it, the elderly and ill have been surrendered to whatever is done. But my parents had been selected for extraordinary practices. My mother was not standard. "Walk where you can melt into the crowd," she always told me. She did not follow her own advice.

"Smile at him, Ma, or else you will be selected for nontreatment." Why argue the merits of feeding tubes, laws of informed consent, and end-of-life decisions when the nursing home and Dr. Himmel, as he will himself admit with a shrug, had not even recognized my mother was malnourished? It never came up. And this obliviousness dated not from her malnutrition but from the day she entered the nursing home. I did not want my mother kept alive at all costs. I did not object when the palliative-care physician, Dr. Chang, removed the feeding tube. I asked for more morphine though it can hasten death. I wanted her to be cared for whether she was living or dying, to have her suffering minimized, and not left to the mercies of nature. As the process continued, it will be obvious that even "keeping a person comfortable" requires intelligence, expertise, and technology. It takes the intelligence of a *chuchem*. My mother's meaning of *chuchem* intermingled the two. There was no goodness without wisdom.

As time passed, and opinions were gathered from everyone except the doctors who had actually been there, what happened to my mother was strangled in the noose of preconceived ideas. How could it be otherwise when everyone's greatest fear was *to be kept alive* by technological means? The Order of Nurses representative consoled me: "At least you were with her – the dying hear everything; she knew you were by her side."

"My mother couldn't hear when she was still alert." All the sentience and intuition my mother was not accorded when she was alive, she had suddenly regained on her deathbed.

"The way to honour your mother is not by remembering either these last six months or these last few years," the *heeger* medical ethicist said, "but all the happy years you spent together."

After I was told she would die, I lay in the curve of her body on the bed.

I lay beside my battling mother who, with every raucous breath, belied the consolations. I lay beside her and I thought, *But now there is nothing more I can do.*

I was wrong. There was never so much I could do as now, in proportion to the amount of pain I could spare her. Each breath of pain, however defined, expanded infinitely as I watched her struggle, so one iota less was worth all the effort so far expended. My mother blew, rattled, coughed, heaved for a week after they told me it might take hours.

When the resident told me she was dying, he asked if there was anything I wanted to request. "I want her to suffer as little as possible," I said. The resident nodded and went away. Then I found we had different definitions of what it meant to suffer.

For a moment I had curled up at the foot of my mother's bed into something like reprieve. I used to curl up next to my mother to savour her even breath. Again, I listened to her breath, which had bored into me for a week and whose every nuance I was to learn in the next days and nights. My ninety-one-year-old mother, who they tell me is dying, is working like a coal miner. She is flailing like a fish out of water.

She is pumping so hard it is pumping her. Her shoulders rise to suck in each breath, sighs are wrenched out of her on the exhalation, and after a deadly silent moment the tremendous effort begins again.

"How do you know she's in pain?" they ask me.

"Pain is when they grimace," they told me. My mother's brow remained smooth, but with every breath her shoulders lift, her chest gasps and tears sounds out of her that I think I will hear for the rest of my life. This was the dignified comfortable result of letting someone die naturally.

"Pain is when the forehead frowns and the person is moaning," the nurse said. In the nursing home they would have consigned my mother to death, but in the hospital they are afraid they might kill her with too much morphine.

"Indeed," my lawyer, M. Lebel, would say later, "long-term-care facilities seem to operate by different standards of care than the hospital and the rest of society."

"But that's insane."

"Yes," he agreed, "yet that's the way it is." Only legal investigation will render my mother the kind of medical review she could have used when she was alive.

"Your mother had apraxia," M. Lebel said, reading our expert's report, "the slowing down which affected her eating function. She did not lose the ability to swallow until the end. That's why she kept swallowing even when you fed her in the hospital. It is true that at the time that her eating slowed down, the question of a feeding tube could have been raised. However, studies have shown that feeding tubes do not postpone the loss of weight any more than hand feeding in patients with progressive dementia. Therefore, the best thing that could be done for her was to have a companion to take time to feed her at her own rhythm and stimulate her swallowing reflex. Which you did."

"Against their will. There was a companion to feed her while I was gone. Only in the last month I hired a physician who took pains to feed her, and the nurse Hilda was horrified."

"It was exactly what your mother needed."

Tears spring up in my eyes. It is unbelievable.

"As a matter of fact, American studies show that it is less costly for an institution to install a feeding tube than to hire a person to feed a patient. The most expensive and most labour-intensive choice is a person feeding another person. Preferred foods and strong tastes are recommended. And then you took her to see specialists. If you had taken less good care of your mother," the lawyer said with a smile, "we would have a better case."

"Don't you think you should inform your sister?" My mother had just been pronounced dying, and I was sitting on her bed watching her struggle for breath. Nadia offered to call my sister. "She thanked me. She said it would have been awful for her to hear this news from an unfriendly voice."

When later I found this in my sister's diary I was grateful: "Mother had excellent care, she was never left alone and was comfortable and in no pain." My sister's excellent mind pierced through the fog nevertheless. "They say Mother's kidneys have failed. From what cause?"

In the coming days when my mother is given morphine, I will badly want to believe in the separability of mind and body. What makes it impossible in my mother's case is that this wordless self in helpless heaving battle is not an exposed carcass with no relation to my mother; it is the self that has always been most recognizably my mother. The reaction to the assault on her leaking cells, the rattling lungs, the choking, that is my mother Chaja. If we are at all our bodies, then we are also our wilted undernourished cells. My mother has her *neshuma*, breath, soul knocked out of her until she catches it, barely, on the next inhalation. The night it coughs itself up out of her in bloody gravel, I hold on to her for dear life. I hold on to her not to run out of the room. Every sigh, gasp, and wheeze rent from her was an attempt to thrust her on the other side of the wire where I would not know her, where I would be afraid to go. I did not want to let what was being done to her make her a stranger to me. I held her, my face supporting hers, as with all her soul and all her might she drew breath again.

A few minutes after my mother began to heave, I had run to the nurses' station for a doctor, and run back. Suddenly Dr. Chang, whom I had seen on the floor, appeared and silently stood in the room.

He listened to the sighing inspiration, the pop of silence before the long collapsing wheezing expiration, then that dead stop that threatened to go on forever until the shrug of her shoulders signalled the gasp that was the beginning of my mother's inspiration. On the expiration, the wheezing rattling guttural release just before the silence that might not be broken again, Dr. Chang said, "If you want to tell her something, when she exhales is the time she can take it in."

My lips are against her temple. "Everything will be good, Mama," I said.

It was a battle to get the morphine. I remembered my mother's capability to abstract herself – this too was *Chaja* – and I requested that abstraction. My mother had been given nothing, she was straining to breathe and I called the resident. I encounter again the strange vagaries of the argument that said the quality of her life was too poor to prolong, but when I ask for morphine to ease her struggle, an entire process goes into play to prove that she is perfectly cozy.

"Perhaps you would like to call Michael," my husband suggested over the telephone.

"Why is she in metabolic acidosis?" Michael asked.

"Because her protein levels are low."

I thought there was no point in calling him now. What else could be done? This is one of those small things with immense effects that I nearly didn't do, because I had also fallen for the idea that a sentence to death meant there was nothing else to be done. I could still do plenty, I was to find out. The telephone call saved my mother forty-eight hours of agony and those forty-eight hours, when they lead to death and not to a recovery that will put the forty-eight hours in perspective, can be obscenely infinite.

"She's wheezing worse than you ever did in your worst asthma attack!" I blurted out.

"Morphine is not only an analgesic; it eases respiration," Michael said.

"Please call the resident and tell him," I begged.

Michael called the resident. The resident prescribed subcutaneous morphine through a tiny pinprick under the skin.

Morphine eased my mother's work for the next forty-eight hours until the resident became nervous about her slow breaths and withdrew it. For forty-eight hours it reinforced my conviction that a few hours, a step left or right, an accident, a favour, a phone call, a fortuitous piece of knowledge can have infinite repercussions. Even to say I wanted her to suffer as little as possible was delusive quantification. As little as possible is still so much, that forty-eight hours of pain were every second a multiple of that other unimaginable duration of her suffering in the *milchume*.

Were each hour a generation – mother to child to mother to child – that is the duration of the coming days when she coughs up her life. She rattles, sighs, moans, and the effort to suck in every breath heaves her shoulders high above her neck.

"She's not feeling it," they assured me.

During one of these hours that is a lifetime, I become aware that a violinist is strolling the halls of the palliative-care unit and stopping by doors to play requests. All I can take in are my mother's laboured breaths but perhaps it is true what they say, that my mother can hear. When the musician gets to our door, I ask, "Can you play 'Black Eyes'?"

I will want to believe she doesn't feel it. There is a surcease in that her eyes will no longer open in fright, they will instead roll up. And for many breaths an hour round the clock for six days this is attenuation. Not counting the coughing up of bloody gravel that resembles coffee grounds, the sore suddenly bursting open on her tailbone and bleeding. *Keriyah*. My mother was being rent and torn. If this heaving, sighing body was also Chaja, and excruciatingly undeniable it was, then she was suffering.

Then the resident counted her breaths per minute, found them fewer as morphine slows down the respiration, and not wanting to be the one to bring them to a stop, cancelled the prescription. At the same time her labour increased. That night her coughing threw me into a panic. Nadia ran out of the room and it was all I could do not to run too. My heart pounding, I held on to my mother. *This is why I am here*, I thought. *My father was looking for his pills the night he died. I am here to give her what she needs.*

We have been off service since we arrived on this floor of my mother's private room. We belong to no bureaucratic niche and seem to have been abandoned except for the lone resident on call.

"Yes, she's dying," I say to the unit nurse in her office. "But dying needs help as much as childbirth sometimes does. Why has nobody checked her blood pressure or come to wash her?"

"Strange that you should find this attitude here," she said, "because this is a palliative-care floor. We have space available for your mother. The palliative-care physician is Dr. Chang."

The night my mother erupts in sounds to rattle the universe, Dr. Chang again appears without a sound by the bed, and silently watches while she coughs up her life in my arms. He stands by the bed and to my infinite relief, he starts ordering morphine. A direct drip is installed, as well as subcutaneous additions every two hours.

One night I have the impression her effort is increasing and that night he affirms it, by raising her morphine level still higher.

"She may have had a small heart attack," he says softly turning over her hand. The silence he creates engenders an expectation that some enormous help is at hand, but that expectation alone is the help. That expectation, the oxygen, the morphine, and the relief provided by the respiratory therapist who comes in the middle of the night to suction out my mother's lungs.

It is fortunate she was brought to the hospital. The nursing home, where she might have been left to die a natural death, has none of these resources.

The breath slows and I hold mine after each collapsing exhalation as she musters for the inhalation. Between each might be her last.

This is the end of pain for gain. We spend so much of our life in training for another gain later on. Comfort care requires a constant weighing of how much there is left to gain. A few days ago my mother forced air out in grunts to throw off toxins. Now she is drowning in fluid. She is given an extra drug, scopolamine, meant to clear her throat, but she is coughing herself into a paroxysm of choking. One of the nurses admits she has withheld the morphine booster to see whether the scopolamine alone would work.

"Give her both," I plead. "Don't even take the chance that it won't work."

The nurse asks her more experienced colleague, who tells her it is too late for the scientific control of variables.

"I am sorry," the nurse said preparing the syringe. "Raissa said that in these circumstances you don't wait and see which works, you give both. I am sorry."

"It's all right," I said dully.

"I suppose it's natural to suffer when somebody with your genes is suffering," she said, adjusting my mother's oxygen mask.

Hélène, the secretary who used to delight in my mother's beautiful smile when she was on the long-term-care ward, now works on this floor. Two and a half years later, Hélène comes in to see my mother. She stands across the room from the bed and looks at her. Through her shocked distance I know my mother has become another, an "other," unrecognizable and terrifying. Whoever she is now is a person in her death agony.

"She was such a beautiful lady!" Hélène walks out with a handkerchief to her eyes, leaving me with a numb resentment at the *was*.

"Mama," I whisper, "*allst vet zayn git*" (everything will be good). I, who have no voice, sing in Yiddish in her ear. I make up a lullaby. "Mother loves you, father loves you, and the little children love you."

That night she vomits up reddish-brown pellets; the nurses throw her around like a rag doll, her eyes roll up, and I hear vocalizations out of my mother that are not my mother's voice.

"Get out!" a nurse orders.

I run out as if driven by a whip. I come back again. The coughing and retching is an assault through which I hold on to her, and between each rattling intake of breath I whisper to her. With her in my arms, I think this is why we invented God. It is too much to hold in our hands.

"It will only make things more difficult for her now," says Dr. Chang softly, as they remove the feeding tube. This is the point at which malnutrition causes no suffering. My mother has morphine and oxygen. She has become a vessel for breath alone.

Allan has come to be with me and he drags me outside. It is May, the month of blooms, nature, my mother's month. My mother was born in May and is not shy about leaving us during it. She never fetishized her moment in the lifecycle and did not want me to do so either. In our family only my mother was brave enough to love the spring. Her forehead has begun to turn yellow.

All the rituals, but the tearing of the cloth, try to attenuate the gap between the living and the dead. *Keriyah.* She has begun to turn yellow. Nothing will bind up this rent. When we go outside, I am grateful it is cold and raining. Chaja, her name means life. Every leaf and breath is full of her. The birds and flowers weep for her. For as long as I live she will be as present to me as my own breath.

On the morning she dies, they will come in and stand beside the bed as I hold my beautiful mother who is turning cold in my arms. The heart shape of my mother's face free of the oxygen mask relaxes into the slightest smile. I tarry with her. Nadia arrives, Dr. Chang, Dr. Rosenberg.

"What day is the funeral?" he asks.

"I suppose Sunday, May 11. Mother's Day."

"There are no accidents," he says. "I have many Holocaust survivors among my patients," he says to Allan. "They came here, without a penny, without the language, without the family they have lost. And they started over. Because that's what you did. That's what they knew to do."

I remember what my mother said to me, sitting *tsvishen menschen*. Once the anxiety for her mother and father and sisters and brothers and husband and children was taken away, there remained only what she felt in relation to herself.

"Do you think I am afraid of death? I am not afraid of death, not at all," she confided to me in the corridor of the Jewish General Hospital. "Not a bit. Everyone dies. But what I have been through. Two world wars. It is a miracle I have lived so long!"

Epilogue

YIZKOR

In the 1950s and '60s, the scattered survivors of the Jewish communities that had been annihilated by the Nazis began to gather whatever they remembered of their lost shtetl in books. These books were called *Yizkor* (memorial) books, after the prayer in which four times a year Jews recall their dead relatives. The books were collective scrapbooks that might include a short history of the town, any surviving photographs, a description of the way of life before the war, or as in my mother's case, her life during the war.

My mother's contribution is translated from Yiddish in the *Demblin-Modryzc Book*, which was published in Tel Aviv in 1969.

DERTSAYLUNG FUN A GERATEVETE
ACCOUNT OF A RESCUED PERSON

Chaja Zylberberg Wajnberg

Until the Outbreak of the War

My father used to tell that he was born in Bobovrnik, a place that is seven kilometers away from present-day Demblin. In the city there was a large fortress that served as a military base. Jews from the city used to supply the soldiers with food, clothing, shoes, and necessities. In Demblin the Jews were occupied in different trades and professions: businessmen, storeowners, butchers, bakers, real estate dealers, etc. The older Jews in Demblin were very religious – they were all *heis* Chassidim or "hot" Chassidim.

In that city was also the residence of the Modryzc rebbe. The Modryzc rebbe was known all over as a great scholar and also as a great composer of melodies.

While the old Jews were religious, the young Jews became drawn to either socialism or Zionism. In 1905 (the year of narrator's birth), in all the big cities in Russia a revolution began. Workers went on strike and marched with red flags reading: Down with the Czar. Also in Demblin, demonstrators demanded to have their freedom.

The strikes were arranged by students in Demblin who used to fight for human rights. More than once did these students sit in jail and were sent by the Czar to Siberia. Among these were Jewish students: Beirich Eizenmesser – his daughter Fela Puterman now lives in Israel – he studied medicine and later he was a rector of the medical school in Leningrad. My uncle, Shloime Zylberberg, received two doctorates and today he is dean in a Leningrad university. Shmillstein, a student, died at an early age of tuberculosis.

During the First World War the Russians again withdrew from Demblin and the city fell to the Germans. After World War I, the Germans left and it became part of Free Poland. I was at that time a small girl, a *maidele*, and only started going to school. Since there was no Jewish school I went to a Polish school instead. We Jewish students suffered a lot from our Christian so-called school friends. They hated the Jews and only caused us a lot of worries.

Despite the anti-Semitism, Jewish life between the two wars was culturally rich. Demblin was fortunate to have all kinds of Jewish organizations. It had a big shul, two banks, a *gemilut chesed* caisse, a "loving kindness" fund for charity, and a *linat hatzedek*, a committee to provide sleeping quarters for visitors. That fund was primarily financed by Yermei Veinappel, who devoted a lot of time. It is also appropriate to recall a person by the name of Dr. Sochatzki who contributed his services to this organization. Yermei Veinappel was a lovely warm Jew. He used to treat sick people without pay. But an anti-Semitic Polack denounced him and claimed that he was a spy for Russia. So on the first of September 1939, the day the Second World War started, he and his wife Anna were deported to this horrible, cold Polish concentration camp in Kartuz Brzezek where they perished.

Bitter Days for the Jews of Demblin

When the Germans came into town, those bitter days began for the Jews. I with my child, my parents, sister, and brother went into the forest in order to hide. But Polish bandits fell upon us, beat us, and robbed us. Therefore we turned around and went back to Demblin. Even at that time, the city was under the total control of German murderers. The Jewish stores were taken over by Christians, and the Germans took away all the merchandise, so that the stores were empty. They used to take us to do forced labour.

A short time later, in very narrow dark alleys a ghetto was created. On a rainy cold day we were forced into it. Immediately, my child became very ill. She contracted diphtheria, and conditions went from bad to worse. I put my life in danger to escape from the ghetto and call a doctor. This was a very difficult request to make. Also it was dangerous to leave the ghetto, because when the Germans found a Jew outside the ghetto they immediately executed him. This is how they killed a son of Mail Meyer, Ronik. I disregarded the danger and decided that I must do everything to save my child. I arrived at the Christian doctor Gelber. He agreed to come back with me to the ghetto. Thanks to this Dr. Gelber, the child healed.

Two years later, when we were in the camp by the station, the same Dr. Gelber again endangered his life and came to help Nissan Weinapple, because he was very sick. I remember that at that time German and Ukrainian gendarmes surrounded the barracks and we were sure we would all be shot. Dr. Gelber said: I think I will also be killed just like you, and my wife and children wouldn't even know what happened to me. Another time, I again saw Dr. Gelber in the camp accidentally; he was with a sick person named Avrum Schillinger. Unfortunately he died. The wife of Dr. Gelber was terrified and she went to the barbed wire to wait for her husband. The doctor was a great democrat, a great friend of Jews, and a wonderful physician. The anti-Semites ratted on him, though, they said he was a Jew, and the Nazis murdered him.

The situation in the ghetto became frighteningly bad. There was a terrible hunger. People were dying from typhus and other kinds of diseases. The Nazis emptied all the Jewish houses in the ghetto of everything they could get their hands on. Any valuables, any possessions, any clothes. And sadistically they beat and murdered Jewish women, old people, and children.

The Roundup

The 6th of May 1942 was the first round up of Demblin Jews. They drove hundreds of hungry, sick Jews out of their houses, beat them, pushed them into overcrowded rail cars, and sent them to the death camp in Sobibor. They never came back from there.

The young men were driven to forced labour at the Demblin air-field and the train station. My family and I succeeded for the time being in hiding ourselves. The ghetto in Demblin during the first roundup was emptied of many Jews, but later on the city was fully packed again because in the place of those that they deported, the Germans brought in thousands of Jews from Slovakia. The situation was absolutely horrible, the overcrowding and lack of sanitation caused lots of typhus and death.

The second roundup came on the 15th of October 1942. During the second roundup, they murdered hundreds of Jews, young and old, men and women.

I, my child, my mother, and a few other women succeeded in getting into Mayontek Vientshkov on a temporary basis to work. But we didn't remain there very long because on the 28th of October, 1942, very late at night, the S.S. man Wagner let us know that he needed to take us to the Jewish town of Konske-Volye where we would be safe. I understood at that point that he was trying to hoodwink us.

I Jumped through the Window

When the villains encountered a woman or mother with her child, they would regularly, in a bestial way, murder the child before the mother's eyes, and then they would kill the mother. This I was never going to let myself live through. And so, leaving my dear mother, Shayndele, I threw myself out the window, certain that we would both be shot. But after me, the children of my husband's brother, Sonya and Nachman, jumped out after me and also Tzertzah's fiancée. Luckily, there weren't any gendarmes around by the fence. All that we had, we had left behind us in the courtyard. Sitting there in deathly fright, barefoot and half naked, I heard how they led out my mother and the other women. I went back to get something for my child and already there were some Poles standing around there and they warned that the SS man wasn't very far away and if I hung around I was going to get shot. In terrible fear, I grabbed the child in my arms and began to make my way to Demblin, not knowing if I'd find one Jew left in the city. My child fell asleep in my arms, my heart wept with pity each minute death threatened us because the Poles knew and could have turned us in to the gendarmes. I was very, very preoccupied with the fate of my poor mother.

I came to a farm stall and I met there a peasant whom I didn't know before. I laid my child on the ground, I was extremely afraid that the peasant would discover us. It was dark when I set out again, trembling at the barking of the dogs, and I hoped they wouldn't wake up the peasants.

A good peasant who lived not far from Krukovke in a little colony took my child in his arms and led us to a windmill in an old suburb. We went into Weingelechen, and from there Robert took us to the gates of the camp, not far from Dr. Zochatzky. At the gate there were corpses of several Jews lying around. It seemed that they wanted to get into the camp, the gate was locked, and they were shot. We succeeded in getting in. My child and I were able to sneak to the train station where my family was. The barracks at the station didn't have any windows or doors and it wasn't heated, and any Lithuanian, Ukrainian, Pole, or German had the right to kill us on the spot. Winter was horribly cold, and they used to come in with wagons to load up all the sick people and send them to Konske-Volye. Rudolf, Zygert, Peterson, and other sadists used to manage to shoot quite a few people every day. We were terribly hungry and sick there. On one bitterly cold day they took my two little sisters, young blossoming children. I wanted to go to them, but the children started to cry and begged that I should go away because the Ukrainians would shoot me. In Konske-Volye they kept them in open, unheated houses.

And soon, all kinds of diseases started to break out. My little sisters became sick with typhus from lying on the bare ground. The older one, Perla, who was sixteen years old, died. The younger one, Esther, was lying hugging her, not even knowing that her sister was already dead. Later on, we succeeded in getting Esther back to the train station and she told us hideous things that happened at Konske-Volye.

Besides my personal suffering, I saw terrible pain and cruelty at the station.

The 14th of July 1943, there was a deportation to Poniatov. At 12 noon, the SS came with machine guns and gave an order that we should get ready to travel. Knowing that my daughter, Yonah, was more threatened than I was by death, within eyesight of the SS, I tore through the barbed wire and I and my child, both covered with blood, succeeded in getting into the house of a Christian acquaintance near the station. We weren't able to stay there very long because the gentile was afraid that the gendarmes would find us and kill them for hiding Jews. Not having any place to go, I decided to go to the rich peasant, Stachorsky, who lived in the same town as my family, the town of Tsherniov, not far from Lugov. He had helped Jews, given them food to eat without demanding anything in return. The anti-Semites betrayed him to the gendarmes who hung him with his family in Demblin.

Stachorsky's address was given to me by the leader of the public school, Skovransky, who was a great democrat and a friend of Jews. Later, two weeks before the liberation, he was murdered by the A.K. in sight of his wife. This was told to me by Vladeyslav Yarashek, a poor bricklayer, who gave his last bit of bread from his own mouth to Jews. Later he died in 1945 of tuberculosis.

I went away with my child to the Katlavneyah, near the camp, actually, to the airport. And there I was able to meet with my husband and my brother Feivel who had succeeded in running away from the station. My two sisters, Rivkelah and Esterlah, and my brother-in-law, Baruch Perelman, from Pulawy, along with all the Jews from the station, had been sent away to Poniatov and they never came back from there. The 3rd of November 1943, Poniatov and Travniki were destroyed.

Good People Help Us

In the camp, at the airfield, we didn't dare remain very long, because we weren't legal. The same night we spent in the field of rye and were shot at by Ukrainians. Luckily, the bullets missed and before dawn, with our hearts beating, we went back to the Katlavneyah because we had no place to hide. I remember that the woman, Edjsha Ekheizer, brought us something to eat, but because of our great sorrow, we couldn't eat knowing that each minute death was coming closer.

The wife of Doctor came in. She wanted to calm us down and said that people in the camp asked the director of the camp to intervene with the German authorities and let us come in. She also gave me the address of the Pole who she said would take us in if it really got bad in the camp. She, with her husband and daughter, if they were able to, would also go there. At the same time, the director of the camp came with good news that we were going to be allowed to come in. In the camp in Demblin we stayed for a year, we didn't have any money, we were half naked and barefoot, but good people helped us. And a deeply felt thanks should go to the wife of Chaim Taichman for her humane treatments.

In the Dembliner camp, we stayed until the 18th of July 1944. When the Soviets approached the Vistula, the camps' inhabitants were moved in two groups to Czenstachov. In the first group were fifteen children, and these children were murdered, thanks to the brutality of the German Bortenschlager. And a great deal of culpability in this event rests with the director of the camp, a German Jew by the name of Yoles. The second group, in which there were 30 children, they took away to liquidate, and for two days and nights the children were in terrible fear, but after that, they gave them back to us. And why the Nazis didn't kill them but returned them, I still don't know even today.

In Czenstachov we remained until the 15th of January 1945, when the Red Army liberated us. A day before that, the Germans deported 800 Jews to Buchenwald. Among those deported were my husband, my father, and my brother.

In the last days of the War, they sent my father on a death march, and along the way, they drove the Jews into a river. And coming out of the river, my father died. My husband and brother avoided the death march, because they were so sick and swollen with hunger. They remained in Buchenwald until the American and English soldiers liberated them.

And finally the end of the horrible War came. My husband and brother came back from Buchenwald. We lived in Lodz, and after that we left Poland. Now we live in Montreal, Canada.

ACKNOWLEDGMENTS

I would like to thank every one of my parents' Polish Jewish community whose story I heard as a child or who told it to me spontaneously as an adult. Each one of them warrants a book; this is the story of the family into which I was born.

As telling it has occupied so much of my adult life, I should thank every friend who encouraged me along the way, from Susan Potashner who let me fill her mailbox with letters from Paris, to Marie Connors who posted a query to McGill-Queen's University Press when I was too ill to do it for myself. "It's your school, isn't it?" There could be no more fitting publisher than MQUP in Montreal, the city where I grew up with my family and which remains a source of Yiddish culture into the present.

The person responsible for the publication of *Sheymes* is my editor, Mark Abley, who shepherded the manuscript through the arduous protocol of my school's academic press. I will not embarrass him any more than to call him a "mensch."

Thanks also to the press's executive director Philip Cercone, the managing editor Ryan Van Huijstee, and my copy editor Carol Harrison, for taking on a multilingual document.

I would like to thank my once–high school classmate Professor David Roskies for the gift of the title. I heard him use the word *sheymes* once in a lecture and that was enough.

Thank you to my friends who put up with my opinion sound-ings on a text that was too close to me for me to see: Jason Weiss, Dani Hausmann, and Marilyn Moriarty. Thanks to the publisher's anonymous readers for their suggestions and a late fresh eye from Robbi Nester. Thanks to Rabbi Arnie Rachlis for informing my Jewish education and to Arie Galles for confirming that I had not dreamed up my parents' Polish Yiddish.

Thanks to my husband, Allan, for the task of keeping me alive.